The Triumph of Managerialism?

The Triumph of Managerialism?

New Technologies of Government and Their Implications for Value

Edited by Anna Yeatman and
Bogdan Costea

ROWMAN &
LITTLEFIELD
INTERNATIONAL
London • New York

Published by Rowman & Littlefield International Ltd
Unit A, Whitacre Mews, 26–34 Stannary Street, London SE11 4AB
www.rowmaninternational.com
Rowman & Littlefield International Ltd. is an affiliate of Rowman & Littlefield
4501 Forbes Boulevard, Suite 200, Lanham, Maryland 20706, USA
With additional offices in Boulder, New York, Toronto (Canada), and Plymouth (UK)
www.rowman.com

British Library Cataloguing in Publication Data

A catalogue record for this book is available from the British Library

Library of Congress Cataloging-in-Publication Data

Names: Yeatman, Anna, editor. | Costea, Bogdan, editor.
Title: The triumph of managerialism? : new technologies of government and their implications for value / edited by Anna Yeatman and Bogdan Costea.
Description: London ; New York : Rowman & Littlefield International, [2018] | Includes bibliographical references and index.
Identifiers: LCCN 2018024951 (print) | LCCN 2018033974 (ebook) | ISBN 9781786604897 (electronic) | ISBN 9781786604880 (cloth) | ISBN 9781538158302 (pbk)
Subjects: LCSH: Management. | Public administration. | Organizational sociology.
Classification: LCC HD30.12 (ebook) | LCC HD30.12 .T75 2018 (print) | DDC 302.3/5—dc23
LC record available at https://lccn.loc.gov/2018024951

Contents

Chapter 1

Introduction

Anna Yeatman

THIS COLLECTION AND ITS THEMES

This collection had its origin in a workshop held at the Copenhagen Business School in June (23–24) 2016. The workshop was called 'New Technologies of Government and Their Implications for Value'. One overarching theme marked out the context of this workshop: the way in which global structures of public-private networks of governance are subordinating government and its distinctively public responsibilities and tasks – securing and attending to the welfare of a national-political community of citizens. The activity of government is articulated as a specific set of responsibilities for a legally constituted jurisdiction, a public place, including the multifaceted (historical, cultural, social and 'natural') ecology of relationships that mark out the topography of this place. It is this set of responsibilities, and the sovereign power required to sustain them, that has come under question by the imposition on national governments of a global institutional order that is designed to secure private capital rights. Governments have been required to redefine their work within the parameters of governance such that specific public policies addressing specific areas of need pertaining to a place-specific public collectivism are abandoned, and these areas of governmental responsibility are reframed in terms of the abstractions of governance: performance, efficiency, productivity, competitiveness and profit. More and more of the operational work of government is delivered via mechanisms of government contracting (on a commercial in-confidence basis) to private agents, including multinational capitalist corporations such as Serco, Pearson Education and ISS.

As Isabelle Stengers (2015, 54) points out, when the work of government is reframed by governance, politics cedes place to management:

> Governance is well named. It describes well the destruction of what is implied by a collective responsibility with regard to the future, that is to say, politics. With governance, it is no longer a matter of politics but of management, and, in the first place, the management of a population that must not meddle with what concerns it.

Curiously enough the British Brexit referendum was held on the first of the two days of the Copenhagen workshop, and by its second day, the news was coming through of just what had happened: a vote against Britain staying in the European Economic Community. Quinn Slobodian (2018) significantly extends the archival histories of how the neoliberal project was successfully organised in the course of the twentieth century to reframe the work of government. Alongside the histories of the Mont Pèlerin Society and the Chicago and Virginia Schools of neoliberal economics, Slobodian shifts focus to the Geneva School which 'was less a discipline of economics than a discipline of statecraft and law' (Slobodian 2018, 11). The Geneva neoliberal thinkers, who included Hayek from 1962, focused their attention on a legal and institutional framework for the rights of capital that could constrain national sovereignty and the public collectivism that such political autonomy makes possible. They scaled up the ordoliberal idea of an economic constitution for the nation to the global level. In the European case, this is the economic federation that is the European Economic Union. Their intention was not to dispense with bounded territorial states, but to have them sign up to a global order of law and rules such as those that are embodied in free trade agreements: 'What neoliberals seek is not a partial but a complete protection of private capital rights, and the ability of supranational bodies like the European Court of Justice and the WTO to override national legislation that might disrupt the global rights of capital' (Slobodian 2018, 12–13). Thus, the question was one of balancing state power (*imperium*) with private capital rights (*dominium*), with the latter accorded a constitutional right to trump the former (see Slobodian 2018, 10–11, for how these neoliberal thinkers appropriated Schmitt's distinction between *imperium* and *dominium*):

> The nation could be useful insofar as it provided services of stabilization (which would often include restrictions to migration) and cultivated legitimacy in the political sphere. But like democracy, it also bore the risk of tipping into excess. Thus, it needed to be constrained just as democracy did. (Slobodian 2018, 15)

What Slobodian (2018, 15) emphasises is how the neoliberal project deliberately scaled up the idea of institutional order: 'Neoliberals were proponents of an institutional framework in which the world economy would survive threats to its holistic integrity'. It is this scaling up, the substitution of a non-place-responsive institutional ordering for one that is located in place, that distributes power and authority away from the public officialdom of a particular nation state in the direction of 'faceless' technocrats whose conduct and language is managerialist. In this context, the Brexit vote signals a growing problem for the legitimacy of the supranational global order: when entire regions of a nation find themselves locked out of opportunities for regular employment of a kind that enables people to enjoy self-worth, contribute to the building and sustaining of civil community life and believe in their children's future, it is little wonder that they declare their loss of trust in the existing governing order. At the same time, notwithstanding this signal, the British government has no intention of exiting the broader neoliberal global constitutional framework, busying itself with finding alternative forms of supranational free trade agreements to that of the European community. There will have to be a more direct calling to account of this order than can be achieved by revanchist populist projects of nationalism before anything changes.

This collection addresses the present historical conjuncture, one where there is a practical and organisational convergence of several historical forces: the intellectual force of *neoliberalis*m as this offers a blueprint for a global institutional order that secures the rights of corporate capital; a global, corporate and financialised *capitalism* that gleefully affords itself the licence to operate that this order grants it; a scientific *technologism* that is oriented within an ethos of adaptive and manipulative problem-solving conduct, unfettered by 'mere' opinion (culture, politics, history); and, *managerialism*, the ideology of let the managers manage.

The *triumph of managerialism*, then, in the title of this collection, refers not to managerialism considered as a phenomenon on its own, but to managerialism considered as the mode of governance of the entire system of relationships that is constituted by the synthesis of neoliberalism, capitalism and technologism. The a-political value neutrality, the technical form of rationality, the 'fixer' mentality and the a-contextual elitism of managerialist discourse are the *lingua franca* that hold the system of governance together.

There is something further to be said about the historical conjuncture of this collection. Until relatively recently, at least in constitutional democracies, the state and the wider public sector of organisations funded by the state operated in terms of the political rationality of public administration. The central values in this discourse are rule of law, political accountability and transparency, service to the public, public interest and – with reference to how the public is served – an idea of citizenship that is practically specified in terms of how state services make it possible for people to enjoy and share the status of citizen. In this frame of reference, it was possible to call the distinct sectors of the welfare state – prisons for example – to an ethical-civic ideal, in this case, to ask of prison administration that it engage with the practical question of how to re-integrate prisoners into a civil-civic mode of being (the idea of rehabilitation). The neoliberal project was intended to undo 'the administrative state' associated with the twentieth-century project of the democratic welfare state: specifically, to undo the political rationality of public administration. In the name of efficiency, cost-containment and national competitiveness, it offered an alternative: the reconstruction of the relationships between policy agencies and service delivery organisations as private forms of contractual relationships between business enterprises. The New Public Management (NPM) was the 'managerialist' discourse that was the practical vehicle of this profound institutional and cultural transformation (for suggestion of the NPM as an historically evolving phenomenon, see Considine and Painter 1997). Certainly, there is a difference between the neoliberals, who provided the intellectual justification for this broad shift, and the practically minded practitioners who carried it out, but there can be no doubt that the NPM would never have occurred if 'the neoliberal thought collective' (see Mirowski and Plehwe 2009) had not successfully transformed how the state and its role are thought about.

The NPM represents the extension of managerialism, already long established as the *modus operandi* of twentieth-century capitalist corporate organisation, to the state and the public sectors. From this historical vantage point, then, managerialism becomes a 'general', non-sector-specific, phenomenon. Thus, it becomes possible to think about what the phenomenon of managerialism *is*. This is what occurs in the literature on managerialism. For example, consider these two recent definitions of managerialism:

> The central doctrine of managerialism is that the differences between such organisations, as for example, a university and a motor-vehicle company, are less important than the similarities, and that the performance of all organisations can be optimised by the application of generic management skills and theory. It follows that the crucial element of institutional reform is the removal of obstacles to 'the right to manage'. (Quiggin 2003)
>
> . . . there is no generally accepted definition of managerialism, but as a working definition it can be said that management is an ideology based on the belief that optimisation of the productivity and outcomes of all organisations can be achieved through the application of managerial expertise, theories and techniques; this applies to both private and public organisations. (Doran 2016, 81)

Reflecting the current historical vantage point as one where managerialism extends to *all* kinds of organisation, in *both* public and private sectors, Doran comments: 'Analysing managerialism is of crucial importance because in the last twenty years this ideology has risen to a position of intellectual and social prominence, if not dominance, impacting decision making in both the private and public sectors, as well as social policy more broadly'. From this vantage point also it is possible to look back and to consider the precursors of managerialism: the utopian socialist and Marxist ideal of replacing 'the government of men' with 'the administration of things'; the managerial society of Soviet communism, German and Italian fascism (as discussed by Doran 2016, 88); the idea of total mobilisation in relation to the development of twentieth-century mass society (discussed by Hemming, chapter 3, this volume); the managerial structures of mass production and mass consumption (discussed by Costea, chapter 4, this volume); the development of a professional scientific technocracy focused on predictive methods of controlling society thought of as a vast cybernetic system of information flows and networks (discussed by Shalbak, chapter 5, this volume); and the iteration of this technocratic systems utopia in the neoliberal conception of market society as an information processor on a global scale (see Slobodian 2018, chapter 7; Mirowski and Nik-Khah 2017).

From this vantage point, too, it is meaningful to ask, was management always already managerialist, or are we to make a distinction between management and managerialism? This question is not settled by this collection. Costea (chapter 4) suggests that these two phenomena are not separable – they both exemplify a distinctly modern will to power – but Malpas (chapter 1) suggests that we might want to sustain a distinction between management and managerialism, the real question perhaps being one of at what point does the scaling up of social ordering require management to morph into managerialism.

The question of 'the role and interests of managers as a class' (Quiggin 2003) is an important one. The chapters in this collection rather skirt this question, although it might be said that they obliquely broach it. All of this collection's writers are practicing academics who have positioned themselves in a relationship of critique of managerialism. Yet, theoretically at least, at this historical juncture, all of them have had experienced, or will experience, opportunities to participate in managerialist organisational roles in academe or beyond. If they say no, what is the status of this refusal? The power and status of the managerial class is organisationally based; recruitment is based on 'merit' so this class can celebrate its inclusive ethic and 'diversity' (see Yeatman 1997); and entry into this class is marked by gaining ready access to a cross-sectoral set of managerial elites that operate both 'locally' and 'globally'. The global managerial elite has its own insider *patois* and forms of civility, but virtually anyone with a higher education degree, the right point of access and making the right kinds of choices can join this club of insiders who disdain those who cannot, or will not, belong. Such insiders can be found running universities and trade unions and (in Australia at this time) the Labor Party's organisational machine.

What then does it mean for those who might, if they want, have access to the club of global governance managers – to what Isabelle Stengers (2015, 29) calls 'our guardians' (in French, *nos responsables*) – to declare: no? I will return to this question at the end of this introduction. Let me turn now to the chapters in this volume: this collection should be taken as symptomatic of our current context. The contributors are not the only people thinking about and discussing managerialism, but they are just the people who were gathered on this occasion.

THE CHAPTERS IN THIS COLLECTION

The first three chapters are philosophical and theoretical, taking a long view of managerialism as an historical phenomenon, one that is bound up with the project of modernity itself. Jeff Malpas argues that managerialism and technologism are different aspects of the same phenomenon: technologism is itself managerial, and managerialism is part of a modern technological ordering. Malpas raises the question whether a distinction is to be made between management and managerialism. Management, he suggests, is involved in every activity: it is 'the taking of things in hand'. But when management is associated with modern organisational life, it refers to a second-order activity, that directs, coordinates and facilitates other first-order activities, as when, for example, management coordinates the work of doctors, nurses, cleaners and cooks in a hospital. Malpas also suggests that we should be careful not to conflate managerialism with bureaucracy, considered as a hierarchical system of public office. Malpas proposes that management morphs into managerialism when it stops understanding itself as a second-order of activity, one that serves, in the sense of facilitating the first order of activity. With managerialism, all activities are appropriated to the sphere of the managerial. He has in mind the way in which computerised performance auditing techniques penetrate every level of an organisation, directly harnessing workers to managerial modes of conduct, dispensing with the layer of middle management and centralising the managerial regime in the executive layers of the organisation that purchases from private corporations the technological methods of its coordination. The two hallmarks of managerialism for Maplas are genericisation (dis-engagement with basic activities, values and ethos of an organisation) and quantisation. Once quantisation has occurred, a third hallmark enters the picture: monetisation. Malpas suggests that managerialism, considered as a technology, reflects the character of technology more generally: its systematicity. He argues that technology should not be understood instrumentally, as a means to an end. It is an entirely self-referential phenomenon: the only end of managerialism is managerialism. Malpas links technology so understood to the mathematical and spatial understanding of the world that is inaugurated by sixteenth- and seventeenth-century natural science. The spatial designates an unbounded and uniform phenomenon, one that can be expressed only quantitatively and numerically. It is something entirely different from 'place', which is always utterly distinct, and plural, for one place exists only as it relates to other places. Where place, being distinct, is inherently bounded or limited, space, being unbounded, is without limit. It is this absence of limit that Malpas sees as the quintessence of technology/managerialism. Even as the technological world view began with modern science, Malpas suggests that the idea of world that it promulgates is a contemporary phenomenon: place has been evacuated and replaced by 'the idea of the world as a single integrated space – a space of flows and connections in which borders and boundaries are increasingly irrelevant'. This is the systematicity that Malpas attributes to technology/managerialism, expressed in the phenomenon of technological convergence, the reduction of everything to something that can be measured and manipulated within the same space. He points out that the form of contemporary capitalism is shaped by the convergence of the technological with the economic and financial. For Malpas, following Heidegger's *The Question of Technology*, modernity represents the desire to escape from limit. From this point of view, then, technology/managerialism is inherent in modernity. Malpas suggests that critique of managerialism is 'almost impossible' because the all-encompassing (totalising) nature of managerialism means that there is nothing outside it. At the same time, 'because managerialism lies outside of managerialism's own grasp, so it cannot recognise its almost inevitable tendencies to failure and incompleteness'. It is condemned to try again, using exactly the same approach that has brought failure. Malpas ends his chapter by suggesting that attentiveness to place may afford us the foothold from which we can offer a genuine form of critique of managerialism, but this means that we allow place, and its inherent limits, to claim us.

Laurence Paul Hemming's chapter focuses on new technologies of government as an all-encompassing rational ordering. He recognises Michel Foucault's analysis of German ordoliberal thought as one of the first discernments of our managerial condition. Like Malpas, Hemming suggests that the nature of Foucault's insight here is to suggest that today capitalism has assumed a new form: the market economy as 'a planned, ordered and technologically arranged freedom'. Here the distinction between liberal and illiberal forms of government disappears because they share the same technological ordering of the market economy. In agreement with others such as Mirowski (2013, 56), Hemming brings neoliberalism, managerialism and technology into the one historical narrative. Like Malpas, Hemming suggests that the world that neoliberalism seeks to create involves a self-referential and self-reproducing rationality: 'Neoliberalism manifests itself not only as itself – as the attempt to bring an entire world under a certain kind of economic, rational domination and control – but also as the capacity to internalise and absorb its own oppositions and contradictions, . . . appearing to normalise and legitimate everything that attempts to set itself up against the effects of . . . [this] rationalism'.[1]

If economic management was first associated with managing a household economy, it is Hegel's connection of reason with the infinite that begins 'the fascination of the infinite possibility, offered by the absolute advancement of human purposes, by directing them toward their maximisation'. Here we encounter again the suggestion that managerialism is an attempt at domination and control that is governed by 'the dazzling possibility of the realisation of the infinite'. This is the contemporary fantasy of power. The Marxist analysis of capitalism, predicated as it is on a distinction between those who have power (the capitalist class) and those who do not (the proletariat), will no longer do. Because the nature of the contemporary fantasy of power is to implicate everyone. More than this: there is no one set of agents who can be identified as planners or rulers. Everyone becomes a relay or an effect of power: even the planners, which captures nicely the passivity that the managerialists exemplify, they can do nothing other than to follow out the logic of the machinic nature of power. Hemming is being deliberate. His suggestion is that critics of managerialism who arrogate to themselves the status of being a 'we' who is 'always aghast' at a 'they' who has brought about this terrible state of affairs, a 'we' who finds itself both victim and impotent in relation to the systematicity of the managerial regime, is already profoundly complicit. For if the critic denounces the regime in the name of a supposedly alternate will, it is and must be simply another iteration of the managerial will to power. The very notion of transcending, moving on up and for the sake of a better future – the idea of revolution – is already contained within managerialism understood as total mobilisation. Thus, proposals (Hemming considers two) to overcome managerialism and neoliberalism by bringing about a 'fundamental equality' are already contained within the metaphysical equality that inheres in the will to power. This is a subjectivity that presents as the universal subject of which the individual is merely an iteration. This is a managed subject, promising an even fuller inclusion of each in a managerial/neoliberal project of infinite possibility. Hemming concludes his chapter with an interesting provocation. He suggests: 'For as long as the only solution to managerialism is an intensification of everything managerial, there can be no resolution to the questions before us'. His insistence that we can no longer deceive ourselves with a revolutionary promise of overthrowing the system perhaps marks out the political question of our time:

> The underlying thesis of this essay is that we have not yet even entered into the questions with sufficient depth to let them be seen and stand as questions.

> Is it true that we can only enter these questions with cold and sharp eyes? . . . Is there any moving beyond the will to power, as the will that organises a total mobilisation of the world surrounding us? It is not at all clear that we should even be striving for such a 'beyond'.

Bogdan Costea's chapter continues the thematic of viewing managerialism as emblematic of the modern will to power. In this case, the will to power is associated with 'the drive to secure an endless horizon for human self-assertion'. Provocatively, Costea takes the 1962 Students for a Democratic Society's Port Huron Statement as the historical threshold for the contemporary managerialist celebration of an unbounded self-assertion. The SDS manifesto articulated the New Left's ideal of a participatory democracy, where each has the right to participate in the decisions governing their lives. Costea takes this text and shows how, from our current standpoint, besieged as we are by managerialist invocations to realise our 'infinite potential', the Port Huron Statement appears as a paradigmatic version of this celebration of subjectivity. The Statement declares: 'Men [*sic*] have infinite potential for self-cultivation, self-direction, self-understanding and creativity'. The promise of an endless horizon of self-assertion seduces us all: Costea questions whether there is any contemporary idea of self-improvement, self-development, self-expression that is not symptomatic of this seduction. More than a seduction, a command: 'Ultimate empowerment and through it, the perfection of one's self are not offers that can be either ignored, or turned down; in fact, they do not offer a choice, they are commands'. His use of the Port Huron Statement was strategic: Costea is questioning the democratic Left – is its conception of humanity different from that which is implicated in managerialism? Here Costea relies on Nietzsche's analysis of nihilism as this follows in the wake of the death of God: (here quoting Heidegger on Nietzsche) 'The otherworldly goal of everlasting bliss is transformed into the earthly happiness of the greatest number'. What was once the divine power of creation is appropriated as 'the distinctive mark of human activity'. This notion of producing reality is the metaphysical backdrop for business enterprise becoming the modal expression of human action understood as the power of creating or producing reality. Not just production, but self-production! Here Costea relates the productive modality of creativity to mass production and mass consumption. But for mass production to have a horizon of infinite potential, mass consumption had to have this too. It was a new rhetoric of consumption – 'the rhetoric of individualised, self-expressing, self-actualising, individuality' – and a 'will to endless acquiring' that demarcates the historical point at which an already-unleashed modern will to power manifests itself as managerialism.

Ihab Shalbak's chapter offers an historical account of the development of the technocratic episteme, a way of knowing associated with professional intellectual workers whose world view was shaped by the distinctively

American traditions of pragmatism and progressivism. These professional intellectuals were 'defence intellectuals' who participated in the military-industrial complex as it took form in the Roosevelt administration during the Second World War, and, upon the war ending, were recruited to advance US military preparedness in the setting of the Cold War. The institutional form that gathered, articulated and networked this scientific and technological way of apprehending the world was the think tank, a freestanding, private policy research institution, outside the university, but exchanging personnel with the university as well as government agencies. The think tank form was first exemplified by the RAND Corporation. This chapter centres on how the RAND Corporation institutionalised a scientifically authorised technocratic world view. This world view was committed to the technology of problem solving at the highest level of abstraction: that of systems integration. It was an evolutionary and cybernetic view of the world as a system: 'an epistemology of system maintenance guided such intellectual work'. The ethos was technocratic because the orientation of such work was one of problem solving rather than one of interpretation, implicating as it does a politics of different perspectives and questions. Problem solving was best pursued as predictive forms of control. The professionalism in question was one of a 'value-neutral' or positivist and technically proficient scientism, given to mathematical modelling and statistical analysis. Articulating the postwar *Pax Americana*, and the consolidation of the American Century, the RAND Corporation and this mode of epistemic engagement were oriented to a de-politicised and de-historicised, spatial ordering of the world. RAND's conception of data was of something more than empirical, rather, data as operationalised within theoretical constructs, and as a manipulable object. In its orientation to predictive probabilities, RAND was concerned with 'the future rather than the past, and with the negativity of what was absent rather than the actuality of what was present'. The world was now conceived, optimally, as a 'frictionless social', as 'a networked space in which interdependency, indeterminacy and immanence ruled over what was rendered as redundant [national] sovereignties'. Shalbak indicates how within the world so conceived 'political, social and cultural interests become units of information flows within a self-regulating and self-perpetuating system'. It is no accident, of course, that Hayek's re-conception of the market as a giant information processor occurs more or less at the same time as the institutionalisation of RAND's presence and influence (the 1950s and 1960s). RAND's theories (rational choice, cognitive psychology, quantitative economy), methodologies (game theory, simulation, systems analysis, operational research) and technologies (computers, the Internet) became paradigmatic for this technocratic world view, and the project of global mastery that drove it. The authorisation of this world view as the only possible way to think resided in a rationality of decontextualised, scientific-technical and mathematical modelling. Yet in its substitution of models for reality, it invited 'the haunting presence of the unknown', bringing with it 'a permanent sense of crisis'. Here we glimpse the element of panic that inheres within the incessant need of the technocratic (and managerialist) world view to ceaselessly re-produce itself,[2] even as, in sustaining a high level of abstract systematicity, it remains relentlessly intent on ensuring that it can neither heed nor hear the claims of reality.

Anna Yeatman's chapter 'Competition Policy and the Destruction of the Welfare State' centres on the elaboration of competition policy in the Australian context so that it is extended to what were once welfare state services. Competition policy is a central feature of the institutional architecture of the contemporary global market economy. It represents the success of the neoliberals in establishing an economic constitution at both global and national levels, where the global institutional order is designed to secure private capital rights and the nation state is re-designed so that, via trade and competition law and policies, it imposes the primacy of private capital rights in a domestic setting, while simultaneously managing the domestic population (see Slobodian 2018). All government activity is redesigned so that it is placed on a business enterprise basis; publicly funded services are situated within a competitive service market; and any substantive distinction between how public and private organisations operate evaporates. The chapter can be read as a case study of market managerialism. It begins with the 2015 Australian Competition Policy Review that extended competition policy to the historically established welfare state services in the Australian set of jurisdictions (both federal and state). Australian federalism is transformed by competition policy with the governments of the component states and territories losing considerable authority and discretion to a centralised institutional framework monitored and maintained by federal government agencies. The marketisation of welfare services is undertaken in the name of improving the welfare of Australians, but the subject whose welfare is at issue here is the privately oriented market consumer, not the citizen, who was the historical referent of welfare state services.

In the context of national competition policy, 'welfare' is an economic idea that slips between references to enhanced national productivity and consumer choice. This chapter suggests that the evisceration of the welfare state in the name of making Australia more competitive and productive does not go unnoticed by Australian citizens who find that what they have understood to be their entitlement to public services is no longer available. However, the institutional redesign of the state – as no longer a welfare but a competition state – is an arcane development for ordinary citizens. The technocratic language of the market managerialists is an insider game, addressed to politicians and government officials, not to citizens. Technocratic language by its nature is intended to disguise the value orientations and ideas that imbue its advocacy (of competition policy in this instance), and the aim of this chapter is to offer an account of the values and ideas that provide the horizon of intelligibility for competition policy so that it becomes publicly and politically accountable.

Anna Hogan's chapter on the increasing role of edu-business in Australian educational policy offers an excellent example of how competition policy already shapes this core area of welfare service need. She shows how the introduction of standardised school testing in Australia (the National Assessment Program-Literacy and Numeracy, or NAPLAN) is indicative of the shift from government (where the administrative state is responsible for how policy is operationalised and delivered) to governance (where the state enters into different kinds of partnership with private organisations). She suggests that this shift creates the doorway for privatisation of key aspects of educational policy development and delivery. Not least, because as any student of the public administration literature knows, policy design and policy implementation should inform each other. Those responsible for implementation play a powerful role in how policy operates and further develops. Thus, private for-profit organisations, such as Pearson Australia (a division of a powerful multinational corporation selling educational services), are able to assume considerable authority in the educational policy process because they are being contracted by government agencies to deliver an entire suite of educational services. In the NAPLAN case these include trialling of test items, equating of test items, special printing of the test, testing of students, marking of the tests, analysis and reporting of results. Pearson Australia is not the only edu-business involved in the Australian education market, there are three significant others, with Pearson and ACER (the Australian Council for Educational Research) being the two most prominent players. It is not just NAPLAN that involves government contracting with edu-business, but government agencies across both federal and state levels of government are increasingly dependent on contractual arrangements with market-based educational businesses for different aspects of educational policy. Hogan suggests four particular concerns with the development of these educational public–private partnerships. First, there is a 'blurring' between public and private with a consequential blurring of responsibility for educational policy. Second, and relatedly, the contracts between government agencies and private educational service providers are commercial in-confidence, which means, Hogan suggests, there is a democratic deficit: members of the public cannot know how their children's schooling is influenced by for-profit private agendas. Third, and also relatedly, in the context of this public–private partnership and network governance approach to educational policy, there is a conflict of interest: edu-businesses acquire the capacity to influence policy processes in ways that are not just non-transparent and non-politically accountable but from which they also benefit commercially. Finally, and of direct relevance to managerialism, Hogan suggests that the expertise that is drawn on in these networked partnerships between government agencies and edu-business in the field of educational policy is not that of professional educators (teachers, curriculum developers or university researchers). Rather, we are led to surmise, the expertise is technical, that involved both in contract management and in the design, implementation and evaluation of the technology of standardised school testing.

Kirstine Zinck Pedersen's and Anne Roelsgaard Obling's chapter 'Compassionate Care: The Managerialization of Virtue' discusses a further twist of the NPM screw with reference to the contemporary British National Health Service. Here serious scandals, along with a sense that the NPM's focus on performance targets and measurement had fostered a tick-the-box mentality, led to a call for reform. Reform focused on the development of a more compassionate character, not just for frontline nursing staff but for management as well (the idea of a compassionate leadership). Pedersen and Obling suggest that this conception of reform is part of the recent shift to an emphasis on values in public management, exemplified especially in 'public value management', which is the focus of the next two chapters in this collection. In this case, a compassion agenda is intended to correct for 'cold' managerialist and market-based modes of operating. Pedersen and Obling argue that the invocation of compassion involves a highly moralised, abstract and decontextualised conception of this particular virtue. It has no bearing on actual procedures and practice which are role-specific: 'Understood as an abstract meta-virtue, compassion is rarely approached or taught in any context or task specific way'. Rather it signals the expectation that frontline service workers and managers in the NHS develop a more compassionate self or personality both in and out of work. There seems to be a shift of responsibility away from the organisation and the larger funding policy system of which it is part onto the personal shoulders of NHS staff here. Pedersen and Obling suggest that if the compassion agenda is intended to soften and humanise NHS performance, the way in which it has been approached indicates it is one more managerialist technology that continues the 'measure-and-manage orthodoxy'. It is now built into customer satisfaction surveys. Pedersen and Obling are not rejecting the importance of ethical conduct in this area of service delivery or any other. They argue that if ethical conduct is to be practically meaningful, it has to assume a context-related specificity where it refers to a particular role or office. As collaborators with Paul du Gay, they follow his emphasis on office as requiring a specific ethical comportment, which is something other than the personality of the individual, requiring, indeed, that the individual be trained in the persona appropriate to the office. They use the example of Florence Nightingale's conception of how nurses should be trained where, as they put it, 'words such as compassion or empathy are nowhere to be found'. Instead Nightingale offers a detailed description of the office of the nurse, which is enacted as a set of specific procedurally oriented practices, not least of these being the trained skill of observation of patients. Nightingale offered a conception of nursing as a professional calling, as a specific role that was designed to complement other roles within the hospital organisation, a role set within which (quoting Nightingale) 'each does that duty to which he is appointed'.

Adam Dahl and Joe Soss's chapter on public value governance is one of two chapters on this topic, the other being chapter 10 by Justine Gronbæk Pors. Both chapters argue that while the public value approach is presented by its advocates as an alternative to the market governance approach of the NPM, it is just as managerialist as NPM. Here, managerialist signals the instrumentalism and technologism of an adaptive problem-solving approach, focused as it is always on maximising value, understood as a quantifiable and thus abstract entity, in relation to inputs. Dahl and Soss's emphasis is particularly on how the public value approach is emblematic of the shift from government to governance, and in this particular case, as a shift from democratic government to 'managed democracy'. Their enquiry is into the implications of the public value models for democratic theory. They point out that, while public value scholars represent their approach as an alternative to neoliberalism, they misconstrue the nature of neoliberalism: like others, they associate neoliberalism with the regime of laissez-faire, with the freeing of the market economy from state intervention, but, in fact, neoliberalism is concerned with reframing the state as the agent responsible for the institutionalisation and design of markets (a point strongly emphasised by Mirowski and Plehwe 2009; Mirowski 2013; Slobodian 2018). Just as Hogan proposes, these authors suggest that neoliberal governance introduces a 'blurring' of the boundary between state and market with the reorganisation of their relationship. In this context, then, it is not correct to see neoliberalism as outside politics, rather it redirects and manages politics by bringing it within market modes of subjectivity and governance. Neoliberalism, then, should be understood as a particular political rationality. The question is whether public value approaches, that champion a collectivist conception of public interest, offer an alternative to this political rationality. Dahl and Soss suggest they do not: in substituting the concept public value for private value, the public value approach remains just as committed as any orthodox neoliberalism to the conception of governance in terms of the production of value. It embraces the idea of collaboration between state, market and civil society actors understood in its possibilities for the creation of (public) value. The distinction between these types of actors is blurred, and it becomes possible to think of the corporation as 'a stakeholder in global society, together with government and civil society' (as Schwab, the founder of the Global Economic Forum, puts it). The corporation is reframed as a citizen in cooperation with other kinds of citizen. What happens to democracy in the public value approach? Dahl and Soss make two points: first, they argue that the public value proponents offer mechanisms to include citizens in the creation of public value, and in so doing, they draw on ideas of democratic deliberative procedure such as participatory budgeting, and deliberative forums. But, they suggest, these mechanisms of inclusion occur against an unchanged backdrop of managerial top-down modes of governing the public that characterise a system of governance that is built around the convergent interests of powerful elites. Such deliberative procedures 'are unlikely to democratize a broader polity defined by profound inequalities of power'. The second point that Dahl and Soss make in relation to the democratic aspiration of public value theorists is that they conceive what should be a *political* process in instrumental (adaptive problem-solving terms), and this must be, and is, an inherently de-politicising and, thus, de-democratising, conception. Politics cannot be reduced to goal-oriented or instrumental action, and it cannot be ranked in terms of its superior performance value. When politics is approached instrumentally, the fundamental and qualitative distinction between public and private disappears, and, on instrumental grounds, it makes sense to engage the citizenry. In this respect, public value governance is no different from neoliberal governance: citizens are no longer political actors but are re-positioned as privately interested and instrumentally motivated actors (taxpaying shareholders and/or consumers) seeking to maximise the public value they receive. Dahl and Soss conclude that the public value theorists fail to address managerialism as a claim to rule and end up endorsing it.

Justine Gronbæk Pors's chapter on public value uses the Danish case where local government is responsible for the delivery of services to citizens. Danish local government has adopted a public value approach to the reform of the public sector. Pors argues that the allure of the approach resides in its promise to combine doing more with less with increased citizen involvement and participation. The argument is also that a public value approach will correct for the managerialism and market-oriented approach of the NPM. On the contrary, Pors argues, it unleashes an even more intensive form of managerialism, one that celebrates an open-ended and flexible exploration of ever more adaptive responses in what is posited as a context of perpetual and unpredictable change. Here value is always emergent, it is made equivalent to adaptiveness to change and its time horizon is that of an unknown future. This futuristic conception of value makes it possible to entirely discount the question of the present-time relationship between resources and services by making it seem that it is impossible to predict how inputs may translate into value. 'Outcomes' are posited as something altogether different from an input–output relationship so that it is possible to argue that value can improve even when resources are cut. Pors emphasises that the adoption of the public value approach in Denmark has occurred in a context where there is a political and administrative consensus that historically established expectations of welfare services have to change, that is, to be reduced. It is in this context that the proposals to include citizens in more adaptive and innovative welfare services are to be understood. Instead of citizens being permitted to be 'passive' consumers of welfare services (as allegedly true of the traditional welfare state and NPM market models), they need to be engaged as co-producers of public value. What is posited is an untapped and unlimited potentiality of how citizens may contribute in this way. Citizens are to be co-creators of their own welfare, and to take more responsibility for their lives. Like Dahl and Soss, and Hogan, Pors points to how this approach blurs historically established boundaries, in this case, between those who are employed in public office and those who are citizens. She suggests that this new approach to social policy in Denmark is intended to replace established welfare state entitlements that follow upon an idea of citizen rights by the enrolment of citizens themselves in the managerial project of doing more with less. In this shift, the state is no longer responsible for the welfare of its citizens; instead, they are facilitated by public managers in exploring how they can find and harvest the hidden potentiality of both individuals and communities.

Anna Yeatman's chapter 'Reclaiming Professionalism in the Face of Productivism' offers a normative conception of professionalism, as an inherently public and ethical phenomenon. Professionalism is conceived as a form of knowledge that is constructed so that it constitutes a practice of service to a particular human good (e.g. health, education, law). How the professions operate as distinct disciplines or sciences is directed by their theoretical and practical attention to such a good. They are stewards of these goods. This conception of professionalism is an intentional riposte to the general view of the professions as nothing more than particular kinds of technical expertise. It is this view that prevails now within a productivist world view, an orientation to the world that makes it appear as so many resources to be manipulated, exploited and extracted on behalf of a human subject who confronts the world in Heidegger's words as standing reserve. In productivism, the object, be it human beings, other living beings or non-living things, loses its integrity. Productivism can prevail only to the extent that the abstractions of quantification and monetisation take over and displace professional attention to what it is that this person, this community, or this land considered as a living system, needs. Productivism asks of those who would be professionals if they were permitted to be to neither listen to nor heed the claim for attention on behalf of the object, a claim that is revealed after the fact, in evidence of its neglect, damage or destruction, in short, when it is too late. The productivist orientation to the world requires many different forms of expertise, and it is this requirement that repositions professionals as so many different kinds of useful technician. But in this repositioning, professionals are asked to abandon their practical ethics of professionalism, an ethics of service to a particular human good that being so can be practised only in relation to attending to those whose good is in question. This practice of attention is a practice of enabling the integrity of the object to appear as something that the professional then serves in a particular way. The antagonism of the managerial-neoliberal productivist regime to professionalism has been noted by others, for example, Quiggin (2003):

> Managerialism and neoliberalism are at one in their rejection of notions of professionalism. Both managerialists and neoliberals reject as special pleading the idea that there is any fundamental difference between, say, the operations of a hospital and the manufacturing and marketing of soft drinks. In both cases, it is claimed the optimal policy is to design organisations that respond directly to consumer demand, and to operate such institutions using the generic management techniques applicable to corporations of all kind[s].
>
> The main features of managerialist policy are incessant organisational restructuring, sharpening of incentives, and expansion in the number, power and renumeration of senior managers, with a corresponding downgrading of the role of skilled workers, and particularly of professionals.

THE TRIUMPH OF MANAGERIALISM?

Managerialism, understood as the historical symbiosis of neoliberal institutional design, corporate and financialised capitalism, technologism, and managerialism, has seemed to triumph. Yet has it? Bogdan Costea in his 'Afterword' suggests that the essence of modernity is the affirmation of subjectivity itself, and that management and managerialism are the realisation of humanity's claims to power and freedom. The self-assertion that is inherent in subjectivity is realised by bringing to full and concrete realisation the ability to produce anything, anywhere, anytime in any quantity. But here precisely lies the rub. As we are discovering, this extraordinary project of subjugating everything in order to exploit its possibilities for exemplifying this will to power has met its match: Gaia. Gaia is the name James Lovelock and Lynn Margulis gave to the assemblage of relations between living things, oceans, the atmosphere, climate, soils (Stengers 2015, 44). Stengers (2015, 44–45, emphasis in the original) comments:

> To give a name – Gaia – to this assemblage of relations was to insist on two consequences of what could be learned from this new perspective. That on which we depend, and which has so often been defined as the 'given', the globally

> stable context of our histories and our calculations, is the product of a history of co-evolution, the first artisans and real, continuing authors of which were the innumerable populations of microorganisms. And Gaia, the 'living planet' has to be recognized as a 'being', and not assimilated into a sum of processes, in the same sense that we recognize that a rat, for example, is a being: it is not just endowed with a history but with its own regime of activity and sensitivity, resulting from the manner in which the processes that constitute it are coupled with one another in multiple and entangled manners, the variation of one having multiple repercussions that affect the others. To question Gaia then is to question something that *holds together* in its own particular manner, and the questions that are addressed to any of its constituent processes can bring into play a sometimes unexpected response involving them all.

Isabelle Stengers (2015, 47) rightly says of Gaia: 'No future can be foreseen in which she will give back to us the liberty of ignoring her'. It is true that managerialism and the managerialists as 'our guardians' proceed as though there must be and will be a managerialist 'fix'. However, the tenor of our times is declared in the co-existence of two entirely contrary states of being: business as usual, where we are all mobilised as (willing or unwilling) servants of the managerialist regime; and the growing awareness that business as usual does not only not work, but that it is provoking what Stengers (2015, 53) calls 'the brutality of the intrusion of Gaia'. It is provoking also profound social distress associated not just with growing inequality but the increasingly brutal character of the managerialist regime of austerity as demonstrated in appalling cruelty, neglect and lack of respect directed at people who are unable to achieve the standard norms of performativity: people on welfare, prisoners in an increasingly privatised system of prisons, people in precarious work, refugees and undocumented immigrants. Stengers (2015, 30) suggests that 'our guardians' are also aware, they 'dread the moment when the rudder will be lost, when people will obstinately pose them questions that they cannot answer, when they will feel that the old refrains no longer work, that people judge them on their answers, that what they thought is stable, is slipping away'.

We *know*! This sense of knowing infuses the tone of all the contributions to this collection. As Stengers declares, the epoch has changed! 'It is a matter of taking it as a question, and a question that is posed, not in general, but here and now, at a moment when the grand theme of progress has already stopped being convincing' (Stengers 2015, 28).

As Malpas, Hemming and Costea suggest, notwithstanding the still-lingering Left revolutionary agonistic fantasy of overcoming, as moderns we are all implicated in the will to power. If we are to find some other way, we have to not just come alongside Gaia, but to accept that we belong to her. To do this means we give up our profound desire for control, our need to have 'the first and last word' (Stengers 2015, 50), our desire for systematicity. Stengers speaks of 'learning to compose' with Gaia, to orient in the attitude of learning to pay attention, of cultivating awareness of what it is we may experience when we do this, and of learning from this experience. The temptation is always to 'jump' experience by substituting theoretical abstraction for it, and if we do this, we cannot open ourselves to place in the way that Malpas suggests that we might. Yet there is a wealth of plenty in our human inheritance that offers examples of how it is we can compose ourselves, our relationships and our institutions, in ways that dwell within the living system of the earth. Just what it would mean to reclaim these with an attitude of awe for this living system, an attitude of honouring Gaia, an attitude of gratitude for 'human existence as it has been given, a free gift from nowhere (secularly speaking)' (Arendt 1958, 2–3), is a question for how we practice being alive in live company.

NOTES

1. Compare Mirowski (2013, 64): 'The market (suitably reengineered and promoted) can always provide solutions to problems seemingly caused by the market in the first place'.
2. Compare Slobodian (2018, 18): 'Despite their apparent victory, however, Geneva School neoliberals throughout the twentieth century were haunted by a vision of a world disintegrating. Sometimes accused of having a smug confidence in the resilience of capitalism, they instead were troubled by the possibility that the global conditions that sustain a capitalist world economy were fundamentally under threat. The dominant emotion felt by the neoliberals at the heart of my narrative was not hubris but anxiety. They expended all of their efforts in attempting to design fixes to stabilize what they saw as a precarious arrangement'.

Chapter 2

'Taking *Everything* in Hand'

Managerialism and Technology

Jeff Malpas

INTRODUCTION

Managerialism and modern technology are closely connected. This is not merely because managerialism arises in conjunction with the development of accounting, actuarial and audit practices in the nineteenth and twentieth centuries, nor even because of its frequent deployment of modern systems of surveillance, measurement and control (though both are important points of connection). Rather, managerialism has to be understood as itself a part of modern technological ordering, as belonging essentially to it and as unthinkable without it. Indeed, one might even go so far as to say that not only is managerialism a part of modern technology, part of a technological system, but that in its modern form, technology, or perhaps we should say, *technologism*, is itself managerial. Understanding how this might be so, however, requires understanding something of the distinctive character of both managerialism and modern technology.

It might be said, of course, that neither managerialism nor technology can be treated of in general, and that there is no single phenomenon that is 'managerialism' or 'technology' – merely different types of managerialism and many different technologies. This seems a rather complacent response, however, that involves turning one's eyes away from the self-evident commonalities that unite many different forms of contemporary managerialism and many different technologies as indeed instances of the managerial and of the technological. It is also to turn one's eyes away from the, perhaps surprising, degree of *convergence* among what might otherwise be thought of as indeed different phenomena (phenomena that are both very much determining and pervasively present elements of our contemporary situation). This chapter is both a response to the fact of such convergence, and to convergence as a phenomenon in its own right, and an attempt to arrive at some critical grasp of it. My aim here is to sketch out a framework that allows a synoptic view of the contemporary managerial-technological landscape (a landscape that is deeply embedded in the structure of contemporary capitalism, and so is also fundamentally economic or economistic), and, while it does not offer any immediate solution to the ills to which contemporary managerialism gives rise, it nonetheless aims to provide some insight into its essential character. The first task, however, is to understand the character of management, and then also the difference between management and managerialism – since the two cannot be simply identified, and in some respects the latter can even be seen as antithetical to the former.

THE ACTIVITY OF MANAGEMENT

If management is understood as just the 'taking of things in hand' (as might be suggested by the Latin etymology of the term[1]), then management is at work in any and every human activity – at least in respect of those activities that involve human manipulation, direction and control. Yet while one certainly can talk of 'management' in this broad fashion, such talk tends to empty the notion of management of definite content – management and managing just become other ways of referring to any form of directed or purposive activity. For the most part, in fact, management is used more narrowly to refer to a distinct *kind* of activity – to a second-order activity, one that takes other activities as its object (we may sometimes talk of managing people or things, but usually this is shorthand for managing activities or processes in which people and things are implicated), and more specifically, to an activity that is directive, coordinative or facilitative of other activities. If management is indeed a matter of 'taking things in hand', then it is a matter of taking in hand certain things, and not *everything*, and specifically of taking in hand certain activities with the aim of directing and coordinating them.

To illustrate the point at issue: neither the autoworker involved in fitting parts to a chassis on an assembly line nor the teacher involved in explaining calculus to a mathematics class is involved in management – at least not in the activities of assembly or instruction taken on their own. This is so even though both activities are likely to be embedded with a larger set of activities that do involve management, and even though both activities will depend on more basic management skills on the part of the autoworker and the teacher in the organisation of their own life and work practices. The involvement in management comes about not through being involved in just *any* activity but through being involved in having to coordinate and direct different, but related activities – as the different activities on an assembly line or that relate to different parts of an educational curriculum are connected through the larger activities and purposes that they serve.

Because management is indeed a second-order activity, and because it typically concerns the coordination and direction of different but connected activities, management becomes more complex, and itself more distinctive and salient *as an activity*, when the activities to which it is directed form a more complex and differentiated structure that typically extends beyond what any one person may do (and for this reason too, the activity of management becomes more developed and more salient in organisational contexts). Craft production, for instance, is thus less managerially disposed than industrial production (even though both involve management), not primarily because of any difference in the relevant things produced (even though there are significant differences in those things), but because of differences in the processes of production, and the structures within which production is embedded, that give rise to those things in their differences. Industrialised forms of manufacture break down the process of production into different and separately undertaken activities, usually involving a differentiated workforce (whether human or automated), allowing higher levels of output, but this also requires more managerial control precisely because of the separation in the processes at issue. For the craft producer, whose level of output is lower, the process is more integrated and unitary, typically involving a single craftsperson across the entire process (whose work, by its very character, cannot be automated), but also less managerially demanding. Management becomes more important as one moves towards more industrial, and also more technologically complex forms of production.[2]

Since management is an activity among others, though an activity that takes other activities as its object, management has its own distinctive character that sets it apart from other activities, and, so also, its own history. As the task of management has become more important, because the range of activities that make up human life become more complex and differentiated – in other words, as the organisational structure of society develops – management increasingly takes on a recognised character of its own, also developing into new and more distinctive forms. One such form is bureaucracy, which is not peculiar to modernity, but rather appears in various historical circumstances (as Weber 1978 famously documents) in ways that reflect those circumstances and so the social and political contexts that belong with them. What is crucial to note here, however, is that even bureaucracy represents a specific form of management practice, one that is distinguished from other such practices, that has various forms of its own and that is also distinct from other forms of practice and activity.

MANAGEMENT AND MANAGERIALISM

The understanding of management as a second-order activity provides the basis for recognising the distinctiveness of management as an activity in its own right. It is also the essential starting point for any investigation of the proper limits of management – the idea of limit itself being tied, in general, to the notion of that which is differentiated and distinct. Moreover, the idea of management as a distinctive kind of activity is central to the understanding of what separates management from managerialism, and so also to the characterisation of managerialism itself.

Managerialism is not identical with management, nor is it identical with the bureaucratic (though it is commonplace to treat managerialism, mistakenly, as just another form of bureaucracy[3]). What characterises managerialism is a tendency effectively to ignore the second-order character of management, and even to treat management, not always consistently, as if it were itself a first-order activity or, more accurately perhaps, to efface the very distinction between activities as first- or second-order. Moreover, inasmuch as managerialism effaces the difference between managerialism and management, so it also effaces the idea of management as a distinctive kind of activity – which also means, to draw upon the term Weber (2004c) uses, that contemporary managerialism can have no sense of its own 'vocation' (nor, indeed, of any other 'vocation' either).[4]

The way this effacement of distinction occurs is not through any simple denial of the second-order character of management or the straightforward affirmation of management as a first-order activity – managerialism does not deny that there are activities, like auto assembly or teaching, that are ostensibly the objects towards which management is directed. Yet it also tends to appropriate all activities to the sphere of the managerial, effectively extending managerial practice into even those activities that would ordinarily be the object of such practice. This does not occur merely through taking activities that may otherwise have escaped the managerial gaze and making them into objects of managerialism – although part of what characterises managerialism is indeed the encompassing character of managerial attention: nothing is so minute or so seemingly irrelevant that it cannot be made part of the managerial project (something reflected in the concern of so many contemporary organisations to manage their 'brand' down to the smallest detail of organisational operation and presentation). The result is effectively that any and every activity is seen as having a managerial component at the same time as any and every agent becomes, to some extent, a manager or, at least, is seen as having managerial responsibilities (something strikingly in contrast with older conceptions of management, as Paul du Gay 2015 points out).

The way this occurs within most contemporary organisations is through increased reporting, compliance and audit requirements that are imposed across the organisation as a whole, usually in generic fashion, and that are most strongly felt at the lower levels of the organisation, sometimes significantly changing the character of activities at that level. This is most obviously the case in those organisations whose primary focus is on activities that involve high level of human interaction with hospitals, schools and universities being obvious examples, but all organisations oriented to the provision of services are hugely affected in this way, and very few organisations are exempt. Typically, the extension of managerial demands across all activities and with respect to all agents occurs alongside constant processes of 'structural readjustment' that almost invariably lead to reduction in management support at the same time as there is an increase in managerial demands, and that serve to reinforce managerial control through maintenance of a constant state of uncertainty and challenge. This is often experienced by employees within organisations in terms of the need to do 'more with less' and so to increase levels of performance at the same time as both resources and genuine autonomy in the workplace are significantly reduced. The increase in compliance and audit systems usually brings with it a commensurate reduction in levels of trust and respect within organisations, as 'systemic' organising managerialist technologies take over from collective commitments, shared values and the cultivation of interpersonal relations.

The introduction of automated and online systems has made possible such an imposition of managerial work in a way that it would not have been before (and this is one of the most obvious ways in which managerialism and technology draw together). The way this is experienced for many members of contemporary organisations is through an increase in electronically mediated managerialisation of activity – in more online forms and processes, and systems of authorisation and notification. Online delivery has become the standard, and often stand-alone, way to meet various compliance requirements in many areas of staff training and information. The shift to online systems has invariably been promoted as increasing efficiency and reducing costs (including staffing costs). Yet there is very little independent evidence that online systems have the beneficial effects claimed for them, even as they actually operate to proliferate and extend managerial activity.

The extension of managerial practice into all activities and areas of organisations inevitably gives rise to whole new areas of managerial work that did not exist previously – managerial activity typically begets more managerial activity. It is this that gives rise to what has been called empty work or, in David Graeber's (2013, 2018) phrase, 'bullshit jobs' – areas of managerial activity that have no object apart from their relation to other managerial activities, and that themselves generate further such activities, but seem entirely disconnected from any end other than the managerial. Although there is an increasing focus on the loss of employment opportunity due to increasing automation and the rise of more sophisticated forms of 'artificial intelligence', the reality of managerial work over the past half century or so is that it has not reduced but increased the number of managerial jobs. Indeed, it is hard to see how jobs that have no real content – Graeber's 'bullshit jobs' for instance – are likely to be threatened by automation, since, one might argue, there is nothing much to automate in the first place. More significantly, it is important to note that many of these jobs have themselves arisen as a result of automation, or at least, of new forms of managerial activity that are themselves created by the rise of online and automated systems. Online management systems are perhaps best understood as cost-shifting mechanisms (which is why they can give the appearance of being cost-reducing), since they allow managerial work to displace the work of those who were organisational 'managers' onto those filling other, non-managerial, and frontline roles (here is one of the ways in which online systems reinforce the tendency for managerial tasks to become more widespread and pervasive across organisations).

The rise of managerialism has sometimes been associated, particularly in the last quarter of the twentieth century, with 'flatter' management structures as organisations have sought to increase centralised managerial control by removing those middle-level managers who are often seen as a barrier to organisational change (that they are a barrier is directly related to the ways in which, in the past, they represented the key lynchpins between the activities of management and the 'productive' activities at more basic levels of the organisation). One might see this shift as part of the historical development of managerialism, since there was a point at which middle-level managers, because of their communicating and mediating roles, effectively served as a buffer and barrier to the imposition of managerial systems across organisations in their entirety. The shift to flatter structures was thus one of the mechanisms by which organisations became more amenable to a more extensive system of managerial control, but such flatter structures can be seen as merely the preliminary stage to what are often more proliferated and hierarchical managerial systems. At the same time, *ad hoc* managerial positions now seem also to be more numerous, often in the form of outside consultants, but frequently through the creation of one-off advisory or other special purpose positions.

GENERICISM, QUANTITY AND NUMBER

The rise of managerialism has meant that organisations are increasingly driven by generic, determinative and invasive managerial processes and systems that are imposed by decision makers who are typically removed from the specific operational context of the organisation in question – removed physically, but also, in virtue of the generic nature of managerial practice, behaviourally and conceptually. In spite of its obvious drawbacks, the advantage of such an approach is that it centralises control while dispersing and depersonalising responsibility. Managerialism removes the emphasis from the management of the activities that make up the real operational work of the organisation, and the values that underpin those activities, shifting the focus onto processes and systems that are themselves more amenable to manipulation (because more removed from the activities themselves), and that also allow managerial work to be more easily and abstractly represented – thereby reinforcing a sense of control and direction.

Since managerial processes are indeed generic, they are also amenable to generalised descriptors such as 'quality', 'excellence', 'efficiency' and 'accountability'. Since managerial practice aims to exercise control over the discursive and rhetorical structures that function within organisations, managerial activity can be advanced, and managerial success can often be achieved (or so it readily appears), simply by manipulation of those discursive and rhetorical structures. It is thus no surprise that managerialism has been so productive in its constant generation of new discursive and rhetorical strategies, forms and vocabularies – and with this, as many commentators have noted, in emptying out meaning and significance from the very language that it employs (see Watson 2004; Spicer 2018; Holborow 2015). Managerialism makes use of language as part of the larger structure of managerial activity, and as a key means by which managerial systems become part of the very structure of all activity, both through the appropriation of non-managerial language into a managerial vocabulary (so even evaluative concepts that might seem to be antithetical to a managerial frame become themselves 'managerialised'[5]) and through the extension of managerial terms and concepts into all other contexts and domains (reflecting the broader extension and expansion of the managerial itself).

Since managerial practice tends towards the generic in its character and application, including in its discursive and rhetorical operation, it also tends to reduce organisations to processes and systems, often represented in abstract and generic discursive forms that have little engagement with the basic activities or the underlying end values and *ethos* of an organisation. As a result, those individuals who gain managerial advancement within organisations need not have any commitment to those organisations' end values, since managerial effectiveness will come increasingly to depend purely on a mastery of generic managerial forms. The separation of managerial practice from any distinctive organisational values or a distinctive *ethos* makes it more likely that those who do gain advancement within an organisation will have no commitment to that organisation or its values (no interest in what the organisation does as a *distinctive* institution), but will be wholly focused on the management of the processes and systems that are seen as underpinning the organisation's activities – processes and systems that will indeed be largely generic. Consequently, just as managerialism is corrosive of any conception of management as itself a distinctive kind of activity and also tends to be corrosive of the distinctive character of other activities, it is also corrosive of any distinctive character that may belong to an organisation. This is especially problematic for public institutions that have traditionally been constituted around a distinctive organisational ethos – universities and schools, for instance, increasingly have difficulty articulating any sense of educational or research values and commitments that might override or constrain the requirements of the managerial, and the same is true of the structures of government and law. Even businesses may find it more and more difficult to hold onto a sense of organisational purpose and integrity beyond a set of narrowly and purely managerial objectives, and this may even reinforce the already-existing tendencies that favour the success of those businesses that are themselves oriented to purely managerial services (notably those businesses within the audit and finance sectors).[6]

The genericisation that is so characteristic of managerialism is itself related to the managerial tendency to give preference to quantitative over qualitative modes of evidence, assessment and analysis. Indeed, it is partly the focus on the quantitative – and so also the numerical – that enables managerial genericisation. Quantity and number become the universal currency into which everything can be translated; a currency that enables the more effective release of managerial practice from any need genuinely to engage with the first-order activities on which such practice ought properly to supervene. Not only does the emphasis on the quantitative give priority to that which is countable and measureable, but it also effectively leaves out of account, and actively excludes, what cannot be counted or measured. The exclusion is not merely a setting of certain things aside as beyond the horizon of the managerial – thereby recognising a limit to managerial practice – but precisely because managerialism refuses the idea that anything can escape managerial control, such exclusion is effectively an effacing of that which falls outside its grasp. Managerialism takes everything in hand, or so it presents itself, and so what it cannot take in hand is nothing at all. This remains the case even when managerialism plays lip service to the idea that there are some things it cannot encompass – the hegemony exerted by managerialism within contemporary organisations and across much of contemporary, and especially Anglo-American, society means that what falls outside of the managerial is effectively rendered irrelevant and valueless.

In the end, the managerial emphasis on the quantitative draws everything within the orbit of one specific form of quantity, namely the monetary, and it does so because this is the one quantitative measure that does indeed appear to be applicable across the board. Of almost any and every activity that is to be managed, one can ask: what does it cost, and how much income does it generate? It is thus not merely the quantification of activity that is characteristic of managerialism, but its monetisation. This shift to the monetary brings other important shifts in its train. It allows the implicit (and sometimes explicit) repositioning of the values framework within organisations, already hollowed out by the distancing of managers from any more fundamental end values, around purely financial and monetary considerations. This is reinforced by, as well as reinforcing of, the tendency for those at the centre of managerial structures, the executive managers themselves, to have their own worth defined in purely monetary terms (although, as noted earlier, this also happens more broadly across organisations, and is tied to both the individualising and monetising tendencies of managerial practice, see Malpas 2012). Even the language of 'corporate social responsibility' does little to counter this monetising tendency,[7] often serving actually to strengthen it, since invariably the justification of such approaches is in terms of the monetarily or financially advantageous or prudential. Thus 'ethical business' is routinely touted as being 'good business', which is to say that it is to be recommended, not primarily because it is ethical, but because it is in the monetary and financial interests of organisations.[8]

The emphasis on the quantitative here is not countered by the continued use of qualitative language within managerial practice. 'Excellence', 'creativity', 'agility', 'resilience' are all qualitative terms, among many others, that are deployed by contemporary managerialism. Yet their employment does not demonstrate any qualitative commitment that goes against the emphasis on the quantitative, since these terms typically operate, not as giving primacy to some real and irreducible quality that is the focus of managerial practice, but rather (and in line with what was said earlier about the nature of managerial language) as rhetorical devices used to endorse and so to promote certain organisational outcomes that are themselves understood largely quantitatively. Indeed, when terms like 'excellence' or 'agility' function as more than empty signifiers, and are instead tied, even if indirectly, to real outcomes, those outcomes are invariably quantitative in character.[9] Similarly, the dominance of quality assurance processes and mechanisms within many organisations in Britain and Australasia does not demonstrate any concern with the qualitative over the quantitative. Part of what is distinctive about quality assurance is its focus on systems for measuring and tracking quality by means of what are essentially quantitative means. Within the context of quality assurance circles, this is made most evident by the constant demand to justify qualitative claims and the assumption that such justification can be achieved only by reference to quantitative data or to processes that can give rise to such data.

Precisely because management operates as a second-order activity, there will always be a tendency for management to operate somewhat removed from the activities and that are its objects. On this basis it might be argued that the tendency towards the generic and the abstract that characterises the managerial is simply a tendency inherent in the practice of management as such – that such tendencies are inevitable and necessary. There is, of course, a degree of continuity between management, in general, and managerialism, just as one can also find points of continuity between managerialism and bureaucracy, but continuity does not rule out difference, and managerialism does indeed depart from other forms of management practice. This is true especially in respect of the managerialist tendency toward genericisation and abstraction. What marks out the way these appear within a managerialist frame is their completely unconstrained character. Moreover, as will be seen in the discussion that follows, both the genericisation of managerial practices and the associated tendency to quantification and numericisation are closely connected (as are quantity and number as such) with a spatialised thinking that itself effaces any sense of boundary and limit (and so also difference). This also means that even though managerialism has a systematic character about it – systematic because of the way it draws everything together – that systematicity nevertheless lacks any integrity beyond that of mere subjection to an otherwise arbitrary spatialised, and so also numericised, ordering. The constraints that have defined and governed past forms of management, especially bureaucratic management, thus tend to disappear in the face of managerialist practice, since such constraints cannot even be represented within the form of systematicity that operates managerially, and are often erased by it.

It is for these reasons that contemporary managerialism frequently has the appearance of inconsistency, even of irrationality (why, too, it is often antagonistic to notions of formalised process and procedure[10]), and why, once again, it is corrosive of any form of practice, including the genuinely ethical, that depends upon more substantive notions that would limit, constrain and differentiate. The genericisation that managerialism brings to its activities and objects – effectively a levelling-out of everything in which all differences become essentially arbitrary – affects managerialism itself. Any attempt to delineate the character of managerialism has to attend to managerialism's own generic and often-shifting character, its tendency towards the arbitrary and the *ad hoc*. Thus, the very attempt to separate out the managerial as a distinctive mode of management practice has to contend with the fact that part of what is distinctive about managerialism is its resistance to any such attempt and its own blurring of the boundaries between managerialism and other forms of management practice. This means that the critique of managerialism will always have a certain awkwardness about it as it seeks both to reassert the need for distinction and differentiation at the same time as it must also attend to the way in which part of what is essential to managerialism is its own tendency to efface such distinction and differentiation even in its own self-formation.

MANAGERIALISM AND TECHNOLOGISM

Generic and sometimes diffuse though it may be, managerialism can nevertheless be understood as itself a technology, and an especially pervasive and ubiquitous one. Although it draws upon a range of more specific technological systems and devices, managerialism also provides a very particular framework within which such systems and devices operate and are directed, as well as shapes the development of new such systems and devices. Managerialism is thus a specific form of technology, and yet its character as a system of ordering reflects the character of technology more generally: technology just is a system for the ordering of the world, and increasingly, for the ordering of the world *in its entirety*. In this respect, technology is not reducible to any specific device or even any single technique – it is indeed an ordering or assemblage or ordering, and as such, it is essentially *systematic* in the specific sense that it operates at the level of the encompassing structure rather than being identifiable with any element or component within that structure.

That it is systematic thus does not imply any sense in which the technological structure is 'well-fitted' to some purpose or that it is more 'rational' or 'efficient'. Such notions have no absolute or neutral meaning, their content always deriving from a specific context of evaluation, and strictly speaking, such evaluative frameworks lie outside of the technological, do not belong to it and are effectively ignored by it. Similarly, it is a mistake to treat technology as primarily 'instrumental' – such a notion of instrumentality implies a sense of a non-technological 'end' that the technological serves, but any such instrumental relationship is accidental to the character of technology as such (and this is so even though the economic and social context in which technology is embedded is one in which the technological is almost always represented, or *misrepresented*, in instrumental terms). The sense of systematicity that applies to technology involves nothing more than the idea of the constantly expanding operational connection and connectivity of the technological structure as a whole, and this is completely indifferent to any extra-technological standards or ends, and indeed, precisely because of its ever-expanding and encompassing character, it actually tends to overtake, and so also to obliterate or to efface any such standards or ends.

The character of technology as systematic in this way is more significant and salient as technology is more developed – the more developed, the more its systematic character is evident. The simplest technologies reveal themselves as systematic in only a rudimentary fashion – the stone tools used by Palaeolithic peoples are part of a fairly simple system of tools and practices, and any single tool can still function effectively even when the rest of the system of tools breaks down (so a Palaeolithic stone tool can still be used today even if there is seldom an occasion for such use) and in spite of the removal of the tools from their original context. Compare this with a mobile phone or any other sophisticated contemporary device which is utterly useless when removed from the systematic structure of which it is only a part. Significantly, the same points about systematicity also apply to managerialism and its mechanisms: managerialism emerges as a technique or technology only to the extent that management develops in a similarly systematic and ramified fashion, and only amid the larger system of contemporary technologies on which managerialism necessarily draws, to which it also contributes and of which it is an integral part. The technological character of managerialism is thus directly tied to its essentially encompassing and connecting character – and the systematic character of managerialism, already briefly discussed earlier, is not a systematicity subordinated to any end that lies outside the managerial system: the only real end of managerialism is the continuation and extension of managerialist practice.

The inter-implication of managerialism with technology occurs both at the level of a similar 'systematicity' of structure and operation and in terms of the same tendencies towards genericisation and quantisation – tendencies that are, indeed, at the very heart of contemporary technology across all of its different forms. To some extent, such tendencies derive from the character of modern natural scientific practice to which contemporary technology is closely tied and by reference to which managerialism also attempts to legitimate its own practice. The great shift in the rise of modern natural science that occurred in the sixteenth and seventeenth centuries was the shift towards a mathematical, and hence numerical and quantitative, but also *spatial*, understanding of the world. The way space is implicated here is especially noteworthy. The shift from ancient to modern science – from the Aristotelian to the Cartesian or Newtonian, let us say – which is a shift from the qualitative to the quantitative, and from the organic and discursive to the numerical, is also a shift from a world of heterogenous places to a world of homogenous space (see Koyre 1957).

Place possesses a singularity (always amid a plurality, since every place nests itself and nests within other places) that resists quantification and numericisation as well as genericisation. Space, on the other hand, can be understood purely metrically – in terms of what is measurable (the etymology of the term going back to the Greek *spadion*/*stadion* as a unit of distance), and so in terms purely of quantity and number. As such, space possesses neither singularity (nor plurality) other than as might arbitrarily be determined.[11]

The spatial, the quantitative and the numerical belong essentially together – indeed, there can be no conception of number or of quantity without a conception of space. Thus Immanuel Kant argues that even the representation of time requires space and empirical psychological studies suggest that the understanding of number is dependent on space also (De Hevia, Girelli and Cassia 2012). Inasmuch as modern scientific thinking is characterised by a tendency towards forms of *reductive* analysis – understanding things in terms of their discrete components – then spatialisation is an essential element in such thinking, since space provides the necessary frame within which those components can be arrayed alongside one another. Unlike place, which always appears in terms of a plurality of different places, so that every *where* is different, space appears the same everywhere, so that every *where* is the same. Moreover, whereas place brings with an essential boundedness – implied by both the singularity and plurality of place and places (singularity being tied to irreducible difference) – space carries no such limitation within it. Just as every quantity allows of increase, so every space allows of further extension, at least notionally, and there is nothing intrinsic to space, any more than of quantity or number, that implies its restriction – the very idea of a boundary *in space* that does indeed constitute the boundary *of that very space* seems incoherent.

The spatial understanding of the world that characterises modern science extends into modern technology – and is indeed exemplified by the all-encompassing and seemingly boundless reach of modern technological systems. The idea of the world as encompassing a multiplicity of places has nowadays been overtaken by the idea of the world as a single integrated space – a space of flows and connections in which borders and boundaries are increasingly irrelevant. Such an idea, and the rhetoric associated with it, has not only become ubiquitous within contemporary business and politics, but it now also suffuses theoretical and academic discussions from sociology and geography through to art and architecture. The contemporary world, understood as fundamentally determined by contemporary technology, thus appears as essentially characterised by its unbounded, spatial character – an unbounded spatiality that is the exact correlate of the systematic and encompassing character of the technological itself. There is thus no part of the contemporary world that stands apart from the rest, no part that is not drawn into the same web of connection and connectivity. The encompassing systematicity that is at issue here is especially evident in the phenomenon of technological *convergence*: the bringing together of functions and activities within or in relation to single devices and systems – most obviously in the mobile phone or other electronic device – and in the convergence of services and activities within single locations such as the shopping mall, supermarket, airport or gas station (the latter locations being themselves brought together even more through the use of mobile and online technologies).[12] What technological ordering does, in fact, is increasingly to enable everything to be accessed and 'managed' in the same fashion and by the same means – allowing *everything* to be 'taken in hand' – to be positioned, measured and manipulated *within and in relation to the same space*.

Yet it is not merely that technology *enables* such encompassing managerialism: just as managerialism is itself technological – is itself technologism – so also can technology be seen as managerial precisely in its systematic and encompassing character and in its reduction of everything to the status of something that can be the object of a specific technology, device or application. Technology and managerialism are themselves *convergent* phenomena such that there is almost nothing to choose between them. Moreover, given the close relationship between managerialism and the contemporary prioritisation of the economic, the financial and the monetary (the dominance, in other words, of a certain form of capitalism), as well as the increasing convergence of the technological with the economic and financial (perhaps nowhere better exemplified than in the generation of wealth through the 'mining' of cryptocurrencies such as Bitcoin[13]), but also in the very conception of the market as itself a computational system or 'machine'), then so one might also say that all three – technologism, managerialism and 'economism' are not separate, but different faces of the same phenomenon. The convergence of these three might itself be seen as exemplifying the convergence that can be observed as so characteristic of contemporary technology, and so to be driven by technology as it extends into the managerial and economic. But the tendency to convergence – to the drawing together of everything within the same framework of control and manipulation – is just as much at the heart of the managerial and the economistic as of the technological. In each case what we see is the same drive towards constant systematicisation, towards the same integration and connection, that occurs through spatialisation, and through the genericisation, quantification and monetisation with which spatialisation is so closely implicated. Indeed, if it is indeed a single phenomenon that is at work here, then perhaps it is the drive to convergence itself.

The relation between convergence and spatialisation requires some further examination, especially since spatialisation might be thought to involve a setting of things apart rather than a drawing of things together. From the start, however, it should be noted that the very language at work here – of both setting apart and drawing together – is itself spatial, and the same point may be made about the language of connection and of convergence. It is no accident that, over and above the tendency towards spatialisation that is such an inevitable part of modern science anyway, contemporary social sciences have increasingly looked to more developed forms of spatial analysis to understand the developments of modernity itself – the 'spatial turn' in contemporary theory reflects the central role of the spatial in the way the contemporary world itself appears. Spatiality and spatialisation are thus already operative at a very basic level, conceptually and linguistically. When we look to the operation of convergence within contemporary technology, then its close connection to spatialisation is readily apparent. Convergence occurs through both connection and concentration, that is, in the ideal case, through connecting everything up within a single extended space that allows for the effective concentration of the entire space at any one point within it – entry into the whole space is made possible through any one point in the space. One can see how this works in more concrete terms in the case of smartphone technology in which the phone allows access not only to an entire network of other phones (thereby also making itself accessible to that network) but also to a network of sites, information, functions and activities – and all via the one device. It is precisely the positioning of everything within the one network, which is to say, within the one connected space, that allows for the accessibility of things from within the network.

Although it may be less immediately evident, and may also operate differently, the same relation between spatialisation and convergence is evident within the managerial (and, one might add, within the economistic also). Both Fordism and Taylorism, each of which can be seen as instantiating early forms of managerialism, rely very clearly on spatialised modes of organisation and analysis, whether in the form of the production line or the time-and-motion study, that themselves derive from the deployment of essentially reductive approaches. It is this reduction down to discrete components that allows otherwise diverse activities to be understood and organised as part of a larger connected system – spatialised reduction allows connection which in turn allows systematicity which further allows convergence – in other words, the bringing of things into one frame, even a single location or device, for manipulation and control. Even if Fordism and Taylorism have largely receded into the past, the general approach that they exemplify continues in contemporary managerialism. Successive managerialist approaches – Quality Management, New Public Management, Value-for Money – all exemplify the same tendencies towards reductive and genericising approaches that enable more encompassing managerial practice through similarly spatialised modes of analysis.

The way spatialisation underpins the expansion and concentration of managerial practice is not only apparent in terms of the overall style of analysis and approach, but also in the way managerialism is instantiated in the everyday operation of organisations, and in their concrete forms and structure. As already noted earlier, contemporary managerialism typically operates in a way that removes upper-level managers almost entirely from the activities they manage – which means their physical removal from the spaces in which those activities take place – as well as increases managerial intervention into all activities and so into any and every space (and so too the increasing genericisation of those spaces). Indeed, control over physical space itself becomes a key managerial tool. Nowhere is this more evident than in the tendency within some organisations to dispense with dedicated workspaces altogether and to replace them with open-plan areas filled with 'hot desks' that are available for use by any employee as needed. Equipped with laptop or tablet and phone, employees can work anywhere and in whatever way they prefer, but at the same time, they are also made more amenable to managerial surveillance and control, and their work roles are made more generic and flexible. What occurs in such cases is, of course, a shift from a mode of spatial organisation in which there are many different spaces to a mode of organisation in which there is just one managerial space within which all employees are located.[14] This unifying mode of spatial organisation is one way in which convergence operates here; and it shows the same character of reduction (in this case to the individual employee), connection into a larger systematic structure, and concentration of access, activity and function that is evident elsewhere. The fact that such a mode of spatial organisation depends on new digital and mobile technologies merely underscores the way managerialism and technologism are indeed closely intertwined, just as the increasing role of digital technology in the financial sector similarly underscores the intertwining of technologism and economism.

MANAGERIALISM AND THE ERASURE OF LIMIT

One of the key features of managerialism, a feature identified near the very start of this discussion, is its tendency to ignore the second-order character of management, and to treat management as if it were itself a first-order activity or to efface the very distinction between activities as first- or second order. It is this that distinguishes managerialism from management, and so also from particular forms of management such as the bureaucratic, but it is also a feature that can now be seen to be closely tied to the spatialising and convergent tendencies that managerialism exemplifies. In this respect, it is not merely the difference between first- and second-order activities that managerialism effectively effaces, or even the character of managerialism as itself a distinctive form, but all manner of differences and distinctions that would otherwise stand in the way of the encompassing reach of managerial practice. Dave Eggers's novel *The Circle*,[15] usually read as a critique of contemporary social media and the Internet, also provides a striking exploration of this aspect of contemporary managerialism. The fictional company that is at the centre of Eggers's novel – a company that bears clear resemblance to companies such as Facebook and Google/Alphabet – exhibits many of the aspects of the managerialism discussed here, albeit rhetorically positioned to appear benign and friendly, but it is a managerialism that extends beyond the space of the company alone to encompass almost all aspects of the lives of the company's employees and their families and, ultimately, even of the lives of those who use the company's products. In Eggers's novel any distinction between the managerial, the technological and the economic fall by the wayside as everything is taken up into the same encompassing and essentially spatialised frame. At the same time as the focus is placed on the individual, the individual is completely opened up to the entire connected space of digitally mediated interaction and attention.

The basic ideas at work in Eggers's *The Circle* are not new – just as the analysis of the managerial, the technological and the economic that has been drawn upon here is adumbrated in the work of many other writers from Adorno to Weber and Heidegger to Simmel, so Eggers's fictional depiction echoes ideas and themes present in the work of many other dystopian writers from Huxley and Orwell to Zamyatin and many others in between. The phenomenon that I have described in terms of convergence, and its operation through modes of spatialisation, is not always directly thematised in the way indicated here, but what appears in managerial terms as the erasure of difference – not only the difference between activities and kinds of activity, but between work and home, between public and personal, between the managerial and that which lies outside the managerial, between the human and the non-human, between truth and falsehood – is indeed a common and unifying theme across many of these different analysis and depictions. This erasure of difference can itself be seen as a function of spatialisation, and as such it is also tied to the tendency to prioritise quantity and number, but it is also a direct consequence of the disappearance, within any purely spatial ordering, of any genuine sense of bound or limit. It is this that was noted earlier as a key element in the rise of modern science – and one might say that it is perhaps the key idea within modernity and certainly within the 'project of modernity' as that arises out of the Enlightenment. Modernity is precisely the desire to escape from limit.

In any specific case, the overcoming of limitation is not, in itself, problematic. It becomes so only when it is generalised, when the productive power of limit is not itself recognised and when the desire to overcome limit lacks any sense of its own limit – in other words, when the very idea of limit has been set aside. In the case of the managerial, it is its inability to recognise any limit or bound to its range of operation or application that leads to its treatment of all activities as subject to it in the same way, and that can even lead to the sort of extension of the managerial into the realm of ordinary life that Eggers, perhaps unintentionally, presents to us. What is implied here, of course, is that the inability to recognise bound or limit, and even the seeming erasure of limit, does not mean that all limits or bounds are thereby rendered ineffectual or that they are indeed erased. If managerialism could indeed achieve what it implicitly assumes already is the case – namely the taking of everything in hand in a way that can ensure complete and unfailing control or at least moves us significantly towards that end – then managerialism would have no limit to constrain it, and the question of its limits or bounds would not arise. Yet there can be no such all-encompassing managerial grasp, not only because the world itself always exceeds any and every attempt to 'manage' it, but because not even managerialism can extend to encompass its own situation, its own character, its own limits – managerialism itself will always lie outside of managerial control.

This is both the strength of managerialism and its weakness. It means that any critique of managerialism is almost impossible to mount in terms that managerialism will itself recognise, since any such critique depends on being able to understand what managerialism itself is as distinct from other forms of discourse or organisational formation – which is to recognise the limits that define and determine managerialism – but this is precisely what managerialism refuses. Yet because managerialism lies outside of managerialism's own grasp, so it cannot recognise its own inevitable tendencies to failure and incompleteness.[16] Exactly the same point holds for contemporary technologism and economism and is reflected in the almost-complete inability within contemporary discourse to mount effective counter movements to the dominance of any of these. Managerialism, economism and technologism seem able constantly to reorganise and reposition themselves even in the face of the crises that they themselves engender. How they may realise themselves may thus change – different technological devices or systems may appear and disappear, different managerial structures and discourses may displace others, different economic instruments or vocabularies, different modes of calculation, even different markets, may come and go. But these are indeed changes merely in the modes by which the underlying phenomenon at issue – the tendency towards convergence that itself operates through contemporary technologism, managerialism and economism – is instantiated.

Just as the convergence at issue here is directly tied to spatialisation, so the seeming erasure of limit and bound in the face of the connection and connectivity that such convergence entails is also tied to the erasure of place. To invoke place in this context is not to engage in any form of metaphorisation, but rather to take seriously the genuine role of the spatial and the topographic in the constitution of the world and in any and all forms of human engagement with the world (see the discussion of metaphorisation in Malpas 2018, 36–37). This means that what we see in managerialism, in technologism and in economism is a reconfiguration of the way the world appears and so of the places and spaces of such appearance. The idea of the world as an interconnected spatial domain – a field of network and flow – is fundamental to the operation of the managerial and technological structures and systems (as well as the economistic) that have been the focus of this discussion. In contrast, the idea of the world as constituted in and through the singularity of places, a singularity that is complex and pluralistic even as it is also singular, brings a very different mode of world conception and appearance – one that draws attention to notions of limit and bound, including the limits and bounds, and to forms of *divergence* as well as convergence. In terms of the practice of management, such a topographical rather than spatialised conception requires attentiveness to both the placed character of the activities that are the objects of management (and so to the distinctive singularity of those activities even as one also attends to one's generality) and the placed character of management practice itself. Indeed, the Weberian idea of vocation, taking this as representative of an alternative conception of management to the managerial, can be seen to bring with it just such a conception of place: in both the English and the original German term (*Beruf*) we can still hear the sense of that which *calls*, and any such call is always a call to something from somewhere, a call that is possible only within the bounded realm that allows such a call to sound, to be heard and to be responded to.

CONCLUSION

As will be clear the critique of managerialism and of technologism and economism is not intended to imply any wholesale rejection of the activity of management, nor of any particular economic device or system, nor even of economics as a discipline or field of inquiry. Rather the aim is to understand the importance of retaining a sense of the proper limits – *the proper place* – within which each of these operates, and by which each is also constituted. This is also why it is so important to recognise the legitimacy of the very inquiry into what these each might be – why the question as to the nature of management and the managerial, the nature of the technological, the nature of the economic cannot simply be set aside as either too general or too 'essentialist'. To refuse such an inquiry is also to refuse to engage with the limits of things, including our own limits and so our very selves, to refuse to recognise the actual place in which we find ourselves. The inquiry into limit, which is also an inquiry into place, is itself the most fundamental, perhaps the only genuine form, of critique, and it is precisely the loss of any ability to understand limit, or indeed, to allow room for its articulation, that underpins the weakness of much contemporary critical discourse. Thus although managerialism has been the focus of much of this discussion, the underlying issue at stake here is not managerialism, nor technologism, nor economism, but rather the refusal of limit, of bound, of place that these each exemplify, and that is part of their own essential limitation.

NOTES

1. The Latin noun *manus* 'hand' is at the root of the term, but it derives more immediately from the Italian *maneggiare*, meaning 'to handle', and especially 'to handle a horse', and the French *manège* meaning 'horsemanship'. Its extension to the handling of business matters occurred in English in the sixteenth century.
2. There are craft activities that rely on sophisticated technology, but typically those activities remain craft activities because the technology is still secondary to the skill of the individual craftsperson who remains individually responsible for all or most of the process of production. It is precisely the role of the craftsperson over and above the technology (whether it be the technology involved in the form of potter's wheel or a laser-cutter) that makes a certain type of production into craft production. On the character of craft production, see Richard Sennett (2008).
3. This is commonplace in much of the critique of contemporary managerialism, and as a consequence it often tends to overlook the distinctive character of the managerial and the bureaucratic – see Paul du Gay (2015).
4. See Weber (2004). This Weberian idea largely underpins Paul du Gay's (2015) critique of the New Public Management as he develops it in relation to the idea of 'office'.
5. The general phenomenon here is one that I have referred to elsewhere as the 'subversion of the good' – see Malpas (2016).
6. Also associated with this tendency towards the corrosion of organisational integrity and organisational values is the corrosion of genuinely ethical practice and commitment. Even ethics itself has been assimilated to managerialist practice through various audit and compliance mechanisms that often serve to enable unethical behaviour rather than prevent it – in part, because such mechanisms have no grounding in any developed concept of the ethical as such, nor in any form of genuinely ethical culture, but are indeed underpinned by what is effectively a reduction of all value to monetary value. On the corrosion of ethical practice and commitment, see Malpas (2012, 2016).
7. It might be argued, in fact, that it is one of the means by which it is obscured or disguised – see for example, Margaret E. Ormiston and Elaine M. Wong (2013), and Subhabrata Bobby Banerjee (2008). The idea of the triple bottom line fares little better as a way of promoting more ethically attentive or socially responsible business practice in part because the concept is more rhetorical than practical.
8. Even if it were this true, it would remain irrelevant to the ethical imperative as such. One might argue that this is blurred by the dominance of certain forms of utilitarian thinking (which might themselves be said to undermine any sense of the genuine distinctiveness of ethical practice), but utilitarianism aside, the idea that ethical practice in business can be justified or motivated by its efficacy as a

business strategy is both to misunderstand the nature of the ethical and to run the risk of seeming to imply that ethical practice is only justified or motivated when it serves the interests of business (and not justified or motivated otherwise).

9. For a critique of the language of 'resilience' in contemporary discourse, see Jacobs and Malpas (2017).
10. See again Paul du Gay's work on the idea of 'office' and the loss of formality of office within New Public Management.
11. For this reason too there is no genuine nesting of space or spaces – space forms a unitary continuum in which there is neither any non-arbitrary divisibility of space and spaces nor any non-arbitrary sense of within and without. Interiority and exteriority, plurality and singularity, come to be attributed to space and spaces only when they are effectively treated topologically and so assimilated to place – such assimilation being both quite widespread and the fact of its occurrence often going unrecognised and unacknowledged.
12. The sorts of locations at issue here are the same locations Marc Augé has referred to as 'non-places' and that he takes to be exemplary of 'supermodernity'. See Augé (1995). As originally formulated, Augé's 'non-places' are transitional places. Yet their character as transitional may actually be a reflection of their more fundamental character as indeed convergent spaces in the sense suggested earlier. One might ask whether contemporary workspaces exhibit some of the same convergence that is at issue here, and perhaps they do, though in a slightly unusual way – the very idea of the workspace as a distinctive space is itself starting to dissolve as the workspace comes to be identified with the space established by digital communication and computing devices in which all aspects of personal and work life are brought together. Eggers's *The Circle* (discussed later) itself provides a useful illustration of this tendency.
13. And even though such cryptocurrencies might fluctuate in value, the general tendency they exemplify remains clearly evident.
14. In general, the character of human life and experience is heavily dependent on the character of the spaces and places in which life and experience are played out – a point I develop at greater length in Malpas (2018). For this reason, any attempt to shape or direct human life and experience must operate at the level of space and place – and the way managerialism operates through the control of work spaces is a simple consequence of this basic fact.
15. Although most earlier dystopian novels typically focus on structures tied to the state or to large-scale social structures, Eggers's focus on corporate dystopianism is an increasingly common tendency in contemporary fiction. It might be noted, too, that the dystopian is itself an increasingly common theme. A film adaptation of the novel was adapted and directed by James Ponsoldt.
16. For more on the inevitability of failure in any and every managerial or 'governmental' (but especially technological) project, see Malpas and Wickham (1995, 1997). The tendency to failure that is also inevitable within technological systems has also been the subject of considerable discussion but see especially Paul Virilio (1999, 2007) who argues that 'every technology carries its own negativity, which is invented at the same time as technical progress'.

Chapter 3

Managerialism as Will to Power

Technologies of Capital[1]

Laurence Paul Hemming

INTRODUCTION

What do we mean when we speak of 'new technologies of government'? Surely nothing other than the promise for the realisation within the political sphere that technology itself and as a whole holds out: to bring everything that *is* under a rational ordering that simultaneously predicts its future and guarantees its safe and proper ordering. Another way of saying this is that technologies of government must aim to guarantee human freedom (they must be liberal) while at the same time being socially accountable (democratic).

Michel Foucault first drew attention to the realisation of a rationalised technology of government in lectures at the Collège de France of 1978–1979, in his discussion of ordoliberalism, as a German form and variant of neoliberalism. His central insight, quoting Wilhelm Röpke (a founding theorist of ordoliberalism), is that 'the freedom of the market requires an active and extremely vigilant policing' (Foucault 2004, 139).[2] Ordoliberalism and neoliberalism itself are, from Foucault's perspective, not attempts to rescue the one logic of capital and so capitalism as such (he explicitly mentions that this is a 'perspective of the Marxist type')[3]; rather, and quite conversely, for the ordoliberals 'capitalism could only survive on condition that a new form is invented for it' (Foucault 2004, 170–71).[4] What Foucault points out is that, at least for the pure economic theorists, there is no such thing as 'capitalism as such' (he caricatures this as *le capital*): there is thus no such thing as a technology of *capital*, only a *technology for* capital. It is this that every liberal form of government shares: the freedom of the market is at the same time a planned, ordered and technologically arranged freedom. It is for this reason that even totalitarian forms of government can claim (and have claimed) at the same time to be 'democratic' and to be guarantors of 'freedom'. As

Foucault demonstrated, neoliberalism does not stand in opposition to the state, nor in opposition to its most cherished aims, but is in fact one possible form of the state. Not only is it one possible form of the state, but it has also been for some decades that form of the state which actual state after actual state has pursued as being able to achieve for it its most cherished aims.

A contemporary commentator who has recognised this paradox and its consequences is Martijn Konings, citing the way in which neoliberalism has become most recognisable as the capitalisation of almost everything, and citing how 'the welfare state represented less a "balance" between a capitalist economy and a social-democratic polity than an integration of the population into the mechanisms of capitalism in ways that transformed those mechanisms at their core' (Konings 2018, 20).

Neoliberalism manifests itself not only as itself – as the attempt to bring an entire world under a certain kind of economic, rational, domination and control – but also as the capacity to internalise and absorb its own oppositions and contradictions, overcoming them by reproducing them within itself, and thus appearing to normalise and legitimate everything that attempts to set itself up against the effects of the rationalism it opposes. In this sense, neoliberalism – economic rationalism – is both itself and its subversions. To see how this is, we must first be capable of seeing that what we are calling rationalism is itself marked by an extreme irrationality: that is by a constant process of dissolution and disorder *as much as* by a constant ordering. Indeed, we must see that the constant ordering would itself not be possible without its attendant annihilation and disorder. Hegel knew and described this movement as an *Aufhebung*: simultaneously a lifting-up to a higher place and at the same time the cancellation and annulment – annihilation – of what has *been* for the sake of what *is to become*. Rationalism is not only never complete, but it is also necessarily always-incomplete. The rational is a constant drive towards, and 'for the sake of' a very highly specified drive: always pressing out towards the fantasy of an improved, 'progressive', and so 'better' future.

Economic rationalism, as a constant drive towards a higher ordering of that which *is*, occurs from out of its own apprehension of, and capacity to materialise in concrete forms, everything that goes under the name of infinity – endlessly and unendingly. *Ratio*, even before it means 'to think', means 'to count' or rather 'to count-up'. All counting-up is the assembling of whatever-is into the ordered sequences that let us see whatever-is in particular ways, to make it available for specific kinds of manipulation and further, and higher, ordering. The 'economic' as that which pertains to the economy is that which is concerned – especially in its Latin form, *oeconomia* – with the management of the house, and so, management generally. In the transition from Greek οἰκονομία, the apportioning and ordering of the house, the emphasis, especially in later, Christianised Latin, of *oeconomia* is not simply management, but governance, or rather management as *dispensatio*, as arbitrary control.

It is especially since Hegel, since the connection of *ratio*, reason itself, with the infinite, that what we understand by a rationalism that takes economic forms is not simply the bringing under control of the 'household as a whole' – the taking in hand of the economy 'as such', but is the connecting of this control with the fascination of the infinite possibility offered by the absolute advancement of human purposes, by directing them *towards* their maximisation, their absolute maximisation: the infinite. (We should not forget, perhaps, that as least as early as Anselm, as much as it is for Hegel, *Ratio* – a word which Anselm always capitalises – can function as another name for God: that is to say, with the foundational cause of all things, even that which is capable of causing itself.) This 'directing toward', however, is what being oriented on the infinite *already* makes possible. The *directing toward* is not a purpose (precisely because it is an aim without an end – something that is aimed *at*), but an effect of the dazzling possibility of the realisation of the infinite: here, and now, and in this very present. Not to understand that this moment of bedazzlement lies at the heart of all contemporary attempts at social domination and control is not to understand the sheer force of the drive ahead. Purposes, if they appear at all, appear only as *effects* – materialisations – of this drive. We could say, as an at least preliminary way of describing what it is that I wish to speak of, that economic rationalism is the name of that drive to organise and set into order the whole of the household for the sake of an infinite driving-forth, which, because it is infinite, has no goal, and no absolute *telos*, only the maximalisation of everything present inasmuch as it *is* present. To be present means to be open to being *more*.

And yet there is a tendency among the critics of economic rationalism and neoliberalism to present what it is they are criticising as if it were itself already, in advance, the expression of a movement that has been planned. This is precisely why Foucault shifts the denominator of the contemporary social drive away from the Marxist logic of 'capitalism' as such (where there are 'capitalists' who plan the eternal bondage of 'proletarians') in an attempt to show that capital and its servants – at every level in the economic hierarchy – are *all* an effect of the drive to 'plan' and so organise and control. The fantasy, or promise, of power is shared by all – those who supposedly 'have' power as much as those who 'seek' it. It does not matter who has or who wants power, but what matters is that all are equally in its thrall. In fact, 'power' does not simply arrange itself into those who have it and those who do not, but assembles and produces vast and complex hierarchies of the executors of power, who from top to bottom exist as the effects of the power that they at the same time reproduce. Rationalism *is* the planning through which it itself comes to be and *is* effected.

The 'planning' of this rationalism comes increasingly to be named as 'managerialism'; its planners, 'managers'. The taking of everything into human hands, for the sake of its manipulation to a purpose for the express or concealed advantage of some identifiable group – the powerful, the wealthy, the one-per-cent – enables us to decipher and trace the contours in every sequence of events of an agency that is not our own, but that has some locus elsewhere (it always posits a 'them'). At once *we* are set over-against those who plan and who execute the plan on *their* behalf. This has the effect of producing the *us* that *we*, in consequence, become. We experience ourselves always as *effects* of a plan, whose executors are elsewhere. We, as powerless, are at the mercy of *them*, arrogating to *them*selves both the effects and the spoils of the powering-up of power itself.

At its worst, this makes the critics of the 'economic rationalism' of 'neoliberalism' sound like conspiracy theorists since this criticism is marked by a certain voice – the voice of being aghast. *We* are always aghast at what *they* have done in bringing about a present into which *we* have entered, seemingly unwillingly. It is to one of these critics I want now to turn – a critic who, not at all unsuccessfully, attempts to bring before us an answer to the first of our two steps of enquiry. Thomas Klikauer describes neoliberal economic rationalism as 'the managerial society' and notes how 'managerialisation – making something managerial – turns every eventuality of human existence into a manageable issue. Simultaneously it standardises everything while promising individualism and individuality'. In laying out how managerialism proceeds, he names the irrationality which I have also identified as what marks the unfolding of economic rationalism, which he calls 'the irrational element in its own rationality'. He then claims:

1. Under Managerialism, society is engulfed by total mobilisation while Managerialism's missionary character demands that nobody can be excluded and all must adhere to its ideas and concepts. After all, management is 'everyone's business'. This total mobilisation takes shape in all spheres of managerial societies.
2. However, Managerialism not only provides global leadership for business, it also engineers leisure activities and aspirations in different social classes. It fosters a pre-established harmony and the managerial purpose. Managerialism invades the private household by engineering public opinion through corporate mass media. In other words, it opens the bedroom to corporate mass media.

And finally, identifying the capacity of economic rationalism as managerialism to internalise everything contradictory to it, he sums up by concluding:

3. The unification of opposites buries the very possibilities of social change (Klikauer 2013, 24, 41–43).

These three claims encapsulate very well the prevailing view of criticism of managerialism as the effect of neoliberal economic rationalism, of how every area of life down to the most intimate and private is brought under the dominion of the universally rational *as* the economically rational. One phrase in particular stands out: 'total mobilisation', a term that gained wide currency in the early part of the twentieth century, and that Ernst Jünger used in 1930 as the title for the first of his essays on the political form of life itself consequent upon the First World War (Jünger 1930).

Even if we are entirely in agreement with our critic's first statement, and even when we recognise in the second statement an extension of an analysis that was made by (among others) Ernst Jünger (as early as 1932),[5] we see from the third, itself characterised by its own commitment to change, that it is not in fact total mobilisation that our critic resists. He speaks of the need for social change, but as a given, as what (he assumes) we would *already* expect him to say. Does social change stand against total mobilisation? It would be true to say that the social change he envisages stands against the total mobilisation that he describes as managerialism. But it would not be true to say that he stands against mobilisation, even a mobilisation that must be total, of a different kind. He is therefore not against total mobilisation as such.

Indeed, the social change he seeks is itself *also* total, for at the very end of what he has to say, he tells us that 'inactions against Managerialism' would constitute 'a crime against humanity' because 'the survival of humanity' depends on the actions he enjoins (Klikauer 2013, 277). Like most activist opponents of economic rationalism and neoliberalism, this critic accepts, almost without realising it, that total mobilisation is itself the form life now takes. He is simply opposed to those in whose hands he understands this total mobilisation currently to be placed: the managers.

In this third statement we glimpse, then, something even more fundamental either than managerialism (which is to be overcome, at the risk of our own criminalisation) or even total mobilisation: it is that all things are to be determined from out of a fundamental willing. The *already* willed willing of managerialism is to be overcome by the *higher* willing of a better, because not criminal or inculpating, future. What our critic indicates is not even an overcoming of the willed activity of the 'managers', of managerialism as such, but the demand *that we join him in choosing, and so exercising a function of the will* between kinds of willing. Over against the willed world of managerialism, we must will another, better and higher, world. To do other, not so to will, not so to *act*, is the highest crime. Not an individual act, like robbing a bank or fiddling our taxes; not a crime, let us say of violence against a person, but a crime against humanity as such. *The* crime that inhibits the highest will of which humanity is capable.

The phrase 'total mobilisation' was coined by Lenin, perhaps for the first time in 1919, to address the workers of Tsaritsyn (see Ryan 2012, 138) in the battle around that city between Bolshevik and White Russian forces. The phrase reappeared with the German radical nationalist, diarist, novelist and theorist whom I have already referred to, Ernst Jünger, in 1930. Jünger, an arch ironist, was citing Lenin in taking up the phrase, one which in any case belongs to the times. Total mobilisation is as contemporary to us as it was to Lenin and Jünger, either as a slogan for action or as an explanation of the condition of life to which we are all constantly enjoined. This phrase is very far from being exhausted. At its centre lies an understanding of work: work not just as production, but even more fundamentally, as production-in-annihilation: *Aufhebung*. This term is *how* we experience, and at the same time produce, our own self-transcendence: we transcend and move on up, always for the sake of a better, greater, future. Managerialism, economic rationalism, neoliberalism are all forms that total mobilisation can and does take. *Every* form that total mobilisation takes, also, always, and from some standpoint, justifies itself through positing the possibility of a higher form of life. Total mobilisation is a condition: the condition of life itself as *becoming*. Total mobilisation is the condition of the will to power. How, then, are we to understand this phrase, 'will to power'?

THE WILL TO POWER

If the term 'power' is ubiquitous in his work, it is only in a few rare moments that Michel Foucault discusses the actual nature of power itself. One of these can be found in his lectures at the Collège de France of 1976. He rejects the hypothesis, often advanced, that power is best understood as what is held back as pure potentiality, especially in the apparatus of law. This understanding considers that law is the repressed 'stock' of power, and so understands power primarily as repression, as what produces a discursive field by holding back what it can enact. Power, as potentiality, is what is held back – it is the power that the law (for instance) *could* dispose but chooses not to.[6] Under this account, repression lets boundaries appear: above all the boundaries or contours that constitute particular kinds of embodiment and materiality.

Foucault, acknowledging the possibility of this way of thinking about power, concludes that the explanation of power is far from exhausted by understanding it as repression (as a 'stock' of what is always held back). The psychoanalytic account of power is (for him) perhaps a constituent, but nevertheless an insufficient, condition to account for power as such. On top of the account of power as repression, Foucault advances 'a second hypothesis, which is: power itself, this is war, this is war continued by other means. At this point we can invert Clausewitz's proposition and say that politics is the continuation of war by other means' (Foucault 1997, 16).[7]

Foucault argues that 'the notion now so current of repression as characterising the mechanisms and the effects of power is in fact totally insufficient to define them' (Foucault 1997, 18).[8] He proceeds in his definition initially with cautions and negations:

> Do not take power as a phenomenon of massive and homogenous domination – domination of one individual over the others . . . [it] is not something that divided itself between those who have it and hold on to it exclusively and those who do not have it and are subject to it . . . power . . . circulates . . . power functions. Individuals . . . are never the inert or consenting targets of power; they are always its relays. In other words, power passes through individuals, it's not applied to them. (Foucault 1997, 26)[9]

In the exercise and distribution of power there are no bystanders. Foucault reveals the bystander to be a psychic fiction. Such a 'bystander' is best understood through Nietzsche's ironic account of 'the victim', the creature of the 'herd', the one who takes power precisely in the act of claiming to have none. This is because the bystander, who may complain of powerlessness and of disempowerment, is never actually a non-combatant, but is most often one who engages, and is engaged, in the relations of power through its absence or denial. The victim makes a claim (the claim of 'justice') that demands redress ('I must have justice'). This claim takes the form: 'because I have no power, I must be empowered, in order to claim what has been denied me and is rightfully mine'. This 'denial' constitutes an imbalance that must be *re*-balanced, and thus is a claim for a redistribution of power in favour of the powerless. The justified negative nodes of power are the ones to whom power must be transferred. The transfer, as a requirement for redress, functions exactly like a relay in an electrical circuit, across which power is also constantly being distributed.

It is in the course of these essentially negative definitions that Foucault brings us to one of his most fundamental understandings of power:

> In reality, what allows bodies, gestures, discourses, and desires to be identified and constituted as something individual, this is precisely what is one of the first effects of power. That is to say, the individual is not that which stands over against power; the individual is, I believe, one of power's primary effects. The individual is an effect of power, and is, at the same time, and to the extent that he is an effect, he is the relay: power passes through the individual which it has constituted. (Foucault 1997, 27)[10]

'You must empower me' means 'I am a relay of power because I am justified in the claim to power I am *entitled* to make: you must give me what you cannot rightly deny me'. What Foucault is describing, in other words, is nothing other than Nietzsche's will to power. Will to power *not* as individual willing, but as the condition from out of which all things occur and appear as having-been-willed.

In a world which is *already* totally mobilised, the manager might appear or seem as one who initiates and generates plans (who makes plans against 'us'), but in fact he or she is nothing other than an effect of the planning that is necessary for anything to appear at all. The manager is not someone who exercises power (who 'plans', either in secret or in public), but rather the one who, as a relay of power, is at the same time power's own moment of containment. If power is nothing other than the empowering power of the infinite, the bedazzling promise of the infinite which drives everything to be mobilised in its pursuit, power is made manifest in and through what contains it. Power is made manifest by those who can contain it long enough to reveal its finite moments. The manager is not one who plans, but the one who *is planned*, who executes the already-demanded plan: the one who does what is required. This is what Jünger had also understood and explained in his figure, or form, or *typus* of the worker. It is what led Martin Heidegger to say of Jünger: 'Jünger sees whatever is (*das Seiende*) with cold and sharp eyes in general as will to power . . . his thinking itself is a form of the will to power – in Jünger's language, thinking itself has "the character of work"' (Heidegger 2004, 227).[11]

The manager is the one whose work it is to bring out into the open, out into visibility, the finite enactments of the infinite will to power. As such, the manager does not 'represent' power, so much as the manager *is* power's containment. The manager sets power into order, into the orderings that power demands. This is what Foucault means by being power's 'relays'. The question that power poses, therefore, is how to choose between the infinitely great possibilities of power's orderings. How should we choose? Should we choose power's highest ordering? Or its most general ordering? *Who* chooses? Or is it not, because in each case the doer is added to the deed,[12] that the one seemingly enacting is in fact the one produced by the mobilisation of everything around him or her? That *highest* and at the same *most general* which we pursue is the highest and most general possibility of the will to power that makes itself manifest not *for* us but in us as we become the *us*, the *I* that brings this possibility to finite visibility. There is no conspiracy to manage the world through an economic rationalism that is at the same time the marketisation of everything: there is only how the will to power wills *us* and *me*. Every attempt to overcome the will to power on a grand scale is in itself an effect of the very power, of the very will in question.

I want now to proceed to the second of my steps, which is to enquire into two rival possibilities for the overcoming, the 'solution' to the managerialism and economic rationalism that we have now caught sight of and named. In each case, I want to enquire into the extent to which, if at all, each of these possibilities escapes *itself* being a form of the will to power.

If the will to power presupposes and at the same gives rise to – enacts – the persona of the manager, does the will to power formally ground the persona of the manager? If we understand the history of total mobilisation now to be represented by managerialism, does the manager succeed Jünger's 'Typus' of the worker as a figure – perhaps *the* figure – of the will to power? Even if this were the case, it could only be so on the basis that *anyone* can become a worker, anyone a manager. Only insofar as this is true does the will to power as Nietzsche describes it, as Jünger unfolds its workings-out, give rise to the possibility of the manager. In fact, the will to power always projects that highest form of being that is available to the will to will at all: which is precisely why the (unwittingly managerialist) critics of managerialism project a higher level of total mobilisation even than that of managerialism as the overcoming of managerialism. It is here that we can see, at least in outline, the fundamental connection between the metaphysics of Nietzsche's will to power and the metaphysics of Hegel's absolute subjectivity. The will to power always projects as its fulfilment the highest possibility of being (as human being) available from the standpoint of finitude projecting itself towards infinity at any given moment. Will to power *is* the infinite realising itself within the immediate confines of the finite, not as an object, but as the *moment* (this is the metaphysical completion of Aristotle's understanding of τὸ νῦν, the present 'now'): the 'now' that ever-realises itself is Nietzsche's 'doctrine' of eternal-recurrence – *die ewige Wiederkehr des Gleichen*. The fulfilment of the ever-recurring present *as* the constant-becoming of the highest possibility of (human) being is what Nietzsche names as *der Übermensch*, 'the over-soul'. The will to power posits the highest possibility of human being as particular, specified, subjects, but *in* their subjectivity ('worker', 'manager', 'post-managerial') around whom the highest possibility of movement itself, total mobilisation, *mobilises*. This is what Hegel had called 'absolute subjectivity', realised in specified (human) subjects.

Hegel secures and completes the accomplishment of the subjectivity of the human subject on the basis of the simple theoretical possibility: *each* human subject, and *all* human subjectivity, is secured through an absolute and necessary understanding of metaphysical equality. After Hegel, we are unable to account for, or justify, any absolute difference between subjects: all difference becomes relative. Every subject exhibits a subjectivity metaphysically equal, thus identical in value, to every other. This subjectivity appears both as highest possibility (that any given 'now' is capable for realising) and as the specified realisation of that possibility ('in' the 'now' as such). So fundamental is this understanding to Hegel and all who follow him up to the present day that it is difficult to gain access to the extent to which this thought is essentially an innovation – an innovation arising from the collision and hammering-together of an old, essentially Greek, metaphysical tradition combined with ideas that trace their roots back through the three 'Abrahamic' religions (in their multiplicity of forms) of Judaism, Christianity and Islam.

To trace the history of this development would be a task for another day. Our task now, I would suggest, is to understand the ways in which this fundamental equality serves as the inconcussible ground for responses that have consequences for the formation of public policy (since public policy is precisely one of the ways in which the 'now' is capable of being realised – indeed, is the facilitation of that realisation – as part of what any given 'now' contains).

How are we to understand the working-out of this thought, the thought of equality, within the terms suggested? The thought states that every subject, equal in value to every other, needs to undertake an identical form of work to accomplish (fulfil to the highest) its own existence, with the same intention to succeed (actually to attain to its highest), and so doing, is then justified in securing a point of existence in consequence of the work deployed (fulfils the demand of the 'now'). The corollary of this view is quite specific: every difference between subjects, whether of weight, height, build, race, sex, sexuality, background, enablement, education, personal history, advancement or failure to advance, and so forth, is neither necessary nor absolute, but only contingent and relative (to the fulfilment of the 'now' as such). Moreover, and in reverse, every identifiable difference can be reversed or inhibited either by practices which overcome it or the inhibition of the circumstance and practices that caused it (when you deny what is 'now' possible, you commit a crime. When you deny *me* what is now possible to me *now*, you commit a crime against me: but potentially against every given 'me', and so against 'us' – 'us' taken as humanity as a whole). In those cases where this is not possible, compensation, of some kind, is at least potentially, if not actually, due. More strongly put: in *each case of inequality a cause for the inequality is either immediately obvious or remains a possibility that can always be found, and altered with the intention of producing an opposite, and so equalising, effect.* This 'finding' can be by means of a formidable armoury of explanatory practices: from genetics or psychological disposition to equality of opportunity or its lack, with very much in between.

A central question here is, what kind of subjectivity is posited as the universalised subject, which every individual subject sets forth to work towards? To understand the answer to this question, we have to turn to the pages, not of political theorists, but economists: to return to our earlier definition of the economic, 'economists' are those who understand best the realisation of governance as a whole. Put another way: we are yet to abandon – indeed our drive is in the direction of the intensification of the insight – that inequality is essentially a consequence of the distribution of resources that can be quantified economically: inequality is *more than anything else* economic inequality, and every corrective to inequality is therefore in the first instance to be realised through economic means. This remains true even for those who are opposed to the advancement of economic growth: indeed, an acceptance that we must all become *less* wealthy (especially in the West) in order to save the planet requires even more heightened control over the distribution and sharing of economic resources that will in future be organised to become more scant: thus an economics in retreat will inculpate those who have – or attempt to hold on to – more, *doubly*. I want to suggest that the universalised subjectivity posited as both the universalised subject and the mean is essentially a *managed* subject – that is to say, one that is accomplished through the management of the economic conditions that surround him or her.

GLOBAL ACCUMULATION AND DISTRIBUTION

Two theorists in particular have posited how this management is to be accomplished, and what I want to say today is a mere springboard for considering the consequences of what they propose. What interests me about what the very different managerial solutions that each poses is that they make their case on entirely moral grounds (the will to power is itself a moral, and moralising, force: to oppose it is to commit a crime – as we have seen). We can see, therefore, that there is a fundamental connection between the universalised economic equality that is posited at the heart of the bourgeois liberal – or neoliberal, if you like – understanding and an essentially moral equality. The term in question for both thinkers is accomplished through an appeal to what is justified.

Thomas Piketty argues that 'it is urgent, it seems to me, to get beyond the somewhat empty debate about merit and prosperity, which appears to me ill conceived' (Piketty 2013, 708).[13] He proceeds to argue, under the heading 'the moral hierarchy of prosperity', that even entrepreneurial skill and arguments derived from the necessity of freeing people to accumulate wealth 'cannot justify all the inequalities of substance [Piketty says *patrimoniales*]', because 'no matter how justified inequalities of substance may be initially, fortunes multiply and perpetuate themselves beyond all limits and every rational justification in terms of social utility' (Piketty 2013, 708).[14] Thus 'this provides the central rationale justifying the introduction of a progressive annual tax on the largest fortunes worldwide' (Piketty 2013, 708).[15] Piketty is accomplished at manoeuvring within a complex postmodern discourse of relative equality of patrimony (*patrimoniale*)[16]: he remarks that any attempt to construct 'a moral hierarchy of wealth' would be in practice 'an exercise in occidento-centrism',[17] and wants to try to understand 'the general laws that on average govern the dynamics of substance',[18] we presume globally (Piketty 2013, 710–11). We must interpret what 'understand' means in this context: we are not trying by empirical means to identify the underlying laws that are to be found: rather the other way around – we are trying to work out what laws must be imposed on economic accumulation to make them conform to a universal, and so universalisable, practice of (equalised) distribution.

I would not be alone in arguing that a fundamental flaw in Piketty's argument is that he conflates too often the formal difference between capital and money. Capital has to be understood here, not only, as in Marx, as 'accumulated labour', but also what preserves and extends that accumulation. Capital is genuine value because, as capital, it produces an increase – it is the *agent*, that is, active and activating, accumulation of the power of human subjectivity to become and go *on* becoming (and so not a 'stock' of merely dead or inert materiality). It becomes, and as becoming, it preserves in the stock that it is the constant capacity to become *more*. A repeated theme of the fourth volume of Marx's *Capital* (the vast treatise that goes under the heading of theories of surplus value) is that when capital cannot increase it ceases to be *either* capital *or* money. If money is the capacity to purchase capital, the only point at which its notional value can be preserved, money can also be destroyed when it is wasted as mere consumption. Money is an option to purchase value, but until it can turn itself into the capacity to increase, it cannot permanentise itself as value as such.

Consequently, the simple transfer of money (through taxes and subsidies) in any direction does not necessarily preserve its value. We see how this manifests itself in the contemporary problem of all resource wealth. Its value collapses unless it can turn itself into capital. Resource economies are notoriously unable to preserve the value they appear to create over time. Because they lack either capital-intensive industries or they concentrate in too few hands the ownership of capital industries elsewhere, they turn people, who would otherwise be workers invested in the preservation of capital, into clients of the state, despite every effort to the contrary. This can be seen in numerous resource economies from Venezuela to Saudi Arabia. One of the contemporary problems of the global economy is that accumulated resource wealth is difficult to turn into capital, precisely because those in whose hands resource wealth is often concentrated are precisely not 'capitalists', nor even rentiers. 'Accumulation' of this kind is not really accumulation at all and dissipates very rapidly, often across one or at most two generations.

The effect of the kind of redistribution that Piketty envisages is too often the enlarging of the role of the state, since the only effective guarantor for the redistribution of taxation is the state. This is precisely where Piketty ends up. He concludes:

> The modern redistribution does not consist in transferring the riches of the rich to the poor, or at least not in a manner so explicit. It consists in financing public services and replacement incomes more or less equally for everyone, notably in the domain of education, of health and of pensions. . . . The modern

> redistribution is constructed around a logic of rights and a principle of equality of access to a certain number of goods judged to be fundamental. (Piketty 2013, 766)[19]

In other words, what is at issue here is not the demand for violent expropriation as such (we need not have a revolution), but perhaps what is only initially a technology of progressive redistribution – and becomes (benignly) in the end, a practice of anticipated, or regulated distribution. Piketty does not avoid a problem Hegel had already foreseen in the forms and effects of the liberal state (Hegel's predominant criticism of Fichte and Rousseau), which is the tendency of the state, in the name of the good of the community as a whole, to exercise a tyrannical relation (opposing itself) to the individual, because it is forced to intervene in the exercise of individual freedom, at the very point of protecting or guaranteeing freedom (Hegel's so-called 'negative' freedom).[20] The degree to which the extension of the state is required can be seen in the proposals developed as solutions to the problem of inequality by commentators like Anthony Atkinson. Atkinson makes fifteen proposals to overcome the problem of inequality, almost every single one of which involves either an extension of the tax base or a direct intervention by the state in the level and management of personal income (Atkinson 2015, 237–39).[21] This is, I would suggest, also reflected in the increasing interest in the introduction of a universal wage.

If Piketty represents one possible realisation of the metaphysics of subjectivity, one indebted to an interpretation of Marx (rather than Marxism itself), a different approach appears from a more surprising direction. Robert Shiller addresses the issue of the crisis of finance that besets us on a global scale. Shiller was one of the first economists to identify and understand the origins of the present crisis, as one expert in the financial technology surrounding sub-prime loans. Shiller explains that 'financial capitalism is an invention, and the process of inventing it is hardly over' (Shiller 2012, vii). By 'invention' we should hear 'production', but we should hear more than that. We should hear 'capacity for production': production of production. Financial capitalism, finance, is that kind of production that lets production produce. This is exactly what Shiller goes on to describe. As what produces most productively, finance 'is creating the architecture for reaching a goal – and providing stewardship to protect and preserve the assets needed for the achievement and maintenance of that goal' (Shiller 2012, 7).

Far more than many other political theorists who have attempted to revive a political Marxism in recent years (Žižek, Badiou and others), Shiller is already thinking alongside and far more deeply with Marx: Shiller appeals to Marx on the very first page of his recent *Finance and the Good Society* to show how financial capitalism – finance – has already moved beyond the industrial capitalism which was, he argues, Marx's focus, or 'the system of production, banking, and trade that shaped modern society up through the end of World War II' (Shiller 2012, 1). Shiller concludes:

> Finance does not tell us what the goals [of our society] should be. Finance is not about 'making money' per se. It is a 'functional' science in that it exists to support other goals – those of the society. The better aligned a society's financial institutions are with its goals and ideals, the stronger and more successful the society will be. If its mechanisms fail, finance has the power to subvert such goals, as it did with the subprime mortgage market of the past decade. But if it is functioning properly it has a unique potential to promote great deals of prosperity. (Shiller 2012, 7)

What Shiller speaks of, no less than Piketty, is capital: not money as an apparent stock of value but rather money as a technique for the creation, preservation and enlargement of wealth. Finance is thus an architecture and technology for the maintaining and preserving of life and reality. Shiller in one sense – and this is the sole reason for my interest in him – does not present an antithesis to Marx but Marx's fulfilment.

Shiller, then, is a very worthy exponent of what the Heidegger of the 1930s (along with Ernst Jünger and others) might have called 'Americanism', and what we all might call 'world democracy' or global financial capitalism. Marx defines capital in the following way, as a social goal:

> As the ceaseless striving after the general form of riches, capital drives labour out beyond its limits of its natural-neediness and thus creates the material elements for the development of that rich individuality, which is as balanced in its production as in its consumption, and whose labour is therefore labour no more, but appears as the full development of activity itself, in which natural necessity in its immediate form has disappeared; because in place of natural-neediness something historically produced has arrived. (Marx 2005, 244)[22]

What Marx describes here is the overcoming or stabilisation (in an equilibrium) of what in the *Economic and Philosophical Manuscripts* he had called alienation. Alienation (the terms he uses, almost interchangeably, are the same as those employed by Hegel: *Entfremdung*, *Entäußerung*) is not a subjective experience, but rather the estrangement or subtraction from me (from my actual ownership) of the surplus I generate through the labour I undertake. In the *Economic and Philosophical Manuscripts* Marx was interested only in the process of alienation: by the time of the *Grundrisse* he had become concerned with how this alienation could be overcome. Thus Marx asks himself what it would mean if I retained the right to that surplus (if it were not alienated from me), and could exchange it, either actually or theoretically with everyone else in a given economy? This is when alienation is overcome and the full possibilities of species-being are realised: the supposed freedom of the labour contract under capitalism (you are free to work, or starve) becomes a genuine freedom only at the point when each one of us produces as much as he or she consumes, and freely enters into the mutual exchange of the surplus in question.[23] The mass becomes fully self-present to itself through a stabilised, balanced (the word Marx deploys here is an entirely Hegelian word: *allseitig* – where every particular 'side' is identical to the *all*) individuation: each becomes equal in value, both as producer and as consumer, to every other. In truth this is nothing other than the fiction of the 'social contract realised through an economic 'technology' or rationalism that permits such a free exchange to take place. It is a contract, not of rights and duties, but developed out of a notional economic surplus or 'becoming', a surplus that points towards an infinitude of promise.

This is exactly Shiller's goal. While jettisoning what he calls the Marxist extreme (by which we may assume he means the revolutionary mechanism of achieving communism), he wishes to 'expand, correct, and realign finance' by '*democratising and humanising and expanding the scope of financial capitalism*' by developing a democracy and technological infrastructure 'that works together with . . . human arrangements to make it possible for everyone to participate intelligently in the financial system' (Shiller 2012, 3, 5, 12, emphasis in the original). By 'intelligently', Shiller means both 'most consciously' and 'most equally'.

It should be clear that I am advocating *neither* Piketty's analysis and solution *nor* Shiller's. My goal is simply to demonstrate what lies at the basis of perfectly sane, academic solutions to public policy questions which do not *propose* the equalisation of the human race but rather *take for granted that this equalisation is already a social demand that must be fulfilled.* Both, in a sense, oppose what we earlier defined as managerialism by proposing not less, but *different* management of the whole: in reality *more* – so much more that it takes on the form of either a legal (Piketty, in the form of taxation) or moral (in the form proposed by Shiller) universalisation of particular managerial technologies.

Shiller's book began life as his lectures to Yale students studying for the MBA in finance. They have a moral purpose: they begin with the challenge that the task of future bankers and workers in the finance 'industry' is not to make themselves richer (which you might think someone who had arrived in the MBA programme in finance at Yale had rather been looking forward to), but to participate more fully in democratising wealth and capital overall. What Shiller and Piketty have in common is that both believe that through the technological manipulation of the means at their disposal on a global scale, the already-present *reality* that they take for granted and that grounds every present subject can be realised and secured. What we come up against here is the grounding, the *moral* grounding, of the subjectivity of the subject in technology. Not technology as 'the electronic' or the advent of higher possibilities for the future, but rather as that which is maximally – infinitely – manipulable and orderable for entirely human purposes. This is actually, I think, what we mean with the words 'management' and 'managerial'. Managerialism, one could say, is the attempt to secure ('the technology of securing') the controlled enlargement of human possibility, measured against its most absolute maximalisation. Why I am committed neither to Piketty nor to Shiller (but am impressed by the impact of what they have had to say) is because this notion of the technological pitches the humanity it at the same time unleashes into an unending war with ineluctable fate and death: but that again is a question for another day.

Shiller's construction of equalisation is far closer to Hegel's than is Piketty's, since it does not, or not immediately, depend on the enlargement of the state at the expense of the individual, and it does not conflate money with capital (and so assume that the distribution of money is equivalent to the distribution of access to capital). Marx sets up the position of capitalist and worker as an absolute opposition in a way that retreats from Hegel's delicate balance between the state and the organs of civil society (whose aim is the preservation of a freedom that functions not negatively, not where the 'freedom of the other begins', but as, positive freedom, as the enlargement of possibility that emerges *through* what the organs of civil society make possible). This leads Shiller to comment that 'Marx never explains clearly why it is that labourers [workers] do not have access to capital. . . . But in an ideal capitalist system, people with good business ideas can, in principle, do just that' (Shiller 2012, 8). It is this problem that Shiller believes both requires a full democratic equalisation and that has already been overcome, at least in principle, by finance, 'financial capitalism'. If he is correct, he is at the same time entirely correct (in the terms of Hegel's logic) that the distinction between capitalist and worker has already been sublated into a higher possibility.

If Marx sought to overcome the opposed subject-positions of capitalist and worker by drawing *both* through a dialectical transformation of the world into an equalised 'rich individuality', Shiller seeks the (dialectically) same goal by turning every worker into a full, equal participant in (capitalistic) finance. The correct way to hear what Shiller means by the word 'capitalist' is not 'neo-liberal' but 'inclusive'. The technology of finance *includes* the individual in the workings of finance, rather than setting him or her over against them. This would, he says, render Marx's criticism (of 'capital') 'obsolete' (Shiller 2012, 9). I am largely uninterested in whether or to what extent either Shiller's or Piketty's ideas and 'programme' succeed, or fail, or can be questioned. That, we might say, is the subject for a 'political' debate belonging to another day. Shiller is the antithesis to Marx. As Marx's antithesis he seeks no less than Marx, and Hegel before him, to preserve and uphold the same 'historical', metaphysical, outlook.

This chapter has not sought to 'solve' the question of the managerial. For as long as the only solution to managerialism is an intensification of everything managerial, there can be no resolution to the questions before us. The underlying thesis of this chapter is that we have not yet even entered into the questions with sufficient depth to let them be seen and stand as questions. Is it true that we can only enter these questions with cold and sharp eyes? A criticism of Ernst Jünger, and of those modern critics who come in his wake, is that they also fail to understand the questions before us as questions. Is there any moving beyond the will to power, as the will that organises a total mobilisation of the whole world surrounding us? It is not at all clear that we should even be striving for such a 'beyond'. Are we not required by the urgency of the situation in which we find ourselves to be able to propose resolutions to what we find? Or are we not even more urgently required to put the situation in which we find ourselves *into* question?

The contemporary response to the problems of poor technological solutions of the past is that *better* technology will always solve them. Thus the 'bad' technology of neoliberalism can always be succeeded by a 'better' technology, guaranteeing a 'more equal' or more democratic access to the distribution of value. The technocratic 'solutions' to the problems of technology are always 'more technology' – an increase in the mobilisation of life, the totalisation of mobilisation, that technology *already* is – but 'better'. This never puts into question the meaning of technology or why we are so delivered over to the constant and ever-increasing mobilisation that it demands.

Heidegger's writing on technology repeated stresses that there is no such thing as technology as such; technology has no 'essence'. What we call technology is the manifestation of a way of being in the world. This is akin to Foucault's denial that there is capitalism as such (which is merely 'a perspective of the Marxist type'): 'capitalism' is a function of something else. What, or how – and *who*, that something else *is* is surely the question that remains. Who are we, and how are we to be?

NOTES

1. An earlier version of this chapter was presented at the 2016 Whitlam Workshop of the Whitlam Institute in Sydney. I am grateful to Anna Yeatman and Eric Sidoti (then director of the Institute) for the invitation to be in Sydney, and for their outstanding welcome and hospitality on that occasion. Thanks are also due to Aaron Aquilina for his patient work preparing this text for publication.

2. From this same volume, see also note 16, citing the French translation of Wilhelm Röpke's *Die Gesellschaftskrisis der Gegenwart* (1941), 'La libertè du marché nécessite une politique active et extrêmement vigilante'.
3. 'Une perspective de type marxiste'.
4 'Le capitalisme pouvait sur vivre à condition qu'on lui invente une nouvelle forme'.
5. See Jünger (1981, 264). 'Freizeit und Arbeitszeit sind zwei Modifikationen, in denen man von ein und demselben technischen Betriebe in Anspruch genommen wird'. ('Leisure time and work time are two modes in which we are engaged in one and the same technological operation'.) Walter Benjamin has no dissimilar things to say at times (see Rojek 1997).
6. This understanding of power originates with Wittgenstein's (and J. L. Austen's) understanding of the performative, an understanding that has been further developed by theorists like Judith Butler, who have tended to focus on the relation of power to the psychic and psychoanalytic.
7. 'Une seconde hypothèse, qui serait: le pouvoir, c'est la guerre, c'est la guerre continue par d'autres moyens'.
8. 'Cette notion si courante maintenant de répression pour caractériser les mécanismes et les effets de pouvoir, est tout à fait insuffisante pour les cerner'.
9. 'Ne pas prendre le pouvoir comme un phénomène de domination massif et homogène – domination d'un individu sur les autres . . . [il] n'est pas quelque chose qui se partage entre ceux qui l'ont et qui le détiennent exclusivement, et puis ceux qui ne l'ont pas et qui le subissent. . . . le pouvoir . . . circule . . . Le pouvoir fonctionne . . . Les individus . . . ne sont jamais la cible inerte ou consentante du pouvoir, ils en sont toujours les relais. Autrement dit, le pouvoir transite par pas les individus, ils ne s'applique pas à eux'.
10. 'En réalité, ce qui fait qu'un corps, des gestes, des discours, des désirs sont identifiés et constitués comme individus, c'est précisément cela l'un des effets premiers du pouvoir. C'est-à-dire que l'individu n'est pas le vis-à-vis du pouvoir et il est en même temps, dans le mesure même où il en est un effet, le relias: le pouvoir transite par l'individu qu'il a constitué'.
11. 'Jünger sieht das Seiende mit kalten und scharfen Augen überall als Willen zur Macht. [. . .] sein Denken selbst ist eine Gestalt des Willens zur Macht – ; in Jüngers Sprache: das Denken hat Arbeitscharakter'. An almost identical point is made in a letter to a soldier of 1939 from the same volume, 'Aus einem Brief an einzelne Krieger', 277–82, 277f.
12. See Nietzsche (1999, 279). Es' giebt kein "Sein" hinter dem Thun, Wirken, Werden; "der Thäter" ist zum Thun bloss hinzugedichtet, das Thun ist Alles'. ('There is no being behind the deed, working, becoming; "the doer" is merely added in afterwards, the deed is all'.); *Nachlaß 1885–1887* (KSA vol. 12), 136 ('Die Trennung des Thuns' vom Thuenden') (= *Wille zur Macht* §631); *Nachlaß 1887–1889* (KSA vol. 13), 136 ('Daß man Etwas-thun, "das Ziel", die "Absicht" den "Zweck" wieder in das Thun zurücknimmt . . . daß alle Zwecke', 'Ziele', 'Sinne' nur Ausdrucksweisen und Metamorphosen des Einen Willens sind, der allem Geschehen inhärirt, der Wille zur Macht . . . ') (= *Wille zur Macht* §675).

13. ‘Il me semble urgent d’aller au-delà de ce débat souvent caricatural autour de mérite et de la fortune’.
14. ‘La hiérarchie morales des fortunes’ . . . ‘ne permet pas de justifier toutes les inégalités patrimoniales . . . si justifiées soient-elles au départ, les fortunes se multiplient et se perpétuent parfois au-delà de toute limite et de toute justification rationnelle possible en termes d’utilité sociale’.
15. ‘Il s’agit là de la raison centrale justifiant l’introduction d’un impôt progressif annuel sur les plus grandes fortunes mondiales’.
16. Those familiar with Piketty in English will note I have translated several key terms in Piketty’s text rather differently from the standard English translation by Arthur Goldhammer (Thomas Piketty, *Capital in the Twenty-First Century* (Cambridge, MA: Belknap Press [Harvard University Press], 2014)). If, for reasons explained later, Piketty has a tendency to conflate the difference between money and capital, Goldhammer’s translation exaggerates this conflation further, regularly failing to distinguish adequately between the different kinds of capital (patrimony, wealth, fortune, liquidity), let alone making enough of the formal distinction between accumulated wealth (capital) and wealth that consumes (money).
17. ‘Souvent en pratique à un exercice d’occidentalo-centrisme’.
18. ‘Les lois générales qui gouvernent en moyenne les dynamiques patrimoniales’.
19. ‘La redistribution modern ne consiste pas à transférer des richesses des riches vers les pauvres, ou tout du moins pas d’une façon aussi explicite. Elle consiste à financer des service publics et des revenus de remplacement plus au moins égaux pour tous, notamment dans le domaine de l’éducation et la santé et des retraites. . . . La redistribution moderne est construite autour d’une logique de droits et d’un principe d’égalité d’accès à un certain nombre de biens jugés fondamentaux’.
20. See Hegel (1938, 109). ‘Wenn die Gemeinschaft der Vernunftwesen wesentlich ein Beschränken der wahren Freiheit wäre, so würde sie an und für sich die höchste Tyrannei sein’.
21. The pages cited are a summary of 115–236.
22. ‘Als das rastlose Streben nach der allgemeinen Form des Reichtums treibt aber das Kapital die Arbeit über die Grenzen seiner Naturbedürftigkeit hinaus und schafft so die materiellen Elemente für die Entwicklung der reichen Individualität, die ebenso allseitig in ihrer Produktion als Konsumtion ist und deren Arbeit daher auch nicht mehr als Arbeit, sondern als volle Entwicklung der Tätigkeit selbst erscheint, in der die Naturnotwendigkeit in ihrer unmittelbaren Form verschwunden ist; weil an die Stelle des Naturbedürfnisses ein geschichtlich erzeugtes getreten ist’.
23. Thus in the *Grundrisse* Marx speaks of a ‘rich individuality which is as balanced in its production as in its consumption’ (Karl Marx 2005, 244, ‘die Entwicklung der reichen Indi- vidualität, die ebenso allseitig in ihrer Produktion als Konsumtion ist’) often referring in the *Grundrisse* to the effect of such a possibility as a *Gleichsetzung* or ‘equalising’ of economic differences between persons.

Chapter 4

Where Is Value Today?

Managerialism in the Age of Self-Assertion

Bogdan Costea

INQUIRING INTO THE NATURE OF MANAGERIALISM

The twin problems concerning the nature of managerialism, and the reasons why it could triumph over so many contemporary institutional and organisational forms, have shaped debates which are productive but also, at times, frustrating. The more the word 'managerialism' is used as a general diagnosis of the contemporary institutional, political or economic situation, the more it tends to resist settling into a coherent conceptual frame. Perhaps this is because *managerialism* remains, in a sense, *just* that: an interpretation, a shorthand for a denser and more intractable, albeit very real, nexus of phenomena. It seems that its very range has now become so extended that it calls for a shorthand reference yet defies it as soon as it is uttered. It is difficult nonetheless, in the study of contemporary organisational forms, to avoid reaching for a term such as 'managerialism'. It is an almost instinctive gesture when it comes to grasping the global generalisation of an idiom spoken by corporate managers and consultants, state administrators and bureaucrats, politicians and by the institutions they represent. Enteman (1993) and Klikauer (2013, 2015), two decades later, treat managerialism as a novel, yet systemic, *ideology*, that is, as a 'set of principles upon which the political, social, and economic order of the society is based. Ideology in general is, then, all possible such principles' (Enteman 1993, 8). Others identify its emergence with a failure of the political imagination in the wake of the fall of communism in Europe in 1989, especially on the Left, who allowed 'a Trojan horse' to reoccupy traditional political doctrines and subvert them with a new discourse of 'modernisation' based on the universal deployment of a conception of order seen through principles of 'efficiency' understood in economic and, especially, corporate terms; the emergence of 'New Labour' in Britain in the 1990s was its archetypal exemplar (e.g., Fairclough 2000; Dillow 2007). The invasion of the public sector by this manner of reconfiguring what count as 'efficient' public goods (e.g., health and education) became the theme in important sectoral studies of managerialism; for some authors, the novelty of this phenomenon seemed so striking that they used the syntagm 'new managerialism' to mark its distinctive character (Clarke, Gewirtz and McLaughlin 2000; Deem, Hillyard and Reed 2008; Lynch, Grummell and Devine 2012; Willmott 2002; Watts 2017). Historians, like Locke (1996), and Locke and Spender (2011), interpreted the emergence of managerialism as part of a broader and longer social process connected intimately to the consolidation of a new elite of graduates (whose number is, by now, hard to count) of management and business schools around the world. And so, in trying to seize all this complexity with a single notion, it is not surprising that most critical analyses of managerialism have tended, almost inevitably, to rely on two presuppositions: (1) that managerialism is a unified phenomenon, a kind of 'force', which (2) has spread (like a contagion) from out of the corporate milieu into all other kinds of institutional spheres and modes of social order, as well as into the wider body of global politics, economy and culture. This *sui generis* contamination surprised and neutralised its victims, 'the victims of ideological socialization [who] do not rebel but support the given ideology', as Klikauer (2015, 1106) proposes in a recent argument. Moreover, this view of managerialism is also accompanied by a general agreement that it is, from a historical viewpoint, a 'new' and relatively recent phenomenon. Lynch, Grummell and Devine (2012), for example, adopt Boltanski and Chiapello's periodisation in framing their own position:

> Management literature during the 1990s offered ideals, propositions for the organisation of people, and modes for structuring objects and forms of security – all of which were so different in nature from that which had been on offer during the 1960s that it is difficult not to conclude that capitalism has broadly changed its spirit in the past thirty years. (Boltanski and Chiapello, cited in Lynch, Grummell and Devine 2012, 3–4)

While it seems that the 1990s did indeed bring forth a change in the language of management and business, is the historical line drawn here right? Trying to understand this change through such blunt distinctions may in fact weaken the intellectual astuteness required by this process. Because, at the same time, no careful observer can avoid noticing that the language of managerialism has gained significant traction beyond the boundaries of private and public organisations, and of political and managerial elites. It has moved, not without some self-confidence, beyond formal institutions and has become a subtle ingredient of common modes of everyday self-understanding characterising contemporary popular culture and its sensibilities in a variety of social spheres and settings. So, if we stay with the medical metaphor for one more moment, the question this chapter raises comes from a natural reaction to these hypotheses: if managerialism is a new and extraneous infection, why is the political, social and cultural body not putting up a more robust immune response? What makes managerialism so historically effective? What kind of phenomenon is it – if it can indeed be addressed in the singular?

My argument here proposes that *managerialism* is not so easily recognisable as a *singular* phenomenal 'reality' (as it is taken to be in most scholarly debates); rather, it may be more productive to treat it as an entry point into a series of pressing questions whose analysis requires continuous conceptual refinement if we are to get hold of the nature of what seems to be under way all around us, especially if it is 'pathological'. Neil Smelser (1997, 1) gave a helpful contour to the latter position using the term 'problematics':

> By 'problematics' I mean those generic, recurrent, never-resolved and never-completely-resolvable issues that shape how we pursue our work, how we generate theoretical tensions and conflicts in that work, how we converse and debate with one another, and how we engage in that complex counterpoint of simultaneous advance, retreat, and repetition in our scholarship.

I will proceed in what follows by tracing an empirical example. It illustrates a recurrent aspect in debates about managerialism, but one which seems to remain stubbornly resistant to a clear-cut resolution articulated in simple terms. It is the question of origin, of the point in historical time from which we can declare managerialism's inception. As a student of *management*, I am concerned with understanding where the historical threshold of *managerialism* is to be placed (in relation to the overall history of *management*). Should we take as read the one suggested by Boltanski and Chiapello, for instance? And, if the birth of managerialism is indeed to be located in the 1990s, in what way is it distinctive from the 1960s? Digging through the multitude of possible 'archaeological' sources, I recalled a rather substantial and significant statement, part of the famous *Port Huron Statement* (made public in August 1962) produced by the largest and most influential radical student organisation of the 1960s, Students for a Democratic Society (SDS). In the section entitled *Values,* there is the articulation of a conception of humanity emancipated from the conformist demands of postwar American capitalism:

> We regard *Man* [*sic*] as infinitely precious and infinitely perfectible. . . . Men have infinite potential for self-cultivation, self-direction, self-understanding, and creativity. It is this potential that we regard as crucial and to which we appeal, not to the human potentiality for violence, unreason, and submission to authority. The goal of man and society should be human independence: a

> concern not with the image of popularity but with finding a meaning in life that is personally authentic; a quality of mind not compulsively driven by a sense of powerlessness, nor one which unthinkingly adopts status values, nor one which represses all threats to its habits, but one which has full, spontaneous access to present and past experiences, one which easily unites the fragmented parts of personal history, one which openly faces problems which are troubling and unresolved; one with an intuitive awareness of possibilities, an active sense of curiosity, and ability and willingness to learn. (Students for a Democratic Society 1962)

What is interesting about this statement (as a metaphysical declaration) is how, from the 1990s onwards, the conceptual structures of management have shown an almost uncanny capacity to assimilate, with relentless intensity, precisely the premises of this view, especially those asserted in the first two sentences of this passage, into the language through which management itself now conceives of the human subject. The main tropes of management discourses – especially explicit in the explosive evolution of human resource management over the past three decades – are rooted in these premises. In this sense, perhaps the 1990s are not all that disconnected from the 1960s. Quite the contrary: may it be the case that, historically, it was not managerialism that contaminated contemporary cultural and institutional orders, but the other way around? Namely, what if it was management thinking and speaking that was absorbed by the ideas and vocabularies of human essence of the late twentieth century, through which all other determinations of existence were finally dissolved, and which affirmed the conclusive triumph of self-assertive and self-expressive subjectivity as sole primordial authority? Even though it sounds like one, this is not an equally one-sided, inversion of the original proposition. Rather, it is a suggestion that it is difficult to understand the advance of managerialism simply as a one-sided exercise of power, as deployment of pure political force which victimises and silences its victims, even though it may seem to be the simplest explanation.

My proposition is that managerialism – if it is to be understood as unified in some way – is, at least so far, only a name through which we seek to grasp a fluid, eclectic assemblage of cultural motifs, often incompatible with one another, frequently self-contradictory, and nearly always conceptually feeble – and that is why the propositions of managerialism always appear, at first sight, as so much fleeting bombast (Wheen 2004; Watson 2005), or, in more serious terms, as mere *untruths*. What seems less examined and understood so far is the source from which something so suspect and mendacious draws its energy and vitality: if managerialism is so weak, suspect and manipulative, why is it nonetheless so strong and irresistible? The present argument suggests that we can seek an answer by tracing the increasing ability of managerialism – understood, in preliminary terms, as a kind of movement of cultural material – to draw its sustenance from the deepest source of modernity's self-understanding: the drive to secure an endless horizon for human self-assertion in the name of a new faith in the infinite *potential* and *entitlement* of *individuality* to 'posit itself as the meaning and measure of the value of things' (Nietzsche 1968, 14, Note 12(B)). Nietzsche's reference to Protagoras's saying in his explanation of nihilism indicates that modernity has to be understood as 'an event that has transformed the relation between the cosmos, its transcendent source, and its human interpreter' (Dupré 1993, 249). I am making here a bold gesture: managerialism has to be connected, in order to be understood, to the foundational axis of modern self- and world-understanding, to the centre from which modern existence is driven: to human self-assertion (Blumenberg 1983; Taylor 1992; Dupré 1993), to the centrality of the *subjectivity of the subject* as the root of all values and modes of valuation. This is an ambitious claim: that managerialism lends itself to, and actually requires for its proper conceptual articulation, a metaphysical interpretation. But it is not a claim to be dismissed out of hand. In his monumental analyses of Nietzsche's thinking, Martin Heidegger explains *self-assertion* as the principle of an epoch in which humanity sees itself as freed up from any exterior determination:

> The securing of supreme and absolute self-development of all the capacities of mankind for the absolute dominion over the entire earth is the secret goad that prods modern man again and again to new resurgences, a goad that forces him into commitments that secure for him the surety of his actions and the certainty of his aims. (Heidegger 1991, 99)

What is management's place in this historical movement? I am replacing the term 'managerialism' (one of speculative nature) with 'management' (as a set of concrete historical phenomena) for a practical purpose. Whereas managerialism is a category elaborated as part of intellectual efforts to name some of common features of our epoch, management refers here to the practical realities to which we can turn our attention when investigating empirical realities which can, subsequently, be categorised as 'managerial'.

MANAGERIALISM AS A PROMISSORY ENGINE

If the seriousness of the question regarding the nature and historical situation of management is accepted, then the task is one of understanding how this manner of thinking arose, how and where it sets out its propositions and how broad is its purview. In the case of management, the sources for such an exploration are far from straightforward. On the one hand, management does not have a set of foundational texts in which its metaphysical articulation is set out; on the other, writings of, and on, management are almost endless and the genres in which they are produced are themselves vastly different from, say, religious or political programmes. To decide which of management's texts is central to its professed truth is an almost impossible task. How do we even begin? Perhaps, one way is to take the position of an archaeologist and look for all the various empirical instances which could be categorised as practices of management and submit them to just as complex a process of interpretation as we naturally would when faced with new archaeological or archival discoveries.

I will try to offer in this section such an archaeological exercise to substantiate the argument discussed earlier. First, however, a word on *method*. Trying to decipher how the cultural synthesis which founds an epoch is reflected in its iconography is a well-established mode of investigation. The reference point in the twentieth century is the work of Erwin Panofsky (Panofsky 1962, 1982, 1997), followed by a long series of refinements, developments and sometimes departures (Barthes 1977; Mitchell 1987; Mondzain 2005). Whereas the study of artefacts that count as works of art is somewhat easier, when it comes to considering common, often indifferent, objects as our sources, the interpretation is a more difficult, more uncertain exercise. However, I will argue later that the example I am using would immediately draw the attention of any serious interpreter; in other words, I am proposing that if this object were to be found a thousand years hence, archaeologists and cultural historians would know that they have something to ponder, something like a master key to the cultural economy of our time – or, to use Ginzburg's images, they will know that it contains 'clues', 'threads and traces', of 'the cosmos' of a twenty-first-century management subject (Ginzburg 1992a, 1992b, 2012).

Sometime in the spring of 2017, while visiting a business school in the United Kingdom, I had to use a public computer to print a document. The computer I found was one of five or six in an open study space on the ground floor of the school. When I touched the mouse, my eyes were immediately drawn to the mouse mat underneath. And it is this simple object that I want to focus on: a simple, cheaply made, standard mouse mat, but, on it, an utterly compelling image (which, unfortunately, cannot be reproduced here due to copyright law). Even though my description might not be as stimulating as the image itself, the real importance of this artefact lies in the text that grounds the image, rather than other way around. The rectangle of this regular-sized mat carries the logo of the supermarket chain Aldi at the top, and that of the university business school where I found it at the bottom (this detail is important: it is an advertisement for a corporate graduate management scheme produced, however, in collaboration between a corporate entity and a university; I later learned more about the circumstances of its production and there are significant further clues about its significance in that process).

The core image is a photographic portrait taking up the left half of the surface; in the centre is a textbox containing a statement made by the character in the portrait. The background is a colourful, but blurred, view of the interior of a supermarket. The figure in the portrait is carefully chosen: it is meant to represent every possible student who would look at it. The head of a bright, yet anonymous, young woman, it is precisely her studied anonymity that renders her into the nearly universally recognisable, generic, 'face' of current generations of university students everywhere. Dressed in a normal, dark, office suit jacket, with a buttoned-up, pale blue shirt, her expression is telling: head bent slightly to the right, she looks straight at the viewer with a discrete, but knowing, smile, self-assured, yet not arrogant (on the company website, she is the main character in a photographic story of a year in the life of a graduate management trainee at Aldi – Aldi 2018). Above all, however, we somehow know straightaway that it is not a 'warm' gaze looking back at us. This is not the face of a *selfless* soul; to the contrary, it is the countenance of a *self* convinced of its place as source of sense and direction for itself, and the only source at that. This is not to say that there is any hint of aggression or guilt, nor any sense of unease, in the portrait: '"Selflessness" has no value either in heaven or earth' for this truly modern figure (Nietzsche 1974, 243, Note 345); to the contrary, self-centredness is a virtue borne out of the victory of freedom. And this is how the other part of the image acquires its logic and importance. The statement made by this character appears in the box at the centre of the ensemble, to the right of the portrait, and of about the same size as the face. The text is divided in sections, each using a colour from the company's logo, and reads:

> I'm still me, but
> the most confident,
> all-conquering version of me.
>
> It's tough. Tougher than I thought it would be. You're
> taken out of your comfort zone and given a million
> things to juggle. But helping to drive one of the UK's
> fastest-growing supermarkets? It feels utterly amazing.
>
> BECAUSE I'M ALDI. AND I'M LIKE NO OTHER

So far, this description is what Panofsky (1962, 5) would have considered to be the 'primary or natural subject matter'; the next stage should attempt to establish the set of cultural conventions, of common points of reference on which the image relies so that it becomes intelligible for an audience. Some of the motifs have been already alluded to: the image that constitutes the portrait, the alliance between a corporation and a university, the light touch of the material support of a basic mouse mat. But Panofsky (1962, 6) suggests that for an image to draw the viewer into its economy, it has to do more than be *formally* recognisable; it has to be comprehensible in terms of the '*themes* or *concepts*' with which it operates, in terms of what he called 'secondary or conventional subject matter'. I looked around and discovered that throughout the area, on several tables, there were stacks of these mats for anyone to pick up and take home. This thing was not there by happenstance; it was not a minor object, on its own, random, almost invisible against the overall background of the place. This mat was a call to attention; it was actually very present and very active and commanding, as it were. It asked its addressees to consider it as their possible desk 'companion'; it really wanted to be taken seriously into consideration – it asked, in other words, *to be read*. And it did indeed work: no one could have come across it on the desk of that public computer and not notice its presence and message. And so, a modest mouse mat becomes, in this sense, something different: it becomes, like so many (if not all) contemporary objects, an intertextual means of communicating something completely different from its primary use-value. It becomes yet another advertising surface whose appearance in a university is, in a sense, a surprise, but, in another, it is almost expected – what else would university surfaces speak of if not the future of their own students?

I realised very quickly that this was a very elaborate, indeed very intelligent, gesture. The level of thought and sophistication that went into its composition was far from negligible. This object shows, in fact, what a serious statement it seeks to make about the ways in which management operates as a medium for the circulation of very important and very complex ideas. Panofsky himself would probably have also stopped and thought through what this humble mouse mat actually names. His attention would have been drawn, beyond the object itself and its context, to the text inscribed on it. And this is where the central character that connects the entire assemblage of object, image, institutional context and the cultural 'cosmos' which gives them all meaning makes its entrance: the imperious, commanding *I*, the ultimate expression of pure individuality, in whose name the order of values is to be arranged. As a statement of the completion of the empowerment of the 'I' towards its 'all-conquering version', this artefact reveals, as it were, the whole metaphysics of our age. Panofsky (1962, 7) calls at this point for a third level of interpretation of such an image: that of its 'intrinsic meaning or content' through which we may apprehend 'those underlying principles which reveal the basic attitude of a nation, a period, a class, a religious or philosophical persuasion'.

Read in this light, the true importance of this little object becomes more apparent. What it offers is not mere mimicry of cultural assumptions firmly entrenched in the foundation of modern, secularised, self-understanding. Moreover, this particular thing is not an isolated instance, an exception. For more than two decades, we have witnessed the emergence and explosive growth of an entire genre in the graduate recruitment literature, a genre specialised in such statements (Costea, Amiridis and Crump 2012a, 2012b; Costea, Watt and Amiridis 2015). In some ways, this mouse mat might be one of the least impressive examples, partly because its circulation is inherently restricted by the institutional context, and partly because, as an object, it seems so disposable – it is, after all, a mere mouse mat. Yet, if we are interested in the ways in which management has become firmly attached to the core of contemporary culture, it is precisely the relative innocuousness of this little thing that makes it all the more worthy of careful interpretation. What is striking about the statement it makes is not only that it would interest Panofsky, but that it would interest thinkers like Friedrich Nietzsche (whose attention to the details of everyday life was perhaps second to none in the philosophical tradition). Why would the philosopher of the revaluation of all values, of nihilism and of the will to power find anything worthy of careful dissection in a mouse mat? Because Nietzsche, like other philosophers later, understood that such images are not simple moments of mendacity and manipulation. To the contrary, as Barthes (1977, 33) argued later, Nietzsche would have known that 'the image's signification is assuredly intentional . . . if the image contains signs, we can be sure that in advertising these signs are replete, formed with a view to the best possible reading: the advertising image is frank, or at least emphatic'.

And Nietzsche was interested precisely in this: the mechanisms through which promises of the first order are made in a culture, and promises in whose name human existence is guided, structured and instituted. The second essay of the *Genealogy of Morals* (1887) begins with a sentence whose import has not yet been even noticed in the study of management and organisations: 'To breed an animal which *dares to make promises* – isn't this precisely the paradoxical task that nature has set itself with respect to man? is it not the true problem of man' (Nietzsche 2000, 493)?

The thought that making promises is 'the true problem' of being human, on the one hand, and that the appearance of humanity sets 'nature' a 'paradoxical task', on the other, is what the Aldi mouse mat illustrates explicitly and implicitly. Explicitly, it shows just how compelling management has become as one of the sources from which ultimate promises of self-assertion originate today. Ultimate empowerment and, through it, the perfection of one's self are not offers that can be either ignored or turned down; in fact, they do not offer a choice; they are commands. This is the implicit tone both of the image and of the text: 'I am still me', but in my irresistible, triumphant version, that to which *you, the viewer*, cannot but aspire. How else would you be able to claim your own existence at all, and how else would you be able to claim to have lived without 'guilt' and a 'bad conscience' (as the title of Nietzsche's essay names the refusal to take up an epoch's promises)? Later, in section 3 of the same essay, he discusses the psychological mechanism by which promises are to be impressed upon 'the human animal . . . this partly obtuse, partly flighty mind': 'How can one create a memory for the human animal?' he (2000, 496) asks:

> One can well believe that the answers and methods for solving this primeval problem were not precisely gentle; perhaps indeed there was nothing more fearful and uncanny in the whole prehistory of man than his *mnemotechnics*. 'If something is to stay in the memory it must be burned in: only that which never ceases to hurt stays in the memory' – this is a main clause of the oldest (unhappily also the most enduring) psychology on earth. (Nietzsche 2000, 497)

And here we have to grasp the implicit dimension of the mouse mat: it is not that it is *threatening*, but it is certainly *unsettling*. The gaze has to be confronted again and again: it is that of one who *looks like* 'me' but is entirely *unlike* 'me'. It is the gaze of the one who has succeeded to such an extent that she has reached the peak of ultimate individuation and self-realisation: 'And I'm like no other'. Her gaze calls *me*, the viewer, into question and – moved as I am by the same cultural forces and by the same values – I am not able, I am not allowed, to look away: this should be *my promise* too; this *fate* ought to be mine just as much, but what if I, when my turn comes, will not be able to withstand the sublation, and fail? And here 'failure' means falling back to the ground of *normality*, where the faceless mass dwells. Nietzsche (2000, 497) calls this 'the terror that attend[s] all promises, pledges, and vows on earth', and it is this terror, he argues, that makes all serious promises effective. A subtle inversion (which partly explains the 'paradoxical' effect Nietzsche mentions in the first sentence of his essay) accompanies every promise: when *I* am called and have to hear the promise of my own self-realisation, the question is not whether the promise will live up to its side of the bargain, but whether *I* will ever be able to rise up to its imperative. It is now perhaps the time to explain further how not just what the mouse mat says, but also how it was produced. Who speaks this version of the language of management? I was able to find out more about this object and the circumstances in which it was produced. Among the many such artefacts I, together with colleagues, have gathered and traced over the past three decades, this one is somewhat different and I tried to uncover some of the traces leading back to its origins. I had the chance to discuss it with some of its direct authors and – perhaps surprising, perhaps not – it is important to clarify here how the text itself was elaborated. As I said earlier, this mouse mat is not a facile or improvised affair. It turns out that the attempt to capture the spirit of the times through this little object was even more systematic than I suspected: the text itself was produced over a year, through a series of focus group sessions, from preliminary ideas, through their refinement, up to the final version, which was chosen and approved by the members of the focus group. Who is speaking managerialism?

We may shrug off Aldi's mouse mat as a minuscule, insignificant occurrence. But then we would have to discard in a similar fashion the vast majority of management's symbolic structures because so many of them are banalities, so much 'mumbo-jumbo of illusions' (Wheen 2004) that cannot be taken as seriously as we would, say, a religious image or text, or referential text or work of art. My argument, on the other hand, is that we would then place our attempt to understand 'managerialism' in a much less secure intellectual position. If archaeology's principle (and lesson) is to leave no stone, or detail, unturned and unmapped in the historical record of the past, then the attempt to understand the record of the present has to be bound by the same aspiration to rigour. In this spirit, Aldi's artefact sheds significant light on one of the most powerful dimensions of management practices: namely, to take up those places previously occupied by other cultural authorities and become one of the most effective promissory engines of contemporary culture. The programme of emancipation of the Students for a Democratic Society in 1962 sought to awaken the American youth from its conformist slumber under the yoke of corporate capitalism. Five decades later, SDS would have to admit that its programme has indeed not only been remembered, but that it has succeeded, albeit in a completely different way than they could have ever anticipated. The students of the 1960s would have to deal with the surprise: to find their counterparts of the 2000s directly engaged in, and by, the vastly more effective expressions of the same belief in the infinite power of self-cultivation and perfectibility of individuality, this time proposed by corporate capitalism itself. Should we then ask: is Aldi's mouse mat a sign of what this volume is after, namely a sign of the triumph of management over its opposition, precisely by taking over the latter's own programme? Or is the absorption of that programme into management not a sign that its anti-conformist, anti-establishment and emancipatory principles have, in fact, triumphed over management? How would we know?

VALUE AND DEVALUATION IN THE AGE OF SELF-ASSERTION

What is at stake in posing this question is not of marginal interest: what has to be confronted here is the question whether the *truth of human self-assertion* lies with the political programme of SDS or with its current managerial version? When speaking from within the same metaphysical horizon (the liberation of the 'infinite potential for self-cultivation, self-direction, self-understanding and creativity' of the individual), can there be a qualitative distinction between the two modes of *instituting* life claiming this imperative as their own? And if indeed there is, what would such a distinction reveal? Key to this question is the conception of *institution* with which it operates. Hans Blumenberg (in his monumental *Work on Myth*, 1985) provides one of the most coherent (yet completely ignored) definitions of *institutions*:

> What the heading 'institutions' covers is, above all, a distribution of burdens of proof. Where an institution exists, the question of its rational foundation is not, of itself, urgent, and the burden of proof always lies on the person who objects to the arrangement the institution carries with it. (Blumenberg 1985, 166)

So, the question about the triumph of *managerialism*, reformulated in the more operative way as the question of the triumph of *management,* asks: why, in the struggle over the same conception of the nature of modern humanity, does the economy of management thinking prevail over what appears to be the vastly more generous economy of the thinking of the democratic 'Left' (whether it is called socialism, social democracy or indeed liberalism)? Why does the Left carry such a 'burden of proof', when management (as mode of *instituting* the same principles) fared with so much more ease in the history of the past half-century?

To pursue this question, we need some understanding of the conditions in which the institution of the 'business enterprise' prevailed over all its competitors in the twentieth century. While it is not possible to offer a comprehensive historical account here, it is possible to understand the metaphysical process at work in this history. In his exegesis of Nietzsche's thesis 'God is dead' (in 1943), Heidegger (1977a, 53–112) provides the kind of reading that can help us here. In trying to show how 'the greatest recent event – that "God is dead"' (Nietzsche 1974, 279, Note 343) defines Nietzsche's essential understanding of 'nihilism', Heidegger explains what happened to the *institutions* of modernity as a consequence of this epoch-shattering event:

> Into the position of the vanished authority of God and of the teaching office of the Church steps the authority of conscience, obtrudes the authority of reason. Against these the social instinct rises up. The flight from the world into the suprasensory is replaced by historical progress. The otherworldly goal of everlasting bliss is transformed into the earthly happiness of the greatest number. The careful maintenance of the cult of religion is relaxed through enthusiasm for the creating of a culture or the spreading of civilization. Creativity, previously the unique property of the biblical god, becomes the distinctive mark of

> human activity. Human creativity finally passes over into business enterprise. (Heidegger 1977a, 64)

It is important to note the nuances in the original German for the last two sentences and, especially, for the appearance of the words 'creativity' and 'business'. They are not easy to translate into a flowing English, but their original sense is important to grasp the point Heidegger makes here: first, the English *creativity* appears first as the German *das Schöpferische* which means 'the creative as such', or 'the attribute of creativity itself', whereas in the second instance, the rendering 'creativity' is perhaps not as felicitous; the German sentence is more complicated: 'Dessen Schaffen geht zuletzt in das Geschäft über'. This means: 'Its *production* [that is, the bringing forth of creative work – BC] passes over into the realm of business itself'. Thus, Heidegger's thought is something like: 'The attribute of creativity itself, previously the unique property of the biblical god, becomes the distinctive mark of human activity. Its *production* passes over into the realm of business itself'. The reason these nuances are important is because Heidegger did not frequently use the word 'business' when discussing *production*, and in the instances when he does, it indicates a significant intention. And that is why this passage explains substantially (as well as succinctly) how the place of 'business', and therefore of its 'management', can be understood in the context of modernity's metaphysical unfolding. The equation of 'human activity' with the realm of 'business', and the latter's equation with 'the creative' attribute, is decisive for the argument made in this chapter too: *business* and *management* are not simply intrusions into the history of modernity. Rather, they are – for better or worse – its driving forces, its very engine. The faculty of creation, that is, the place for the production of *values*, but also of *valuation* as such, is now their province. This is why Aldi's mat is such an important expression of 'the creative' faculty: it shows how *management* becomes, in itself, the place for the ultimate gesture of *production*: *self-production* and *self-empowerment*. In other words, management is not simply the administration of the production, distribution and consumption of 'goods', but the very crucible in which the ultimate value of the age of self-assertion is produced: 'me, but the most confident, all-conquering version of me', that ultimate one who is 'like no other'. And the corollary becomes equally true: whoever cannot reach this ultimate position of self-valuation has no worth.

Heidegger explains Nietzsche's thinking further: the word 'God' has to be 'thought essentially', that is, thought not as a remote figure of myth, but rather as the principle that orders all values and maintains that order. 'God', in other words, is to be understood as a 'foundational structure' (*Grundgefüge*, he [1977a, 64] names it) which brought the grounding values of the Christian epoch into a stable and meaningful hierarchy. But with the death of *this* god, and the dwindling away of its values, that hierarchy is shattered, is it not? Surely, it cannot be possible to posit *values* any longer without a principle to order them? Is this not Nietzsche's (1968, 9, Note 2) definition of 'European nihilism' itself? 'What does nihilism mean? *That the highest values devaluate themselves*. The aim is lacking; "why?" finds no answer'. Heidegger's answer is 'no', because *business*, as the realm of 'the creative', steps onto the empty stage *prepared*. The actor able to take up the mantle was ready and had been ready for a long while before the twentieth century. But *business* is not a new 'god', and it refuses to take that position because with it comes an unbearable responsibility. *Business* is merely the new principle of movement that allows the entrance in history of a new 'all-conquering' subject, but, this time, this is a very different kind of historical being and a different kind of producer and consumer of *value*. Something else is under way in history now, and perhaps this is the moment when we can truly read into the rise of business and management as modes and sources of valuation one of the facets of Nietzsche's diagnosis of nihilism, as a destructive, resentful and decadent movement.

Who is this *destroyer* of the highest values, and what does this have to do with business and management? The paradoxical answer is that this *destroyer* is, in fact, the most effective *producer* of all history. And this is where the thesis about the triumph of managerialism needs one further qualification: what does business *produce*, and why has management been so successful in reoccupying the place vacated by the vanishing authorities hitherto? The world-changing success of the system of mass production, based on the progressive assembly line invented by Henry Ford in 1908, is not only a material, administrative or technological accomplishment. It is all these, but it is also the condition of management's own cultural success. Mass production in itself is not sufficient to guarantee its historical effectiveness; on its own, it is always a problem for itself. Mass production needs something else to sustain it, and that is an ingredient of a completely different order, one which the twentieth century took a while to create and consolidate. It needs its consuming counterpart: mass consumption. But not any kind of mass consumption: however massive, the finite stock of needs of a finite mass does not resolve the real *metaphysical* problem of an economy able to *physically* produce everything, in any amount. The apparently infinite power of mass production created a well-known euphoria with the new human power: the ability to make anything, anywhere, anytime, in any quantity and, at the same time lower, the cost of everything. But this model can only be short-lived; there are no infinite needs, there are no infinite populations and there is never infinite demand. Surely, the proposition of infinite production is as untenable as any that denies finitude and 'erases limits' (as Malpas shows in this volume)? Infinite production should simply not work as a *promise*, because even modern humanity must surely know, *with certainty*, that it is mortal and finite. In an age that claims reason as its defining faculty, infinite production can only be an irrational proposition, the most anti-economic one, is it not? The *economy*, as the realm of modern practical reason, cannot be entertaining the illusion that it is rational to produce anything infinitely.

But this is precisely what did happen: not only is the physical machinery of production a *perpetuum mobile*, but contemporary culture has given birth to the infinite *consuming subject* now driving a metaphysical *perpetuum mobile* too. It turns out that there indeed was a solution to the problem of finite consumption. And it came from an apparently paradoxical source: it was, as I have already indicated, the 1960s that provided the answer to this quest. It came from ideas that shaped the political, social and artistic movements of anti-corporatism and anti-capitalism, united against what appeared to be a joyless, conformist, consumer existence. It soon was no longer acceptable to be a simple cog in the middle-class, bourgeois, social machine which had mapped so simply the path of an individual's life: education, corporate employment, the formation of a suburban middle-class family, with a predictable (and measured) pattern of consumption, a linear lifestyle in a uniform, faceless society. The motto in 1966 was, Timothy Leary's 'Turn on, tune in, drop out'; in the 1970s, it was Abraham Maslow's 'self-actualisation', the Esalen Institute and Werner Erhard's EST Training (Heelas 1996); in the 1980s and 1990s, it was Tony Robbins's 'Do not settle for anything less than you can be! Make your life a masterpiece!'; in 2017, it is Aldi's 'become the all-conquering version of yourself! Be like no other!'

What emerged from this process turned out to be nothing against business or management, but exactly what the economy of mass production needed: a new kind of infinite mass consumer. This time, however, this new mass consumer does not see himself or herself merely as a member of a faceless 'mass'. Each individual is entitled to understand himself or herself 'like no other' and to demand to be treated in this way. And so, a new rhetoric of consumption took hold with increasing (and unrelenting) intensity: the rhetoric of individualised, self-expressing, self-actualising, individuality. In other words, the very act of consumption found a new form of presentation: to consume is to search endlessly to express one's sense of a unique self. Every product, every service, every act of shopping has become an act of self-performance, an act of positioning oneself through consumption as a singular, special, unparalleled individual. The machinery of mass production has now found its most important driver: an endless consumer who no longer seeks objects to satisfy limited needs, but infinite desires. Therefore, the production of any object is no longer under threat from finite consumption, but rather made possible by infinite requirements. And this consumer has a name – it is the name of a *promise* in Nietzsche's sense, an endlessly sustainable *metaphysical proposition*. One more – apparently minuscule – archaeological fragment from the history of the present century might probe yet more the depths of management's roots in the contemporary soul. I discovered it in the mid-2000s, as the Internet commerce revolution was in full swing; it is a clothing retailer whose original name and motto would (and ought to) be as striking if found in an archaeological dig of the future as Delphi's 'know thyself' was for us: 'Spoiled Brat: Who says you can't have it all . . . '. This is one of the most serious statements in which both the 'triumph' and the peril of business and management are expressed. Indeed, the retailer itself has since removed the tagline, while retaining the name; they may have realised themselves how enormous that promise was. When Nietzsche (1968, 3, Preface) announced 'the problem of man' as 'daring to make promises' in 1887, he may not have anticipated just how much the concrete act of promising itself would triumph over, and become the basis for, all other social bonds of 'the next two centuries'. But that would be to overlook how profound his intuition was about the two centuries he had in sight. The promise 'to have it all' is not simply the promise of having access to the possession of all 'things'. Max Scheler (1980, 133) explained this in 1924, after almost a century of modern consumption had already begun to show its essence: 'Capitalist *economy* is based in the *will to endless acquiring* (as an act), *not* in the will to *acquisition* (as a growing *possession* of things)'.

And the promise of contemporary life reaches even further than that; it goes as far as Aldi's promise of access to the ultimate possibility of total validation (and valuation) of the subjectivity of any subject: to become the measure of all things, and the measure of all measures that can apply to 'me'. Isn't this to have reached the highest possible place? Nietzsche (1968, 380, Note 713) explains value itself in precisely these terms: 'Value is the highest quantum of power that a man is able to incorporate – a man: not mankind! Mankind is even a means sooner than an end. It is a question of the type: mankind is merely the experimental material, the tremendous surplus of failures: a field of ruins'. Aldi's offer, in other words, is the offer of the epoch itself: what type are you? The valuable one or one for the ruin heap? The possibility, the promise, is there and it cannot be refused – to refuse it is to deny the very premise of modern existence: self-assertion.

CONCLUDING REMARKS

In his explanation of 'European nihilism', Nietzsche (1968, 12–14, Note 12 [A] and [B]) sees it as 'Decline of Cosmological Values', by which he means the devaluation of the categories of 'aim', 'unity', and 'being'. He makes a clear historical reference: he is talking about *modernity*. And he sees modernity as a process of decline with three 'psychological states', three states of the soul. It is the combination between the first and the second that offers a way of reading the metaphysical plane on which managerialism may be said to have triumphed. The first 'psychological state' of 'European nihilism' is the loss of faith in a sense of purpose for existence as could be articulated in the precepts of the Christian synthesis. The second, however, is more subtle and more revealing for the question addressed in this volume (in what way can we speak of a triumph of managerialism?): with the loss of a sense of purpose comes the loss of a sense of bond that may *unite* humanity into a meaningful whole, but, with this, there also comes the greatest triumph of modernity – freedom *from* all transcendent authorities. The annihilation of the bonds of purpose and unity marks the great liberation of which modernity is so legitimately proud. But, Nietzsche argues that, at the very same time of this conquest, the modern soul – who knows itself to be finite and, therefore, unable to carry the burden of fate on its own – is, immediately, haunted by an unrelenting anguish and a desperate search for a uniting principle, for a new 'whole', a new 'totality' to which every 'one' can once again belong. He explains it in the following manner:

> Nihilism as a psychological state is reached, *secondly*, when one has posited a totality, a systematization, indeed any organization in all events, and underneath all events, and a soul that longs to admire and revere has wallowed in the idea of some supreme form of domination and administration (if the soul be that of a logician, complete consistency and real dialectic are quite sufficient to reconcile it to everything). Some sort of unity, some form of 'monism': this faith suffices to give man a deep feeling of standing in the context of, and being dependent on, some whole that is infinitely superior to him, and he sees himself as a mode of the deity. 'The well-being of the universal demands the devotion of the individual' – but behold, there is no such universal! At bottom, man has lost the faith in his own value when no infinitely valuable whole works through him; i.e., he conceived such a whole in order *to be able to believe in his own value*. (Nietzsche 1968, 12, Note 12[A])

With uncanny foresight, Nietzsche outlined here the political, social and economic history of the twentieth century, and could do so because he understood the structure of the modern soul – he was, in this respect, a true 'psychologist' unlike any who succeeded him. If the succession of experiments with political formulas meant to provide both total organisation and the revaluation of humanity in the wake of the death of god could be summarised in one statement, this one of Nietzsche's is probably as close as any could be. Communism, Bolshevism, socialism, national-socialism, fascism, and liberalism were so many crucibles which tried to forge, to the extreme, one and the same material: a new cultural synthesis in which modern humanity could function in a world freed from transcendent authority, but also one in which the individual would not have to bear the weight of responsibility that came with modern freedom. While all the political systems of the twentieth century promised to create conditions for the rise of the 'new man', most failed to articulate a convincing proposition that did not require some new form of unconditional submission of *individuality* (as the essence of modern humanity) to either party, state, class, race or fatherland. None turned out to be credible. It was *business* and *management* that inherited the problem of freedom (metaphysically understood) and began, after 1989, to provide the most compelling programme of the empowering of individuality, to the point that their institutional formula seems to provide the most subtle articulation of 'a whole' within which the production of *values,* that is, the production and contestation of *power* itself, has been handed over to the individual subject who, now '*able to believe in his own value*', has but one struggle to face: to be 'still me, but the most confident, all-conquering version of me'. The triumph of the language of management seems to require further elucidation in this respect, that of the 'psychological state' to which it corresponds historically, as much as it requires elucidation in terms of its institutional and organisational forms and evolution.

Chapter 5

The Birth of the Think Tank

RAND and the Development of a Technocratic World View

Ihab Shalbak

INTRODUCTION

The establishment of RAND Corporation after the Second World War in the United States introduced a new institutional form – the think tank – and a new kind of intellectual persona, the professional knowledge entrepreneur and broker. While new, it also continued an established American tradition of pragmatist and progressivist thought that brought capitalism, democracy and science together in the form of the philanthropic foundation. Central to this tradition was a faith in scientific problem-solving as this is translated into technological intervention of one kind or another. Such faith relied on a reconstruction of American society and its place in the world not as a contingently historical phenomenon but as an evolutionary one where the American mode of modernity represented not just the most successful but the exemplary form of adaptation. It was this technocratic world view that authorised American hegemony, turning the twentieth century into an American one. While today we have reason to question the continuation of American hegemony, the technocratic world view now underwrites a global system of governance that has displaced the authority of national states and the responsibility of national governments for attending to the welfare of their citizens. It is the think tank that is the institutional form of technocracy. In this chapter I examine how RAND came to be the paradigmatic think tank, and how it inaugurated a distinctive set of intellectual practices and forms of knowledge given over to the imperative of systemic order.

Although, after 1941, John Dewey, and with him Pragmatism, went into a long abeyance, Dewey remained 'a patron saint of American thinkers' (Kuklick 2006, 8). His philosophy, with its instrumental bent, remained the inspirational logic of an educated and professional class determined to preserve its status and fulfil its destiny. Dewey's reconstructive philosophy had this to say to this professional class:

> *If* ideas, meanings, conceptions, notions, theories, systems, are instrumental to active reorganization of the given environment, to a removal of some specific trouble and perplexity, then the test of their validity and value lies in accomplishing this work. If they succeed in their office, they are reliable, sound, valid, good, true. If they fail to clear up confusion, uncertainty and evil when they are acted upon, then they are false. (Dewey 1920, 156)

By the 1940s, generations of students had read and absorbed Dewey's call to employ the 'method of intelligence' and his argument that knowledge must be 'active and operative' (Kuklick 2006, 8). Strategic policy intellectuals of all stripes, including the newly founded RAND Corporation theorists, were 'steeped in these writings . . . [and] largely agreed with the dominant credo of their time' (Kuklick 2006, 11). In becoming functionaries of the American National Security State, these disciples of Dewey turned the intellectual and institutional structures developed to address the social question of the Progressive Era into the framework with which to address the geopolitical question of the Cold War.

From the 1950s to the 1970s, the RAND Corporation represented a distinctive mindset and style, generating techniques for tackling geopolitical and sociopolitical issues. RAND focused on organisational techniques and methods that would provide economic and technical policy solutions to military problems and, later, to social and political ones. RAND's intellectuals worked in teams, prioritised quantifying disciplines and methodologies and declared themselves above politics. Due to appeals to instrumental notions such as 'efficiency', 'manageability', and 'competence', RAND appeared to be an innovative institutional form that effectively employed the 'method of intelligence' and had worked out the right formula for making knowledge 'active and operative'.

RAND provided a new institutional setting for the production of a distinctive form of reasoning and authority, which perfected and extended the Pragmatist coupling of naturalism and empiricism. As a style of thought, as Robert B. Brandom argues, pragmatism was shaped by the spread of Darwinian evolutionary and statistical explanations as the principal forms of intelligibility. In a society in a state of flux:

> Evolutionary and statistical explanations explain *contingent* happenings, by displaying conditions under which they can be seen to have been *probable*. Both are ways of making intelligible the contingent emergence of collective order from individual randomness. (Brandom 2011, 5)

Armed with these two pragmatist ways of seeing, naturalism and empiricism, RAND's theorists engaged in developing cybernetic and informational technologies of codification that rendered the Cold War order visible and articulable. Based on the ability to codify contingencies and turn them into controllable probabilities, the RAND Corporation provided knowledge workers with a space in which they could enact and assert an authority that did not rely on established traditions. It provided a space for the instrumental reorganisation of scientific and intellectual inquiry, and for formalised procedures shaped by evolutionary-statistical forms of explanation.

RAND was a turning point in the history of the policy research institution. This institutional form began in the Progressive Era, but before RAND it had a marginal existence and a limited role. By the early 1970s the institutional form of RAND, its intellectual practices and its claims to scientific objectivity and authority, established the think tank as the modal form of policy research institution which proliferated from this time.

The birth of the RAND Corporation represented the crystallisation of a new complex of scattered investments: a nexus of institutions that, according to Edwards (1996, 47), is best understood as 'the concept of the "iron triangle" of self-perpetuating academic, industrial, and military collaboration'. The conventional story of the RAND Corporation starts with the American war effort and the military-industrial complex, without connecting this story with the American tradition of thought and style of thinking that shaped the development of knowledge in the United States.[1] The emergence of RAND exemplifies the intersection of the intellectual and institutional investments of the Progressive Era with the emerging dynamics of the Cold War.

PROGRESSIVE PHILANTHROPY: A FRANCHISE TO GOVERN

From roughly the 1890s to the 1920s, American intellectual, social and private energies coalesced around efforts to lay the cultural and institutional foundations of a rapidly urbanised industrial society. This period of intense reform effort is called the Progressive Era. A notable feature of this era is the contribution of newly established philanthropic foundations to social reform, through their support of scientific social research.

The American political system and social structure enabled the rise of the philanthropic foundation. The 'tradition of federalism – the unwillingness of Americans to give their national government the authority to set national standards of social well-being, let alone to enforce them' created the conditions for the emergence of 'a system of national philanthropy – privately devoted to increasing the welfare of mankind' (Karl and Katz cit. Roelofs 2003, 12). In the early twentieth century, benevolent people with vast resources began the trend of turning their philanthropic attention away from pious charitable activities to focus on the 'social questions' afflicting American society, such as social dislocation, mass migration and poverty. The shift in focus points to new social and ideological roles that the philanthropic foundations of the Progressive Era began to seek. The primary mission of the Progressive Era foundation was to provide a 'private-sector alternative to socialism' (Hall 1992, 43).

The Russell Sage Foundation pioneered the new approach: it was established in New York in 1907 for 'the improvement of social and living conditions in the United States' (Russell Sage Foundation n.d.). The Russell Sage Foundation supported the professionalisation of the charity movement in order to promote a rational approach to solving social problems. In this context, professionalism became a distinctive American ideology. At a time in which European and third world intellectuals were joining radical political parties and contributing to the destabilisation of the *status quo*, the trajectory in the United States was towards the incorporation of intellectuals into the structure of power through professionalisation. As an ideology of social stratification, professionalism constituted the framework in which social mobility, access to power and prestige could be attained. This ideology was at once reformist and conservative.

Within this framework, the steel magnate Andrew Carnegie funded the founding of two major philanthropic institutions, the Carnegie Foundation for the Advancement of Teaching in 1905 and the Carnegie Corporation in 1911. Given the size of its endowment, the Carnegie Corporation signalled the birth of a new politics of knowledge on a grand scale. As Lagemann (1992, 6) puts it, 'The Carnegie Corporation's self-imposed mandate to define, develop, and distribute knowledge was, in a sense, a franchise to govern, in important indirect ways'. The new politics of knowledge allowed the Carnegie Foundation and Corporation to contest the monopoly of the state over the provision of public goods; moreover, it gave them latitude to claim that the American population at large fell within the moral jurisdiction of their benevolent actions; finally, it allowed the Carnegie Corporation to enlist intellectual workers, and their knowledge and methods, in the effort to improve and maintain the social *status quo*. The outcome was a reconciliation of private wealth and public welfare. This reconciliation had profound implications:

> [O]nce industrial capital was accepted by professionals as the framework in which betterment and progress would occur, social issues became technical problems with these ideational assumptions embedded therein. Then the

> professions could perform latent ideological functions while correctly claiming a manifest value neutrality. (Arnove 1982, 78)

A new socio-professional identity was born that, while appropriating the codes and roles of established socio-professional identities like the expert, the activist, the adviser and the academic, was distinct in its public intellectual performative role, which rivalled the role of the public intellectual of the Left.

The relationship between these professional intellectual workers and capital was structured by the institutional form of the foundation. The foundations increased their credibility by attaching themselves to groundbreaking research and authors, for example, the Carnegie Foundation financed the writing of Gunnar Myrdal's *An American Dilemma*, the Carnegie Corporation supported the writing of David Riesman's *The Lonely Crowd*, and the Ford Foundation supported both Hannah Arendt's work on 'totalitarianism' and Daniel Bell's *End of Ideology*. All these books had profound impact in the United States and beyond.

The funding arrangements of the foundations implicated, rather than directly coerced, intellectual workers and their academic institutions in a process of knowledge production that met the foundations' world views. In a seminal 1927 essay, *Foundations, Universities, and Research*, Harold Laski (1930, 174) argued:

> The foundations do not control, simply because, in the direct and simple sense of the word, there is no need for them to do so. They have only to indicate the immediate direction of their minds for the whole university world to discover that it always meant to gravitate swiftly to that angle of the intellectual compass.

The new regime of philanthropic patronage transformed the rules and logic of knowledge production, with market-like mechanisms facilitating the generation of prestige, recognition and legitimacy for the benefit of all participants.

The ideology of a value-neutral professionalism created a *functional* understanding of the self and the social world. As Trent Schroyer (cit. Arnove 1982, 18) puts it, 'A technocratic self-understanding of contemporary society – specifically, the ideal of rationally managed social change – now functions as both the principle of justice and the practice of domination'. For these intellectuals, reform was conceptualised as enabled by an alliance with those in power. For example, when in 1915 the Walsh Commission questioned Mackenzie King about his research on industrial peace on behalf of the Rockefeller Foundation:

> He argued that his work for Rockefeller was technical and did not affect his impartiality. However, when . . . asked if the technical expert in a democracy

> should use his talents by placing the facts as he sees them before the public or by advising those in power and influence, King indicated his preference for serving power: [as he put it] more will come about'. more quickly 'than . . . years spent . . . trying to focus [popular] opinion'. (King cit. Arnove 1982, 73)

At the theoretical level, the philanthropic foundation promoted the construction of a systemic and functionalist view of society rather than one that views society as an instantiation of contingent historical forces. The new disciplines of American social science, now largely supported by foundations, became implicated in the effort 'to contain the implications of historical change and salvage the [American] exceptionalist vision. Their exponents sought to reveal the operation of natural laws – laws of liberal progress and social equilibrium' (Ross, cit. Isaac 2007, 733). An epistemology of system maintenance guided such intellectual work. At the level of practice, intellectuals – social scientists in particular – were asked to provide technical solutions to social problems rather than developing interpretive or explanatory understandings of these problems. The effect of this orientation was the proliferation of tools and methods for prediction:

> Social Scientists . . . were asked to develop predictive capacity while organising data in ways that pointed to solutions of current social problems. Knowledge of the future gave leverage for control. (Arnove 1982, 64)

The systemic theoretical stance facilitated the development of formalised mathematical methodologies that transformed empirical data so that the real conformed to the ideal. As E. R. A. Seligman (a former president of the American Economic Association who was closely associated with the Department of Economics and Sociology at the Carnegie Institute) said, 'As the science itself becomes more complete, it . . . will be in a better position . . . to explain . . . the true method of making the real conform to the ideal' (Seligman cit. Arnove 1982, 64).

PROJECT RAND: THE EMERGENCE OF THE THINK TANK FORM

At the end of the Second World War, demobilised knowledge workers who had contributed to the military effort looked for new settings in which to use the knowledge they had gained during the war. This search turned them into partners of the military-industrial complex. The 'military-industrial complex' is best viewed as a condensed reference to a wide range of processes, procedures, institutions and events that, to appropriate Edward Said (1997, 380), 'methodologically unite[d] a practical need with a theory, an intention with a method'.

The RAND Corporation came into being in this environment. In 1945 the commanding general of the American Army Air Forces, H. H. Arnold, tasked his scientific advisor, the Austro-Hungarian *émigré* Dr. Theodore von Karman, with gathering 'a group of practical scientists for all the new things' (von Karman n.d.). Karman went on to author the well-known report *Toward New Horizons*, which called for 'the establishment of a new kind of scientific community, a nucleus for scientific groups such as those which successfully assisted in the command and staff work in the field during the war' (Abella 2008, 11). The report responded to the directive of General Arnold to establish forecasting capabilities, ensure US military readiness and prioritise scientific approaches over experience. The most important document that illustrates such thinking is the 1945 report of the director of the Office of Scientific Research and Development (OSRD), Vannevar Bush: *Science, the Endless Frontier*. As President Roosevelt states in the letter to initiate the report, 'There is . . . no reason why the lessons to be found in this experiment [war] cannot be profitably employed in times of peace' (Bush 1945, 3). Both Karman and Bush's reports are part of the effort to maintain the operational structure that gave the United States the upper hand during the war. As Joel Isaac (2007, 14) puts it, at the end of the Second World War and the beginning of the Cold War, '[t]he task at hand . . . was to fashion new institutional forms that could consolidate the links between the defense industry, the incipient national security state, and the scientific establishment'. It is within this context that Vannevar Bush convinced General H. H. Arnold, to initiate Project RAND, with the stated mission of '[a] continuing program of scientific study and research on the broad subject of air warfare with the object of recommending to the Air Force preferred methods, techniques and instrumentalities of this purpose' (Abella 2008, 14).

For Vannevar Bush (1945), 'the generation in uniform must not be lost'. The war offered a platform on which the charismatic figure of the scientist could emerge. The American theoretical physicist J. Robert Oppenheimer, head of the famous Manhattan Project that developed American nuclear weapons, personified this new socio-professional identity. The war effort enabled the emergence of a new socio-professional identity and status for the 'specific intellectual' of the national security state.[2] The most important function of these intellectuals was their assumed practical and symbolic ability to turn urgent political and military concerns into technical ones. The 'scientists in uniform' not only contributed to the advancement of scientific knowledge and its application, but their military service also legitimised the theories, and technologies that they were proposing, thus helping to create a self-referential form of knowledge.

In the United States, the specific intellectuals of the war worked closely with the private sector. In its early days Project RAND was not hosted in a military or public base but at the Douglas Aircraft Company, a major supplier of military hardware to the Air Force. This is not surprising, since the US government traditionally 'opted to contract out its scientific research development to private concerns' instead of nationalising military industries as countries like Britain and France had done (Abella 2008, 14–15).

Ralph Nader (in Guttman and Willner 1976, x) argues that within the new institutional development 'a career triangle with Government and business [had formed], which features a continual shuttle of personnel from one to the other'. This shuttling is an early example of the revolving door phenomena that is so common today. The triangulation of social relations as forms of exchangeable capital played a double role in shaping the functions and determining the subject matter of the knowledge field and in altering the ways in which intellectuals perceived themselves, talked about their work, and justified it. In short, the war created a trading space where bodies of knowledge and experiences were converted into theories, methods and technologies under the directives of capital.

In 1948 the Project RAND was incorporated as an independent institution. This decision was made for practical and commercial reasons, among which the most important were the concerns of competing military suppliers over the advantage that Douglas Aircraft Company could gain from hosting the Project RAND. Formal independence gave RAND further legitimacy and set in motion a new mode of fluid movement between government, business and the academy. The new arrangements allowed knowledge administrators to occupy a brokering position. Scientists or science brokers were appreciated for their ability to 'move freely through the corridors of the Pentagon and the State Department rather as the Jesuits through the courts of Madrid and Vienna three centuries ago' (Kaplan 1983, 11, citing a British journalist's description in the London *Times Literary Supplement*).

H. Gaither personified the new function and profession of a think tank administrator. He presided over the drafting of the RAND articles of incorporation in 1948 before he became the first president of the RAND Corporation and the chairman of its board for more than a decade. Using his connections, Gaither managed to secure transitional or seed funding from the Ford Foundation to support the newly formed institution. The mission of the RAND Corporation, as drafted by Gaither, was '[t]o further and promote scientific, educational and charitable purposes, all for the public welfare and security of the United States of America' (RAND Corporation n.d.). This mission resonated with the Ford Foundation's Cold War reorganisation, which aimed 'to lend financial support for world peace and the advancement of scientific knowledge' (Abella 2008, 32). Gaither's activities exemplified the intersection in the 1950s of two established American practices, philanthropic funding and research contracting. This intersection provided material support for the founding of the RAND Corporation, creating a mesh of military and civilian values as never before.

The emergence of RAND's 'defense intellectual' as a distinct socio-professional identity is inextricably intertwined with its adherence to pragmatic problem-solving methods guided by the values of efficiency, security, order and stability. In the tradition of civic virtue, RAND's defense intellectuals were seen to have raised themselves above the constraining contingencies of their own disciplines. Through training, engineers, economists and physicists all became 'weapons systems analysts'. They promised 'the country efficient production and wise choices by planning not only the hardware of weaponry, but the methods of operating and maintaining the weapon during its full "life cycle"' (Guttman and Willner 1976, 85). In effect, the military-industrial complex facilitated two interrelated developments: it elevated the position of the *specific expert* in the public eye, and at the same time it helped shape these experts' conceptions of themselves as virtuous crusaders.

FROM THE SOCIAL QUESTION TO THE GEOPOLITICAL QUESTION

In constituting the RAND Corporation, the forces of the military-industrial complex brought into being the institution that would reproduce, project and embody the material and ideological constitution of the United States. In the context of the Cold War, this constitution, to echo Hardt and Negri (2000, xv), was a logic, practice and structure of rule intent on expunging the murderous legacy of old Europe by instituting 'a perpetual and universal peace outside of history' that encompasses the spatial totality of the universe.

The RAND Corporation symbolised the mode of action of the Cold War and acted as an expression of Cold War politics and culture. In comparison with earlier policy research institutions, the primary significance of RAND, in comparison with earlier policy research institutions, is that it was not simply a newly *instituted* or formalised organisation – rather, it was the *instituting* process of a new paradigmatic institutional modality.

RAND championed scientific methodologies, introduced techniques of economic management and contributed to the development of the game-theoretic approach to organisation theory that focused on how people make decisions and act under given constraints. Operations Research methodologies, for instance, began in the military field but were refashioned by RAND as systems analysis and deployed in almost all possible fields. Operations research 'gave to policymakers an economist's approach to battle. War was a production process where the outcome is a killed and wounded soldier on the other side. The question was how to kill them more effectively'

(Kuklick 2006, 20). Operations research, systems analysis and other similar approaches developed by RAND became dominant methods, establishing bodies of knowledge, transforming their objects of study and formulating social and political choices or policies.

RAND's theoretical paradigm had its genesis in the distinctively American amalgamation of pragmatic, utilitarian and empiricist approaches. This pedagogical approach, according to David Kaiser (2007, 101), forged close ties between 'theorists and the "empiricist temper". Some program-builders . . . worked hard to make the contact between theorists and experimentalists even stronger, designing new laboratories and even sketching . . . architectural drawings'. Unlike the early empiricists, who claimed to decipher truth from empirical data, RAND operationalised empirical data within theoretical constructs, not simply to establish the identity of this data, but rather to establish it as a manipulable object. RAND, as an institution of theoretical knowledge, was concerned with predictive probabilities, with the future rather than the past, and with the negativity of what was absent rather than the actuality of what was present.

Viewing RAND in context of Progressivist intellectual currents reveals the extent to which RAND's theoretical orientation to reality was built upon the naturalistic epistemological foundations of the American social sciences, which, in the hands of theorists like Dewey, emphasised the functional unity of American society. According to Reinhold Martin (2005, 4), the defining epistemology of the military-industrial complex 'coalesce(s) into an organism that operates on the model of a total, if pliant, system'. This epistemology had a levelling effect: different phenomena, including social and technological processes, were abstracted from their institutional and social contexts so that they expressed the world now conceived as a networked space in which interdependency, indeterminacy and immanence ruled over what was rendered as redundant sovereignties. Modelling, formalisation and simulation methods like systems analysis provided analytical and cognitive models that turned the world into a pliable and manipulable environment. From their offices in Santa Monica, California, RAND's intellectuals were convinced that the more they refined their models, the more they mastered a world with no history.

This new version of a frictionless social did not just appeal to those interested in annulling or denying the historical dynamics of social conflict but also to those who had experienced the self-destructiveness of European metaphysics and the failure of its normativity in the wake of the two great wars. Many intellectuals, particularly European *émigrés*, imbued with a tragic sense of history, came to loath 'historicism' associated as it was with a nationalist public collectivism expressed in national sovereignty. These displaced intellectuals brought with them not just their skills, but also their intellectual angst. American pragmatism provided a hospitable refuge for

European logical positivists, despite their intellectual differences with it. As Kuklick (2006, 11) puts it, 'The identical emphasis on the experimental method that promised to give us a purchase over nature minimized these differences. . . . Positivists and pragmatists often united in disdain for soft, humanistic inquiry, and in their respect for methodological precision and statistics'. Institutions like RAND provided space for these refugees to ponder the European 'gods' that failed and to look for recipes for eternal peace. They championed a pared-down epistemology that concerned itself with the maintenance of social order through processes of control without 'centralized governmental and civic authority' (Martin 2005, 7).

The tracing of the intellectual, institutional, professional and epistemological making of RAND and its forms of knowledge provides a revelatory framework for understanding the order of knowledge of which think tanks are an integral part. In constructing a frictionless world, RAND offers a cybernetic conception of the evolutionary relationship between organisms and their environment. In this universe, political, social and cultural interests become units of information flows within a self-regulating and self-perpetuating system. When cybernetics takes over the theory of evolution, it is information and the communication of information that become the central parameters for conceiving a global homeostasis.

AMERICAN THEORY: REORDERING THE WORLD

The RAND Corporation acted as a site for the development and circulation of a number of significant *theories* (rational choice theory, cognitive psychology, quantitative economy), *methodologies* (game theory, simulation, systems analysis, operational research), and *technologies* (computers, the Internet). Lydia H. Liu calls these theories 'American theories'. This is not to say that only American scientists and institutions developed these theories, but to emphasise that they 'became hegemonic with the rise of the American empire' (Liu 2010, 293–94).

Among the American theories, cybernetics occupied a primary position. In his paper *A Mathematical Theory of Communication*, Claude Elwood Shannon, known as the father of information theory, published a landmark paper in the field 'A Mathematical Theory of Communication' in 1948. At the same time Norbert Wiener was calling information theory cybernetics (from the Greek *κυβερνητική, kybernetike*) which meant 'steersman'. He 'borrowed the Greek word . . . to name the new interdisciplinary study of control and communication in the machine and in the animal' (Liu 2010, 294). As a thread running through most of the new theoretical approaches, cybernetics became the logic that underpinned the foundational categories of life, labour and language. Its influence was far-reaching, becoming a methodological and heuristic figure of thought that has shaped much thinking about the human/ social world. Heidegger was one of the first to recognise in this mode of thinking a logic of a totalizing, all-inclusive system. In *The End of Philosophy and the Task of Thinking* he wrote: 'No prophecy is necessary to recognize that the sciences now establishing themselves will soon be determined and guided by the new fundamental science which is called cybernetics' (Heidegger cit. Dolan 1990, 93).

Cybernetics reduces the world to a technological ecology. It dissolves history and society and replaces them with information and communication. It has fostered the proliferation of theoretical constructions that focus on systems integration, harmony and equilibrium. Jamie Cohen-Cole (2008, 110) recounts the profound effect of cybernetic thinking on the formulation and production of knowledge since the 1950s:

> By emphasizing how systems of whatever type were organized, cybernetics, and the new information sciences of the mid-twentieth century generally, encouraged research that ultimately linked neurology, the biological sciences, electrical and mechanical engineering, political science, psychiatry, operations research, game theory, economics, sociology, anthropology, mathematics, psychology and philosophy of science. Doing away with distinctions between the disciplines, cybernetics did away at the same time with other, more entrenched distinctions – between nature and artifice, things and ideas, values and rationality.

Cybernetics led to a process of 'de-differentiation' in which the relationship between the categories of the social and material world was levelled and internally reconstituted.

In Foucault's terminology, cybernetics was a new episteme. Foucault (1972, 191) used the term 'episteme' to refer to 'the total set of relations that unite, at a given period, the discursive practices that give rise to epistemological figures, sciences, and possibly formalized systems'. Epistemic transformation finds a corresponding expression in institutional transformation. The modern university was the manifestation of an earlier episteme, the University of Reason and the University of Culture, associated especially with the German tradition of *Bildung*. This episteme unified knowledge on the basis of the humanities (especially philosophy and literature), producing distinctively social and historical ways of thinking that shaped the modern university and its nation-building role in the nineteenth century. The cybernetic episteme, with its preference for modelling over historical, literary and sociological studies, corresponded to the think tank form of institution which began to rival the centrality of the university in knowledge production.

As Jean-Paul Sartre (cit. Liu 2010, 292) observed, developments in the United States in the 1960s produced 'a technocratic civilization [that] no longer holds a place for philosophy unless the latter turns itself into technology'. Science now displaced philosophy as the knowledge unifier. RAND was the institutional form that legitimated and embodied this turn in science's mission and function. This turn represented a global epistemological revolution that progressively reordered the whole regime of signs, in the Foucaultian sense, to optimise the operation of command, communication and control in an ever-expanding, open global site. The economic and mathematical formalism of the RAND Corporation did more than just advance scientism. It also articulated a mode of thinking that was promoted as the only possible one.

RAND, then, as an institutional site that gathered different cognate theories, methods and technologies contributed to a profound change in the structure of knowledge of the mid-twentieth century. Symbolic domination now 'relies on the authority of science' (Bourdieu 2003, 20). The birth of the new empire and its institutions were intertwined with a post-historical move beyond culture understood as a crucial constituent in 'the birth of the modern university and that of the nation state' (Readings 1996, 53). 'Presentism', the perception that the current moment is both radically different and self-sufficient, and 'de-referentialization', the doing away with reference points in time and tradition, are characteristic of this post-historical mode of knowledge.

This reordering of signs enabled a fluid exchange between social structure, intellectual action and epistemological reproduction. It gave rise to a particular mode of determining the objects of knowledge, which unsettled and reconfigured the conceptual foundations of the social sciences. For example, the idea of *interest*, which once served as a primary conceptual tool in the sociology of class and social stratification, now morphed from being a social and public phenomenon to being solely a personal and private one, an attribute of a possessive individual. Rational choice theory, developed by RAND theorists, introduced the methodological individualism of 'the rational actor'. This concept 'holds that self-interest, unleavened by collective concerns such as religion or patriotism, is the hallmark of the modern world' (Abella 2008, 6). The 'rational actor' displaced the 'social act' as the unit of analysis in the social sciences. One manifestation of this theory was RAND's 'psychology of communication' during the Vietnam War, which assumed that the Vietnamese would operate in terms of a self-interested calculus as understood and defined by RAND. According to this logic, the war dragged on because of the Vietnamese failure to understand the relationship between their self-interest and American intentions. Therefore, the prolonging of the war was either a function of Vietnamese *irrationality* or a tragedy of *miscommunication* between rational actors.

Another manifestation of this privileging of individual self-interest is the (now ubiquitous) 'prisoner's dilemma' which was developed by RAND mathematicians, Merrill Flood and Melvin Dresher, as a game theoretical model of rational actor calculation. The prisoner's dilemma is a peculiar iteration of the 'state of nature' notion. The prisoner's dilemma posits that the self-interest of individuals is mutually destructive in that it precludes the possibility of mutually beneficial cooperation. The axiom is to kill or be killed. Social order comes about as a result of coercive bargaining (Amadae 2003, 293). The significance of the prisoner's dilemma, according to Sonja Amadae (2003, 293), resides in the substitution of disaggregated social action for Jeremy Bentham's famous panopticon. That is, instead of centralised societal control over individuals by institutions, in the prisoner's dilemma, 'each person is seen to participate in a decentralized game in which efficient resource allocation is replaced by potentially suboptimal equilibrium of actor's strategies' (Amadae 2003, 293). In this state of nature, social order emerges as a self-enforcing cybernetic world composed of rational actors engaged in strategic coercive bargaining games.

Rational choice theory became established as conventional wisdom, and the prisoner's dilemma operated (like Bentham's panopticon) as 'a historical perception or sensibility, as much as a discursive system' (Deleuze 1999, 42). The guiding question for RAND was not how man was *formed* socially or informed pedagogically but how he or she would *perform* in formally modelled conditions. The epistemological questions regarding the historical and relational making of man shifted to an ontological question about a ceaseless metamorphosis of man, guided by self-interest, in interactive events of adaptation to a constantly changing set of information flows.

In game theory simulations at RAND, all participants, including the Russians, were conceived as rational actors, performing roles based on rational criteria of constraints and preference. Those who constructed the simulation discounted not only Russian history but also their own history even as the rational actor was conceived on the model of a mid-twentieth-century American. Here RAND's contribution to a new episteme helped to make the second half of the twentieth century 'American'.

Theoretical science did not just displace the historical sciences, but it also impacted on the idea of science itself as an essentially experimental and empirical procedure for establishing the truth of things. As Sam Schweber (cit. Kaiser 2007, 99–100) argues, in the mid-twentieth century 'physical theories need neither be right nor true, merely useful for the job at hand'. Daniel Bell (1999, xxxix) considers this development part of the dawning of the 'post-industrial society' in which knowledge becomes the source of innovation and change through what he called the 'codification of theoretical knowledge'. This form of knowledge is intrinsically related to 'the creation of a "new technology of intelligence" with its panoply of tools such as systems analysis, games theory, decision theory, and so on' (Mattelart 1994, 130), all of which are engaged in fashioning probabilities and simulating possible scenarios. Here instead of science refining its method in order to establish the nature of reality, data is generated and constituted within the theoretical model which involves a profound degree of abstraction from things as they appear.[3]

When objects of knowledge are determined solely by formal theoretical methods and models, 'the function of establishing identities, of imposing determinations and of enforcing lines of demarcation can only be conceived as an effect of what we call "institutions" and of "institutionalization"' (Weber 2001, xiv). This profound and multifaceted reordering of intellectual practices, theories and technologies served to do away with history: 'Society appears as incessant, perpetual movement . . . any fact turns out to be an event; any agent resolves into action; any state is only a phase in an ongoing process' (Sztompka 1993, 190). Here the dissolution of the social corresponds to the rise of the rational actor. And finally, with the rise of the theoretical sciences, the *unknowable other* is already provided for within their categories and therefore there is no need to engage in work of translation and hermeneutics.

RAND AS A SITE OF STYLE

Perhaps the most representative example of RAND's mode of intelligibility was a statement by United States secretary of defense Donald Rumsfeld, himself twice chairman of Board of the RAND Corporation. During the build-up to the war on Iraq and to the amazement of the global audience, Rumsfeld announced: 'There are known knowns. These are things we know that we know. There are known unknowns. That is to say, there are things that we now know we don't know. But there are also unknown unknowns. These are things we do not know we don't know'. Overwhelmingly, this statement was greeted with puzzlement and mockery. Understood in context of RAND's epistemology, however, Rumsfeld's statement becomes legible. Shorn of its own history and the history of the theory that informs its appearance, the *unknown* 'becomes, as it were, the element or *medium* of knowledge, not merely its negative other' (Weber 2001, 230). In its ruthless concern to model reality, excluding what the model is unable to incorporate, formalism gave us discourses such as 'overload', 'complexity' and 'non-representability'.

The haunting presence of the unknown invites a permanent state of crisis. Crisis becomes the basis of politics in peacetime and wartime alike. The social sciences, which functioned as technologies of progress or evolution within the framework of the modern institution of knowledge, focused on utopian conceptions of a possible good society for all. In contrast, the social sciences of RAND, driven by unknowns, were dystopian and pessimistic. The proliferation of unknowns gives us the 'risk society' (Beck 1992). Rumsfeld's seemingly baffling remarks operate within a discourse of risk according to which 'society is driven by the distribution of "bads" or dangers, in contradistinction to industrial society, which was principally concerned with the distribution of material "goods"' (Ericson and Haggerty 1997, 86). The unknown serves as the pretext for the constant call for law and order, or, during the Cold War, the call for a world system resting on American control. In analysing RAND's contributions, Frederick M. Dolan (1990, 105) argues:

> [T]he ideological context of the demand for a vocabulary of the political system in general is the post-war international crisis, the Cold War. Such doctrines as 'rollback', 'containment', and 'counter-insurgency' might be read as sketches for a metaphysics of contemporary world history as a permanent crisis requiring constant supervision and, if necessary, intervention.

Lacking the intention and skill of historical, sociological and cultural translation, this American enterprise is held together by fear. At the hands of RAND's *bricoleurs,* fear reached epic proportions during the first two decades of the Cold War. Stanley Kubrick's 1964 black comedy *Dr. Strangelove or: How I Learned to Stop Worrying and Love the Bomb* is based on the character of RAND Corporation analyst Herman Kahn, who was also the founder of the Hudson think tank and the author of *On Thermonuclear War*. In his lectures to the public, Kahn exploited to the limit the language of scenario games that RAND had put in place. As Cockburn (1987, 161) describes, Kahn instilled fear in his audiences. 'Businessmen and housewives would head for the exits . . . engaged in rapt conversation about "intrawar deterrence", "credible first-strike capability" or the professor's notions on the best ways to avoid epidemics of vomiting in the aftermath of a nuclear exchange'. This type of fear evades questions of political representation and deliberation while invoking existential concerns and meanings.

RAND fashioned 'a site of style' during the Cold War, by operationalising 'the complex of relations between appearance, recognition, and identification' (on style see Benjamin 2006). Kahn's performances stem from a particular understanding of the existential, epistemological and moral status of his audience. The structure of recognition in question is tied to how the self and others, political order and morality, are perceived from the perspective of the rational actor. Against a background of American patriotic fever, Kahn presented a terrifying, but cost-benefit, case for a cosmic war.

ENCLOSING THE WORLD: THE WORLD-AS-NETWORK

In his study of the colonial political process that accompanied the capitalist transformation of Egypt, Timothy Mitchell (1988, xii) suggests that when 'power relations become internal [they] appear to take the form of external structures'. For example, in colonial Egypt, 'the geographical hierarchy of schools [is] arranged to represent the structure of a nation-state'. For Mitchell (1988, xiii), new methods of organisation and institutional arrangement generate 'new effects of structure'. The modern colonial conceptual-architectural form of the school came to embody an operative discursive formation that projected a particular synthesis of power and knowledge. As the archetypal think tank RAND projects its own particular synthesis of power and knowledge. Structuring effects similar to those Mitchell describes are clear in the way Alex Abella describes and compares RAND's old and new buildings, which both retained the same structuring logic. According to Abella (2008, 4), 'The old building is designed to be like a campus without students':

> Even the long hallways that had to be negotiated to access common areas were meant to get people out of their rooms and interacting with another. [In t]he new RAND building . . . One thing remains the same: it is still hard to go in a straight line from one point to another, everything is interconnected, with the specific purpose of promoting the flow of people and information.

Mitchell (1988, 40) analyses the 'principle of order [that] made it possible to "fix" men in place, to keep them "steady in the performance of their duty", and to coordinate them as the separate parts of a single . . . machine'. Abella's description evokes an image of constant movement, a space in which participants connect and network, at ease with exchanging information. For Mitchell (1988, 131), 'such techniques have given rise to the peculiar metaphysics of modernity', which he terms the *world-as-exhibition*: 'mechanisms . . . that served to introduce a modern and mysterious political metaphysics'. In the case of the era of which RAND is an integral part, structures, functions and relations have come to be seen as all in flux, becoming fluid vectors of exchangeable and interchangeable flows, divested of the weight of any referential entanglement or fixity.

In his book *The Closed World: Computers and the Politics of Discourse in Cold War America*, Paul Edwards outlines the ideological imperatives that powered much of RAND's activities. According to Edwards (1996, 8), 'Language, technologies, and practices . . . together supported the visions of centrally controlled, automated global power at the heart of American Cold War politics':

> Closed-world discourse, through metaphors, techniques, and fictions as well as equipment and salient experience, linked the globalist, hegemonic aims of post-World War II American foreign policy with a high-technology military strategy, an ideology of apocalyptic struggle, and a language of integrated systems.

In this closed world, RAND's concept of integrated systems had two major effects; on the one hand, it provided an operational logic for emulation; on the other hand, it provided a reality effect in which objects shorn of their history and social context become sheer information, situated by a logic of informationalisation as malleable and manipulable bits and bytes.

Methodologically, RAND developed many formalistic techniques that aspired to divide its object of study 'into an ever-finer set of indefinitely variable (yet enumerable) regulating codes' (Martin 2005, 5). All the formalistic technique and methods developed by RAND that we have encountered (cybernetics, decision theory, game theory, etc.) were designed to operate in a closed world using methodologies based on an information calculus of inputs and outputs. For RAND, information became the foundational principle of the universe.

Informationalisation pervades society as a process of de-differentiation. Social and physical spaces are flattened and recoded within what is depicted as presentist flows of information, that operate in terms of the organisational logic of the world-as-network. Reinhold Martin (2005, 3–4) suggests that since the early 1960s a distinctive organisational complex of networks emerged as an 'aesthetic and technological extension of . . . the 'military-industrial complex'. From the 1960s onwards, the 'network has become a common form that tends to define our ways of understanding the world and acting in it' (Hardt and Negri 2004, 142).

In the 1950s and 1960s RAND provided a structuring narrative for what was seen to be a chaotic uncontrollable world. In the 'world-as-network', unity is achieved through aesthetic and representational devices of order. As Samuel Weber (2001, 16) suggests with networks, 'The question of a cohesive factor then becomes increasingly associated with the stories that hold together, or at least define, a network as a structure distinct from other, more hierarchical forms of organization'.

INFORMATIONALISATION OF SOCIALITY AND INTELLECTUAL PRACTICE

According to Peter Burke (2000, 44), 'Intellectual debates owe a good deal to the forms of sociability and so to the social frameworks in which they take place'. Within the framework of informational network sociality, intellectual debates and practices take place as a process of convergence on targets. In contrast to the modern university logic of organising intellectual work in discrete disciplines, the RAND Corporation was organised in programmes around *problems*.[4] RAND carried out its work project by project, driven by concerns about practical ends and focused on means of achieving objectives.

The methodological reorganisation of intellectual practice around *problems* contributed to the dissolution of disciplinary boundaries and to institutional reorganisation. In this environment, the institutional status of scholars of knowledge is downgraded in comparison to the knowledge manager or administrator who manages research through the internal allocation of resources to projects that respond to external demands. The birth of RAND, then, was part of a displacement of one structuring organisational form by another. As Manuel Castells (2011, 187) explains, the shift was from:

> organizations for which the reproduction of their system of means becomes their main organizational goal; [to] . . . organizations in which goals, and the change of goals, shape and endlessly reshape the structure of means . . . the first type of organizations' bureaucracies; the second type, enterprises.

As a consequence, institutional and intellectual autonomy are profoundly transformed. No longer is each discipline governed by its own norms, rather external forces come to define research purpose and direction. Intellectual workers have to continuously (re)form themselves around or converge on *problems as moving targets* of research. And all disciplines and their workers are forced to evaluate themselves in terms of utilitarian efficiency.

Emerging from the restructuring of research around *problems* are the phenomena of interdisciplinary and multidisciplinary programs. There are two notable consequences of this shift: first, multidisciplinary approaches 'are rooted in the idea of unity and synthesis, evoking a common epistemology of convergence' (Klein cit. Readings 1996, 127). As such they signify 'a desire for final consensus, the consensus that would permit the determination and transmission of "the conflict" as a unified object for professional discourse' (Readings 1996, 127). Multidisciplinary teamwork at RAND served the dual purpose of providing a cognitive model for perceiving the world and an intellectual technology for making it. The second consequence of this shift to team-based multidisciplinarity is that, in joining activities and disciplines that once were separate, '[k]nowledgeability becomes systemic, operating at collective and institutional more than individual levels . . . knowledgeability is collective and institutional rather than individual' (Ericson and Haggerty 1997, 13). Being a team member is more important than disciplinary affiliation and accreditation.

In the multidisciplinary team, working is at the same time networking. Here we are not talking about 'labour value' or 'knowledge value' but 'relationship value'.[5] The *revolving door* phenomenon in the United State, according to which think tanks actors move in and out of multiple roles, or occupy multiple professional roles simultaneously, is an example of the blurring of distinctions between *what* one knows as a scholar and *who* one knows as a team worker. In the 1960s, the epistemological and methodological mindset of RAND enticed Defense Secretary Robert McNamara to appoint many of RAND's scholars as his advisors. Since that time, members of RAND and other think tanks have continuously been shuttling back and forward between different roles. As such, RAND scholars were precursors of what the anthropologist and public policy scholar Janine Wedel (2009, 1) calls the "*flexion*": a social type 'who serves at one and the same time as business consultant, think-tanker, TV pundit, and government adviser [who] glides in and around the organisations that enlist his services'.

In this context, as an innovative reorganisation of the institution of knowledge, RAND is a precursor of a wider *enterprising-up* of social relations and practices, according to which a commodifying and entrepreneurial logic came to underpin the very functioning, methods, practices and organisation of the knowledge institution. The form of sociality and intellectual practice that RAND set in motion was a precursor of the late twentieth-century neoliberal think tank and its ethos, one that assumes an entrepreneurial and economically competitive rational actor and invites its members to act accordingly.

CONCLUSION

In *The Modern Prince*, Antonio Gramsci (cit. Said 2000, 130) observes that 'reality (and hence cultural reality) is a product of the application of human will to the society of things'. Edward Said (2000, 130) concludes from Gramsci's observation that 'in the realm of culture and of thought each production exists not only to earn a place for itself but to displace, win out over, others'. Consequently, as Said (2000, 130) puts it: 'All ideas, views and texts aspire to the consent of their consumers'. The fashioning of RAND as a particular institutional modality of knowledge is precisely that – an act of displacement of one modality by another in order to advance a new order of things. RAND performed this task by transforming historical reality into a cybernetic one. The cybernetic logic provided a new scaffolding for social thought and intellectual practices oriented to systems integration, harmony and equilibrium. RAND turned theoretical informational forms of knowledge and their economical and mathematical formalism into the conventional modus operandi of *Pax Americana*, an institutional complex that was hegemonic not only within America but also in the new international institutional order constructed after the Second World War.

The emergence of RAND would not have been possible without the intellectual and institutional structures of the Progressive Era. The imperatives of pragmatism, which privileged technical expertise, and oriented professionalism in service to social harmony and integration, remained the subterranean current that animated RAND's intellectual ethos and formulations. RAND expressed what Dorothy Ross (1991, xiii) argues are the familiar features of twentieth-century America: namely, '[i]ts liberal values, practical bent, shallow historical vision and technocratic confidence'. The military-industrial complex was the catalyst through which human will and social forces coalesced to create the RAND Corporation, the informationalisation of social life, and the world-as-network. In the Foucaultian sense, the military-industrial complex was an *enunciative ensemble* that designated a field in which only certain statements could be made. These statements were based on an epistemology that brought into being a particular state of relations between things and people. Within the context of the Cold War, RAND institutionalised a newly constituted field of visibility. It identified an increasing number of unknown or incommensurable qualities, things and objects as theoretically fungible information, while at the same articulating formalistic statements of probabilities about security using aesthetics tropes. In this sense, the RAND Corporation brought into being a particular way of seeing, saying and knowing. It is for this reason that RAND came to be seen as the archetypal think tank.

NOTES

1. For example, Paul Dickson (1971, 51), in the often-cited first book on think tanks, describes the RAND Corporation as 'Mother RAND' because it was the example other think tanks followed as they emerged after the Second World War. See also Diane Stone's *Capturing the Political Imagination: Think Tanks and the Policy Process* (1996, 19). See also the official RAND Corporation history page which states that RAND's roots are in the Cold War competition with the Soviet Union.
2. Michel Foucault (1980, 127–28) suggests that 'perhaps it was the atomic physicist – let's say in a word, or rather a name: [Robert] Oppenheimer – who acted as the point of transition from the universal intellectual to specific intellectual'.
3. On the profound effect of abstraction on the possibility of a meaningful human communication and interaction, see Anna Yeatman (2018).
4. For more on postdisciplinary developments see Mario Biagioli (2009).
5. On the new forms of sociality, see Andreas Wittel (2001).

Chapter 6

Competition Policy and the Destruction of the Welfare State[1]

Anna Yeatman

INTRODUCTION

In March 2015 a panel of four people headed by Professor Emeritus Ian Harper, a partner at Deloitte Touche Tohmatsu,[2] presented the final report of the Competition Policy Review (CPR) to the Minister for Small Business (Bruce Billiton) of the Australian federal government. As the panel declared in its opening 'message', their recommendations 'comprise an agenda of reinvigorated microeconomic reform' that it believes 'is necessary if Australia is to boost productivity, secure fiscal sustainability and position our economy to meet the challenges and opportunities of a rapidly changing world' (Harper et al. 2015, 1). The panel declares in the 'executive summary': 'Competition policy is aimed at improving the economic welfare of Australians. It is about meeting their needs and preferences by making markets work properly' (Harper et al. 2015, 7). The task of the panel was to review whether Australia's competition laws and institutions are 'fit for purpose' – see Box 6.1. They make a number of recommendations to all levels of government and offer a road map for implementation.

Competition policy represents the marketisation of the public sector, and the loss of its identity in relation to the private sector. Competition policy redefines all government agencies and activities as businesses, and in so doing, places them on a business enterprise basis. From which point it makes sense to ask how these government businesses, like all business enterprises, should come under the framework of trade and competition policies. It also makes sense to propose that government enterprise should not have an unfair competitive advantage with regard to its now-constituted private sector competitors: this is expressed in the principle of 'competitive neutrality'. The inexorable direction of this restructuring of the public sector is one of marketisation: the bias is against the continuation of government ownership

Box 6.1

BOX 1.4: FIT FOR PURPOSE (HARPER ET AL. 2015, 9–10)

A competition policy that is 'fit for purpose':

- focuses on making markets work in the long-term interests of consumers;
- fosters diversity, choice and responsiveness in government services;
- encourages innovation, entrepreneurship and the entry of new players;
- promotes efficient investment in and use of infrastructure and natural resources;
- includes competition laws and regulations that are clear, predictable and reliable; and
- secures necessary standards of access and equity.

and for the privatisation of erstwhile government enterprises (see Goot 2010); and where government funding is still required for welfare services, the relationship is contractualised as one between the funding agency and private (for-profit and not-for-profit) agencies that competitively tender for government business. Public service turns into contract management and becomes a form of 'market managerialism' (Considine and Painter 1997, 10). Competition policy, more precisely, refers to the institutional framework for the marketisation of the public sector. In this context, those (like the team who produced the final report of the CPR) who engage in the formulation of competition policy, and those (like the Australian Productivity Commission) who implement and evaluate it are market managerialists writ large.[3] The following chapter should be read as a case study of contemporary market managerialism.

The CPR is of twofold significance. First, it confirmed and built on the national competition policy framework that was established in Australia in 1995 following upon the Hilmer Report (see Box 6.2). In so doing the CPR further systematised the institutional architecture of competition policy, definitively turning it into the principal framework for Australian government and public policy. In line with the transformation of the Australian state into a 'competition state' (Cerny 2010), the Australian Productivity Commission was given responsibility for the reception and implementation of the CPR. The central place of the Productivity Commission in contemporary Australian public policy represents the ultimate triumph of the 'economic rationalists' whose rise to power in the bureaucratic architecture of the federal (Commonwealth) government Michael Pusey charted in *Economic Rationalism in Canberra: A Nation-Building State Changes Its Mind* (1991).[4] It represents also the thoroughgoing convergence of the technologies of managerialism and neoliberalism.

Box 6.2

BOX 1.2: NATIONAL COMPETITION POLICY (HARPER ET AL. 2015, 17)

In 1995 Australian governments committed to a set of agreements under the NCP, which:

- extended the *Trade Practices Act 1974* (TPA) to previously excluded businesses (unincorporated businesses and state, territory and local government businesses);
- established independent price oversight of state and territory government businesses;
- corporatised and applied competitive neutrality principles so that government businesses did not enjoy a net competitive advantage as a result of public sector ownership;
- structurally reformed public monopolies to separate out industry regulation and, where possible, further disaggregated potentially competitive parts of the monopoly;
- established a third-party access regime for significant bottleneck infrastructure;
- reviewed all legislation restricting competition;
- applied the competition agreements to local government;
- established the National Competition Council (NCC);
- imposed conditions on governments seeking to exempt conduct from the competition law; and
- provided financial assistance to the States and Territories conditional on progress implementing the NCP.

The second point of significance of the CPR is that it extended the reach of competition policy to the human services. This term is explained by the CPR in the following way: 'The human services sector covers a diverse range of services including health, education, disability, aged care, job services, public housing and correctional services' (Harper et al. 2015, 218). While the CPR placed some caveats on how competition policy should be applied in the human services sector, the intention is clear: competition policy should apply to the services that have constituted what historically we have referred to as the welfare state. What this means is that principles for the competitive ordering of private action (consumer choice and firms or business enterprise) are to apply to the human services. The distinct service sectors of the welfare state are now lumped together as (human) services – as in the conception of a (goods and) service market – thus making it unnecessary to consider the substantively distinct nature of such phenomena as education or health. 'Welfare' is homogenised, economised, and marketised. It is no longer a question of state provision for civic need (for an elaboration of this idea of the welfare state, see Yeatman forthcoming 2018).

Here is the recommendation at issue.

Box 6.3

RECOMMENDATION 2 – HUMAN SERVICES (HARPER ET AL. 2015, 36)

Each Australian government should adopt choice and competition principles in the domain of human services.

Guiding principles should include:

- User choice should be placed at the heart of service delivery.
- Governments should retain a stewardship function, separating the interests of policy (including funding), regulation and service delivery.
- Governments commissioning human services should do so carefully, with a clear focus on outcomes.
- A diversity of providers should be encouraged, while taking care not to crowd out community and volunteer services.
- Innovation in service provision should be stimulated, while ensuring minimum standards of quality and access in human services.

In *Markets, Rights and Power in Australian Social Policy* (2015), Gabrielle Meagher, Susan Goodwin and their collaborators argue that the principles of marketisation have been at work in the area of social services for some time, and that the adoption of National Competition Policy by the Keating Labor government in the early-mid 1990s (Meagher and Wilson 2015, 37) laid the groundwork for this set of developments.[5] They define 'marketisation' as 'the importation of characteristically private sector ways of doing things into the public sector' (Meagher and Goodwin 2015, 3).[6] They point out that while Australian social services especially since the 1970s have involved a mixed economy with significant historical reliance on not-for-profits, which continue to play an important role, the logic of marketisation means that for-profits become an increasingly powerful player in the sector: 'For-profit provision now dominates long day care for children and some forms of residential care for older people, and has a growing presence in other fields, including job placement services and community care'. They continue: 'Meanwhile, public sector provision has stagnated, declined or disappeared altogether, depending on the field' (Meagher and Goodwin 2015, 2).

In this context the significance of the extension of competition policy to human services becomes clear: now as a matter of principle and systemic approach, Australian governments are to adopt this framework for social policy and social services. This is a declaration that the philosophy and institutional architecture of the welfare state is to be replaced by the neoliberal philosophy and institutional design of marketisation.

Meagher and Goodwin suggest that marketisation in this area has gone largely under the public's radar in contrast to the more visible instances of asset sales or 'privatisation'. This is true enough. But the July 2016 Australian federal election, with the Labor Party's apparently successful use of 'Mediscare', suggests that Australian voters may have become educated by the proposed de-regulation of university fees, the disaster of the application of competition policy to the TAFE (vocational education and training) sector and the proposed co-payment for GP visits.

However, it is difficult for the public to understand the *institutional pattern* of these proposed changes, a pattern in which the Labor Party is as implicated as is its conservative party opponent. It is also difficult for the public to find the ideas and the language that enable it to discover and articulate the significance of their resistance to these changes. Their protest is anticipated by the decision-making elites who have adopted the institutional design of competition policy. Even if the public does not buy the line that 'the age of entitlement is over', the decision-making elites do. They are determined to ride out the public's attachment to what is portrayed as unsustainable expectations of public support, and to continue what they see as the necessary work of remodelling the relationship between state and society in terms of neoliberal principles and assumptions. The gap that has opened up between these elites and the public now constitutes a primary fault-line in Australian society that, as elsewhere, is eroding trust in the political class and the institutional order.

The public inherited the achievements of the welfare state. Like all those who inherit past achievements, the public has tended to take them for granted and to be incurious about what values and ideas these achievements were designed to serve. At the same time, the practical rationality of these achievements, especially in the form of the right of the child to have access to good quality primary and secondary schooling, and the right of all people to have access to good primary health and hospital care, has entered into the public's DNA. For this reason, it would not be difficult to invite the public to embrace an explicit articulation of the philosophy and institutional design of the welfare state, and to do this not in a reactive sense but in an agenda-setting way.

The *idea* of a civic entitlement to welfare needs to be positively articulated and defended. But if this fundamental idea is to be reclaimed and re-articulated on the terms of our present this can occur only in relationship to a critical examination of the *idea* of neoliberal institutional design. We have to recognise in neoliberalism a political and social philosophy albeit one that does not appear as such because it denies the distinctive nature of the political and the social in collapsing them into 'the economic' (on 'economism', see Malpas 2016). We have to refuse to neoliberal institutional design the appearance of a value-neutral technology that has as its aim the improvement of our welfare. It is not just that we are more likely to find how we need to reclaim the idea of the welfare state if we examine how the idea of neoliberalism deprives us of the shared and inclusive civil mode of being that the welfare state made possible. It is also to call those who formulate, communicate and buy into neoliberal political philosophy to political account for the way of being that they are imposing on us.

I proceed then on the assumption that it is not enough to critically arraign neoliberal institutional design but that its full import for how we live together and treat one another can emerge only if such arraignment occurs in context of an enquiry into an alternative political and social philosophy that is offered in the spirit of public discourse and communication. If we are to do this, we have to refuse the idea that if one set of institutions replaces another it is because the former is more in sync with 'history' than the latter as though there is some kind of natural historical process to which we have to adapt. As Hannah Arendt never tired of reminding us, history concerns the freedom associated with action to begin something new: 'History is a story which has many beginnings but no end' (Arendt 1994, 320).

COMPETITION POLICY AND NEOLIBERAL MARKET DESIGN

Competition policy offers the institutional architecture for the remodelling of the institutional architecture of the nation state as a juristically constituted society[7]: it is transformed from being a political society into a distinct jurisdiction of regulated global society understood as the embodiment of a competitive order. Competition policy is the quintessential expression of the economics imperialism that is the hallmark of neoliberal thought (Nik-Khah and Van Horn 2012; Mirowski and Nik-Khah 2017).

Competition policy is the domestic institutional architecture that intersects with the global architecture of a market economy that is expressed in the private law constitutionalism of free trade agreements. The model of economic development that is presupposed in this architecture is that of export-led growth (Palley 2011), which replaced the import-substitution/domestic demand-led strategy associated with the postwar Keynesian welfare state. As Palley explains, export-led growth (of the kind associated with the North American Free Trade Agreement in 1994) brought 'the beginning of the modern era of corporate globalization', where growth 'is no longer a purely national strategy' (Palley 2011, 9). National competition policy facilitates the access of multinational corporations to investment opportunities within the nation but on terms that suit these corporations rather than a national strategy for economic development that is focused on domestic and citizen needs.[8]

While it retains a role for the state in the authoritative establishment of this institutional architecture, the logic of competition policy is to bring both public and private sectors, as they have been historically demarcated, within the ordering principles of a globalised competitive market economy. Where this is not possible, the proposition being that there are some aspects of government activity that should not be subject to these principles, these areas do not just have a residual status, but their distinctly public character is placed ever on the defensive in relation to the question of why they cannot or should not be subject to the norm of market competition.[9] The effect of competition policy and the institutional order to which it belongs is to cancel the distinction between public and private sectors, thereby bringing about a situation where the *sui generis* nature of 'publicness' can be neither talked about nor comprehended.

Edward Nik-Khah and Philip Mirowski (2017) see the distinctive feature of neoliberal economic thought as residing in the idea of market design where economics provides the theory of market design and the state institutes it. It is for this reason that they have always insisted that neoliberal economics, as key figures such as Hayek have emphasised, is different from a libertarian or classical laissez-faire economics. A strong state and state intervention are needed to do the work of institutionalising markets and ensure that they are properly maintained.

The ascendancy of neoliberal economics belongs to the era that began in the 1970s when, as the new economics orthodoxy, micro economics displaced or, perhaps more aptly, subsumed, macroeconomics (Rodgers 2011, chapter 2). Macroeconomics had been dominant in the 1940s, the heyday of welfare state thinking: 'The macroeconomy . . . was the arena where market inadequacies and public governance met' (Rodgers 2011, 47). It was central to the political conception of the welfare state where the objective of 'full employment in a free society' (as William Beveridge, the architect of the British Welfare State after the Second World War, conceives it) was not just a way of ensuring freedom from want but made possible a labour market that was 'a seller's market rather than a buyer's market' (Beveridge 1944, 19). This was desirable, Beveridge explained, on ethical grounds:

> The reason is that difficulty in selling labour has consequences of a different order of harmfulness from those associated with difficulty in buying labour. A person who has difficulty in buying the labour that he wants suffers inconvenience or reduction of profits. A person who cannot sell his labour is in effect told that he is of no use. The first difficulty causes annoyance or loss. The other is a personal catastrophe. The difference remains even if an adequate income is provided, by insurance or otherwise, during unemployment; idleness even on an income corrupts; the feeling of not being wanted demoralizes. (Beveridge 1944, 19)

By the mid-1980s, the term 'full employment' had 'all but disappeared from economic theory' (Daniel Rodger's 2011, 55). This fits the periodisation offered by Mirowski and Nik-Khah (2017) regarding the progressive association of economics with market design from the 1980s. Now:

> Any problem, economic or otherwise, has a market solution, given sufficient ingenuity: pollution is abated by the trading of 'emissions permits'; inadequate public education is rectified by 'vouchers'; auctions can adequately structure exclusionary communication channels; poverty-stricken sick people lacking access to health care can be incentivized to serve as guinea pigs for privatized clinical drug trials; poverty in underdeveloped nations can be ameliorated by 'micro-loans'. (Mirowski and Nik-Khah 2017, 57)

This new orthodoxy had reached such heights by 2008 that the then Australian Labor Deputy prime minister and Minister of Education, Employment and Workplace Relations, Julia Gillard, identified it with 'the new politics of the progressive centre':

> The next generation of reform challenges are all about how the power of the market interacts with the surrounding framework of institutions and the actions of individuals themselves. That means we are focusing on the fundamentals of market design. . . . How can we develop markets which interact productively with strong public institutions and empower users to participate successfully in them. (Gillard 2008, cit. Meagher and Wilson 2015, 62)

The Competition Review Report Panel could not have put it better themselves. Their first recommendation regarding 'competition principles' sets out what Gillard calls 'the fundamentals of market design' as these are to be instituted by the state:

Box 6.4:

RECOMMENDATION 1 – COMPETITION PRINCIPLES (HARPER ET AL. 2015, 33)

The Australian government, state and territory and local governments should commit to the following principles:

- Competition policies, laws and institutions should promote the long-term interests of consumers.
- Legislative frameworks and government policies and regulations binding the public or private sectors should not restrict competition.
- Governments should promote consumer choice when funding, procuring or providing goods and services and enable informed choices by consumers.
- The model for government provision or procurement of goods and services should separate the interests of policy (including funding), regulation and service provision, and should encourage a diversity of providers.
- Governments should separate remaining public monopolies from competitive service elements, and also separate contestable elements into smaller independent business activities.
- Government business activities that compete with private provision, whether for-profit or not-for-profit, should comply with competitive neutrality principles to ensure they do not enjoy a net competitive advantage simply as a result of government ownership.
- A right to third-party access to significant bottleneck infrastructure should be granted where it would promote a material increase in competition in dependent markets and would promote the public interest.
- Independent authorities should set, administer or oversee prices for natural monopoly infrastructure providers.

Applying these principles should be subject to a public interest test, such that legislation or government policy should not restrict competition unless:

- the benefits of the restriction to the community as a whole outweigh the costs; and
- the objectives of the legislation or government policy can be achieved only by restricting competition.

Just how we get past this technocratic jargon and open it up so that we can understand the conception that underlies it is assisted greatly if we understand something about the intellectual genealogy of competition policy. It should be obvious by now that in this form of competition policy we find a comprehensive political economy. It centres not just on how to curb anti-competitive practice as in traditional competition policy but on the principles for the institution of a market economy understood as a competitive order across not just the private sphere of economic production but the public sphere as well. It is surely unprecedented in reach and scope. What then by way of the history of political economy may assist us in understanding this kind of competition policy?

Neoclassical economic theory certainly emphasised competition. As the Wikipedia entry (as of 15 April 2018) on 'competition law theory' has it, a 'simple neo-classical model of free markets holds that production and distribution of goods and services in competitive free markets maximizes social welfare'. This premise is found in the Harper Report's (2015, 7) declaration: 'Competition policy is aimed at improving the economic welfare of Australians'. However, neoclassical economic theory does not offer the systemic political economy that appears to be at work in Australian competition policy. Neoliberal economic theory, especially that of Hayek and the German ordoliberal political economists (see Kolev 2015; see also Ptak 2009), does.

I have no evidence that Ian Harper and his colleagues, or indeed their predecessors in the development of the conception of Australian competition policy, understand themselves to be intellectually indebted to Hayekian and German ordoliberal economic thought. However, German ordoliberal thought, especially in its post-classical period, influenced European competition policy (Behrens 2014; Felice and Vatiero 2013) and the Organisation for Economic Cooperation and Development or OECD (in its earlier incarnation as the Organisation for European Economic Co-operation which was established in 1948 to administer the Marshall Plan and which provided the framework for negotiation that set up a European Free Trade Area in the 1950s). Australia joined the OECD in 1971.[10] In the 1970s Keynesian thought in Australia was placed increasingly on the defensive in relation to the promulgation of Milton Friedman's monetarist economics, sparked by a business-sponsored visit of Friedman to Australia (Courvisanos and Millmow 2006).[11] Hayek's core ideas have been widely distributed in the Anglo liberal democracies, and the Chicago School of neoliberal economic thought (Van Horn, Mirowski and Stapleford 2011) has both trained and influenced various individuals who have contributed to the development of a neoliberal framework for public policy in Australia since the 1980s.[12] But, more to the point, Mirowski and Nik-Khah (2017, especially chapters 7, 8, 9, 10 and 14) show how neoclassical economics in the second half of the twentieth century increasingly converged with neoliberal economics: the neoclassical and humanist idea of the individual as a rational utility maximiser was left behind in the conception of the market as a vast machinic apparatus of information processing.

In this connection, Michael Pusey's (2017, 13) analytical construction of 'economic rationalism' as the discourse that took over Australian government and policy from the 1980s is instructive. He indicates that in this takeover we have an entire institutional nexus of global and national agents at work:

> Economic rationalism is an ideological project that was foisted on Australia by four powerful institutional groupings: 1. The international peak business organisations such as the World Bank, the OECD, the World Trade Organisation and the IMF and the international credit rating houses; 2. The National peak business organisations most notably the Business Council of Australia; 3. The New Right libertarian business funded think tanks (the freedom fighters!) notably the Centre for Independent Studies, the Institute of Public Affairs and others; 4. The four large Accounting Houses who are the thought police for major investment. The neo-liberal takeover of Australia could never have been successfully accomplished by any one of these institutions or by the new [neo-classically trained] econocrats in the public service acting alone. Economic rationalism was always a political project aimed at the re-engineering of a whole nation society.

The Harper Review has to be seen in a direct line of inheritance from a number of Australian Commonwealth Government–commissioned policy reports that begin with the Garnaut Report of 1989. The Garnaut Report (*Australia and the Northeast Asian Ascendancy*) began the public policy approach that seeks to align Australian domestic institutions of government with global competitive forces especially those of the rising new Asian economies. The Garnaut Report was followed by the Hilmer Report in 1993, which placed competition policy 'as the centrepiece of Australian public policy' (Beeson and Firth 1998, 223). Beeson and Firth (1998, 224) argue that the 1995 Karpin Report (*Enterprising Nation: Renewing Australia's Managers to Meet the Challenges of the Asia-Pacific Century*) 'is a comprehensive blueprint for promoting the agenda of market-driven reform, especially at the micro level', with a strong focus on promoting enterprising attitudes and values in the Australian population:

> The Karpin Report is a seminal example of the way in which public policy was increasingly directed toward making health, education and the public service contribute to re-making 'Australia' as a globally competitive economic space. The underlying rationale is to break down the boundaries between state, society and economy in pursuit of greater integration and overall efficiency. (Beeson and Firth 1998, 224)

Finally, the 1996 Report 'on aspects of the management and financial activities of the Commonwealth Government' of the National Commission of Audit (NCA) Report established a key axiom of competition policy: that 'elected governments should not own businesses' (Goot 2010, 77). This axiom is offered in an historicist narrative that makes it seem that if once governments had to be involved in business enterprise, now governments do not need to be involved because '[p]rivate markets had matured and could provide many services' (NCA Report cit. Goot 2010, 77) once provided by government.

The genealogy of the Harper Review lies in these reports as well as in the major de-regulatory reforms that the Hawke-Keating Labor government began in the 1980s (see Humphrys and Cahill 2016) and that were continued by following governments. This being so, it is useful to consider the *ideas* that lay behind this institutional and policy process of the dissemination of neoliberal doctrine. For there can be no doctrine without ideas even if they have been taken over as undeclared assumptions in what otherwise appears as a neutral technical pragmatics of adaptation to current realities.

THE HAYEKIAN AND ORDOLIBERAL IDEA OF 'THE COMPETITIVE ORDER'

There are three key ideas that underpin the technocratic discourse of Australian competition policy. The *first* idea is that of *consumer sovereignty*, an idea that occurs especially in the Harper Review's justification of the extension of competition policy to the human services. The idea of championing individual user autonomy over, and indeed against, 'provider priorities' has been at the centre of all Australian policy discourse regarding human or welfare services since the 1980s. While Australian policy intellectuals like to make it seem that all they are offering is an obvious technical solution to a practical set of problems, there can be no doubt that they are influenced by the normative conception of 'economic freedom' that underlies the idea of consumer sovereignty. Economic freedom is a key posit in neoliberal thought, especially that of Mises, Hayek and the ordoliberals. While economic freedom 'includes producers' freedom to compete as well as consumers' freedom of choice' (Behrens 2014, 5), it is consumer choice that is the normative cornerstone of the whole edifice. Mises's subjectivist economics, where market prices are explained in terms of a general theory of human choice (Behrens 2014, 9), is the first historical elaboration of this idea of freedom of choice. In this passage from his treatise *Human Action* we see how consumer choice is made to be the driving force of a competitive market economy:

> The direction of all economic affairs is in the market society a task of the entrepreneurs. Theirs is the control of production. They are at the helm and steer the

> ship. A superficial observer would believe that they are supreme. But they are not. They are bound to obey unconditionally the captain's orders. The captain is the consumer. Neither the entrepreneurs nor the farmers nor the capitalists determine what has to be produced. The consumers do that. If a businessman does not strictly obey the orders of the public as they are conveyed to him by the structure of market prices, he suffers losses, he goes bankrupt, and is thus removed from his eminent place at the helm. Other men who did better in satisfying the demand of the consumers replace him. (Mises 1949, 269–70)

The *second idea* is that *state action is needed, and the role of the state is to provide and secure the institutional framework for the market economy.* Contrary to Mises's libertarian orientation (see discussion by Kolev 2015, 435–36), both the ordoliberals and Hayek emphasise the activist role of government in what came to be called market design. As Kolev (2015, 425) suggests, 'For the ordoliberals exchange needs an elaborate foundation for its proper functioning, and an important part of this foundation is to be provided by the state'. The state was responsible for providing the institutional design for 'the competitive order'.

It is the idea of *the competitive order* that is the *third* of the organising ideas of Australian competition policy. The idea of the competitive order as the institutional frame for human conduct was central to Hayek's reformulation of liberalism in the 1940s as he left technical economics behind for questions of social philosophy (Kolev 2015, 433). In his programmatic riposte to the idea of the welfare state – *The Road to Serfdom* (1944) – Hayek's alternative proposal is that of the competitive order (Kolev 2015, 433). Kolev (2015, 435) suggests that not only was this term, the competitive order, 'a clear sign of intimate intellectual proximity' between Hayek and leading ordoliberal scholars, but the ordoliberals and their idea of the competitive order were symptomatic of a new interventionist liberalism that took form in the first meeting of the Mont Pèlerin Society in 1947.[13]

Behrens (2014, 11) argues that 'classical liberal concepts such as those developed by Adam Smith and later by von Mises and the subjectivist school of economics set the stage' for the ordoliberal school of thought which started out as the Freiburg School. The hallmark of this school was its insistence that 'institutions matter' (see also Ptak 2009). It was an emphasis on legal institutions that Behrens identifies as the first innovative element of this school's way of thinking. Competition is the alternative to state intervention, but if it is to exist it has to be instituted: 'The fundamental insight was that in practice there can be no freedom and consequently no competition unless it is granted and protected by law' (Behrens 2014, 12). Franz Böhm, an eminent jurist in the Freiburg School, argued in 1933 'that participants in competitive markets must be empowered and at the same time controlled by legal rules which grant equal freedom to all (consumers as well as producers), private property rights pertaining to economic resources, freedom of contract, enforcement of and full responsibility for obligations resulting from contractual agreements as well as liability for damages inflicted upon others' (Behrens 2014, 13). These legal institutions are 'constitutive elements of markets and competition' (Behrens 2014, 13). Behrens emphasises what is at issue here: 'They represent nothing less than an "economic constitution" largely based on private law' (Behrens 2014, 13). Here we glimpse the radical reconstruction of the tradition of public law constitutionalism (Loughlin 2010) so that instead of public law preceding and containing private law, it serves private law. Behrens continues:

> [These legal institutions] turns market participants into legal subjects and the market society into a 'private law society'. It follows that competition is the result of individuals making use of their rights to freely engage in market transactions. (Behrens 2014, 13)

The second innovative element of the Freiburg School's thinking was 'the emphasis on the systemic nature of a competitive exchange economy' (Behrens 2014, 14). It constituted in Walter Eucken's conception an entire economic order. The coordination of this order resided in decentralised individual planning through market transactions (Behrens 2014, 14).[14]

Contemporary German ordoliberalism, Behrens (2014, 16–17) suggests, has continued the key 'focus on individual economic freedom (i.e., producers' and consumers' sovereignty with regard to economic planning) as the legally protected basis for a system of decentralized planning (i.e., a system of competition)'. At the same time, it corrected and refined the Freiburg School's thinking on some key points, and it has done this in ongoing dialogue with Hayek's thinking.[15] For instance, it moved away from the model of perfect or complete competition to one of 'workable' competition, a move also found in Hayek's thinking and the development of the Chicago School of neoliberal economics. The important thing was to protect competition rather than competitors, and market power as such should not be punished unless it gives rise to anticompetitive conduct:

> It is generally accepted that where market power or even monopoly is the result of success in the market there is no justification to punish it. Contemporary ordoliberal thought recognizes that market power, even where it gives rise to a 'dominant position' in the market, cannot be held illegal per se. . . . Market dominance must, however, be acquired by lawful means. (Behrens 2014, 19)

The second point of refinement was borrowed from Hayek, his idea of competition as a dynamic process of discovery, 'which produces all the information necessary to determine consumers' wants, their demand for specific goods and services and their willingness to pay as well as all the information necessary for producers to determine what to produce at what costs' (Behrens 2014, 20). This idea of the market as an information processor is now a fundamental assumption of neoliberal economics (Nik-Khah and Mirowski 2017). Behrens (2014, 21) also says that this idea of the market was 'complemented by adoption of the Schumpeterian idea of rivalry as "creative destruction", i.e., a process of constant emergence and erosion of market power, where one or more innovative firms strive to outcompete others who are then challenged to overtake the lead by more effective innovation'.[16]

The third point of refinement concerned the proposition that the state had a role to play 'in order to compensate for the limits to competition' (Behrens 2014, 20). There has to be a system of competition rules (Behrens 2014, 21) that govern market agents, and protect their economic freedom.

The institutional emphasis of ordoliberal thought on competition law and rules as the condition of a competitive market system is precisely what we find in Australian competition policy. The aim is to institute a competitive market order. Positive welfare or efficiency is equated with whether individual business strategies 'pass the test of "consumers' choice" in the market' (Behrens 2014, 27): 'In the end, any business conduct that appears efficient on the micro-level of the individual firm(s) must pass the efficiency test on the macro-level of the system of competition where consumers decide what they want' (Behrens 2014, 28).

AUSTRALIAN COMPETITION POLICY AND ITS EXTENSION TO THE HUMAN SERVICES

Here my focus is on the Harper Report's extension of Australian competition policy to the human services. But first we can remind ourselves of what I began with in this chapter that, in going back to first principles, this report offers a restatement of the institutional architecture of competition policy understood in terms of the idea of competitive order as an entire systemic frame for social life. We can glimpse the core neoliberal idea of competitive order in the four questions that the review panel asked in consideration 'of whether Australia's competition laws are fit for purpose':

- Does the law focus on enhancing consumer well-being over the long term?[17]
- Does the law protect competition rather than individual competitors?
- Does the law strike the right balance between prohibiting anti-competitive conduct and not interfering with efficiency, innovation and entrepreneurship?
- Is the law as clear, simple and predictable as it can be? (Ian Harper et al. 2015, 9)

The extension of the idea of the competitive order to human services is a radical shift in Australian public policy. If we look at the Australian Treasury's National Competition Policy Report 2005–2007 we can see that the assumption that this sector would be exempt from competition policy still prevailed. Thus in the section discussing 'competitive neutrality', the idea that government business activities should not be publicly subsidised or protected so that they have an unfair competitive advantage vis-à-vis private competitors, this report clearly indicates that it does not regard the human services as falling into the category of government business: 'Further, where public funds are removed from the provision of goods and services considered best left to the private sector, and those remaining activities are provided more efficiently, a greater proportion of total public funds can be directed towards the provision of social policy priorities such as health, education and welfare' (Treasury 2007, 47).[18]

Harper et al. (2015, 218) express awareness of the radical nature of this shift, and they indicate that there may be limits to the extent to which human services can be made subject to competition policy:

> Governments at all levels have traditionally played an important role in delivering human services. A number of human services serve important social objectives (for example, equal access to education and health services) and users of human services can be among the most vulnerable and disadvantaged Australians. Because of these characteristics, the scope to use competition or market-based initiatives may be more limited than in other sectors.

Yet there can be no doubt of the systemic intention: 'There is growing interest, both in Australia and overseas, in competition-based instruments to secure better outcomes for users of human services and better value for money' (Harper et al. 2015, 218).

The Harper Review's Report occurred in an 'austerity' climate where government at both federal and state levels of Australia has cut back human service funding. Austerity is built into the core command of the public sector managerialism that took over the Australian state from the 1980s onwards: do more with less. Meagher and Goodwin (2015, 9) rightly propose that marketisation is 'a policy frame that positions social policy systems . . . in conditions of "permanent austerity"'. While government is responsible for the institutional framework of competition, it is no longer responsible for welfare understood as a public phenomenon. This makes it possible for Harper and team to back off from any consideration of government funding responsibility for human services even as it acknowledges that governments must have a continuing role in this area:

> The Panel makes no recommendations regarding overall levels of funding for human services – funding decisions are a matter for governments and are

> generally determined through budgetary processes. However, funding levels and methods can have important implications for choice, diversity and innovation in human services markets. (Harper et al. 2015, 226)

The keystone, as always, in the legitimation of the application of the principles of a competitive market economy to the human services is the expansion of user choice. The report continues in the discursive tradition first begun in the 1970s that portrayed the welfare state as paternalistic where bureaucrats and service providers made decisions for service users: 'Traditionally, governments have decided which human services would be delivered, in what quantities and to whom. One result of this practice was that individual needs were rarely reflected in the standard service offering' (Harper et al. 2015, 230). Here in one swoop is dismissed the delicate multipurpose and multi-stakeholder calibration in public policy of budgetary allocation, population-based needs assessment in relation to the public value of universality, service rationing, professional judgement concerning need and the orientation of this judgement to how the individual presents and tells his or her story. The irreducible complexity of a *public* system of human services is waved away in the adoption of a market form of populism as this legitimises the private ordering of human services.

To be sure the Harper Review recognises that in some cases vulnerable service users will need others – 'intermediaries or purchase advisors' – to help them make decisions and that policies will be needed 'to align the incentives of purchase advisors with the best interests of users' (Harper et al. 2015, 239). They also recommend that service users must have 'access to relevant information to help them exercise their choices, including, where appropriate, feedback from previous users of services' (Harper et al. 2015, 239). The user information system they have in mind, however, is one where users have online access to comparative performance data (about schools, hospitals, etc.), there being no acknowledgement of the perverse incentives these systems create for risk averse (e.g., client 'creaming') and standardised service provision. Nor is there any genuine acknowledgement of the desirability of the asymmetry in both information and knowledge as this characterises the relationship between service provider and service user where the latter is dependent on the former's professionalism.[19]

The Harper Review (Harper et al. 2015, e.g., 247) states frequently that it does not want a competitive order to displace the historical role of not-for-profit providers in service provision. It also acknowledges the approach that Gary Sturgess (an advisor to the Review) recommends where contestability is distinguished from compulsory competitive tendering (Sturgess 2015, 12). Sturgess argues that a collaborative, relational and continuing relationship between government funders and providers is normally desirable. What keeps the providers on their toes in such an arrangement are the two mechanisms of performance benchmarking and the possibility that under- or poor performance would mean that they lose their contract:

> Contestability . . . often involves providers agreeing [*sic*] long-term contracts with public purchasers on the basis that the contract remains in place if the quality of the service is maintained and improved at a reasonable rate. The key point about contestability is the latent but real possibility that services can be switched to other organisations, acting as a continual incentive for providers to consider how they can improve their performance. (Sturgess 2015, 12)

While the Harper Review mentions that 'newer approaches to commissioning focus more on collaboration and contestability rather than strict competitive tender processes' (Harper et al. 2015, 240), it emphasises 'diversity of service providers' and makes the point that 'where there are economies of scale, good quality services may best be achieved by having a few large providers' (Harper et al. 2015, 244). It also states that for-profit providers 'can bring particular strengths to human services markets': 'They are likely to face stronger incentives to minimise cost, including through adopting new technologies and innovative methods of service delivery' (Harper et al. 2015, 246). As Considine (2018, 27), among many others, remarks, 'The welfare market model provides an almost irresistible motive to reduce staff costs as a way to enhance profit or maintain a sustainable presence in the market'; with the reliance on less qualified and increasingly casualised staff, quality of service provision declines. It seems also difficult to escape the conclusion that the logic of the situation that is created by competition policy means that more powerful for-profit providers crowd out especially smaller, close-to-the-ground, not-for-profit providers and provoke the bigger of these to consolidate, centralise and begin to behave like for-profit providers intent on building market share.

The separation of funding, regulation and provision is a lynchpin of competition policy. These are declared to be distinct interests that should not be mixed. The effect is to disaggregate what used to be called the policy process (see Yeatman 1998, chapter 1) where policy design, implementation and evaluation constituted distinct stages of a complex feedback-learning loop.[20] It enables the funding agency to assume the interest of the funder narrowly conceived in terms of a focus on cost containment and value for money. It enables the regulator to conceive a system of regulation that is abstracted from funding realities and on the ground delivery issues. It positions the provider in a formal contractual relationship to the funding agency and a relationship of compliance with the regulatory agency. And it enables the substance of the contract to assume the aspect of 'commercial in-confidence', thus evading political accountability and transparency. Competition policy has destroyed the heart of public service as it resided in programme management.

In so doing, it represents the success of the economic rationalist central agencies of government in not just bringing the line departments which had been responsible for programme management to heel (see Pusey 1991), but actually destroying any authority they may have had in representing a grounded knowledge of citizens' need. The public service ethos of the providers has been eroded in placing them in a competitive relationship with each other, and in destroying the peak body access they used to have to a collaborative stakeholder policy process that characterised public administration reform in the 1970s and 1980s.

The Harper Review is being implemented. On 29 April 2016, Scott Morrison, treasurer of the Commonwealth government, instructed the Productivity Commission to 'undertake an inquiry into Australia's human services, including health, education, and community services, with a focus on innovative ways to improve outcomes through introducing the principles of competition and informed user choice whilst maintaining or improving quality of service' (Australian Government Productivity Commission 2016, iii). This inquiry, now complete, has issued in a report (Australian Government Productivity Commission 2017) which has offered support for the extension of CP to human services, recommending, in particular, that it apply to end-of-life services, social housing, family and community services, services in remote Indigenous communities, public hospitals for elective care following a referral from their general practitioner, and public dental services.

CIVIC NEED AND THE WELFARE STATE

This is not the place to expatiate on the idea of the welfare state. Suffice to say that the idea of the welfare state is guided by a civic conception of need. This is a category of need that has to be met if the individual is to enjoy the status of freedom (T. H. Marshall's phrase discussed at length in Yeatman, 2018). To enjoy the status of freedom means that the individual cannot be treated as a slave, a thing or the property of another. The status of freedom is a relational condition: it bears both on how the individual internally regards himself or herself and on how he or she treats and is treated by others. The status of freedom, then, brings people into relationship with each other as individuals in their own right, who are free to claim their lives as their own, and as equal in this respect. Together they constitute a political community that is committed to securing and enabling the status of freedom as the fundamental principle of a public and civic collectivism.

There are four things to say of civic need. Firstly, it is because it entails an equality of status that the services it warrants must be designed and delivered so that they articulate this equality of status. It is for this reason that T. H. Marshall with reference to the British Health Service thought it so important that, regardless of class-based differences of wealth, all citizens had access to provision for their health needs in such a way as to constitute a common experience for them. This idea is not unlike Pierre Rosanvallon's idea that the French revolutionary practice of voting in assemblies 'created a novel type of social relation between individuals of different conditions'. He (2013, 39) continues: 'Distinctions were effaced by proximity and hidden by the neutrality of alphabetical ordering'.

Secondly, attending to and providing for civil need is the fundamental constitutive element of what we call public service and its ethics. If need is private, no longer constitutive of civil status, but instead the expression of consumer sovereignty, it is hard to see how the idea of public service can continue.

Thirdly, it is because civic need implicates not just the status of the individual, which is always relational, but also the existence of a political community of individuals that is committed to securing this status for everyone, that design for and implementation of services that meet civic need must have a universal and communal aspect. This can take different forms ranging from the association of such services with local community building to the invitation at the level of national design for services to all the stakeholders to come together to participate in the task for design.

Fourthly, how services provide (or do not) for civic need is something that has to be accountable both within administrative and public law and the political process. How such accountability operates is a political and a civil process governed by appropriate procedural norms.

CONCLUSION

Contemporary competition policy is not just an arcane, technical, economic process that is happening somewhere over there in the margin of our existence. It is reframing the nature of our lives both as individuals, as individuals in relation to each other, and as communities. It is turning our existence over to market principles that invite us to have no collective existence beyond family life, and to be privately oriented and privately interested. As the epitome of the neoliberal redesign of social life in terms of a competitive order, competition policy was and is designed to destroy the idea of civic need as this informs the conception of the welfare state. If we do not attend to the ideas that lie behind competition policy, it is impossible to understand just what it is that is happening to us, the nature of what it is that we are losing and to grasp in the face of this loss how we might reclaim a public and a civic collectivism.

NOTES

1. This is a revised version of a paper first published as A. Yeatman (2017).
2. The other three members of the panel were Peter Anderson described as 'a national business leader' who 'recently stepped down from the position of chief executive of the Australian Chamber of Commerce and Industry'; Su McCluskey, CEO of the Regional Australia Institute, who has had senior public sector roles in regulation, small business and tax reform, and who is a beef cattle farmer; and Michael O'Bryan, a Queen's counsel who 'has practiced extensively in the area of competition law' (Harper et al. 2015, 3).
3. The managerialisation and marketisation of the contemporary form of the constitutional-democratic state follows out the path dependency of the history of state formation in a particular country. Thus, it is arguable that Australian competition policy sustains the state-centric character of the Australian state, and the increasingly centralised nature of its federal system. In this respect, this chapter should be taken as a national case study of competition policy not as a general description of competition policy at this time.
4. In his book, Pusey shows how the central agencies of prime minister and Cabinet, Treasury and Finance, adopted an economic rationalist world view in the 1980s that converged with that of government ministers who shared a background in economics and who were in the Right faction of the Labor Party. The rise to prominence of the Productivity Commission represents the success of a project to de-politicise policy and turn it over to econocrats, so much so that the Productivity Commission now rivals the Department of Treasury in influence. Jones (2016, 181) remarks: 'The Productivity Commission . . . in Australia has a comprehensive mandate for government policy inquiries, a near monopoly probably unparalleled in any other country'.
5. It is important to note that in Australia and New Zealand it was Labor governments that made over the policy settings to a neoliberal approach in the 1980s. See Humphrys and Cahill (2016) for this important corrective of the view of neoliberalism as a 'right-wing' or conservative government project.
6. This actually goes back to the 'first wave' of managerialism in the Australian public sector in the 1980s (see Considine and Painter 1997).
7. As Martin Loughlin (2018) proposes, the three constituents of the juristic conception of the state that came into being in the early modern era in the West are territory, people and governing apparatus. The state understood as the juristic entity of a political society that is territorially based, and subject to the institutions of government, is an inherently public and civil phenomenon.
8. Palley (2011) offers a clear account of how the export-led growth model is exhausted. He (2011, 18) recommends a return to domestic demand-led growth which includes: 'Build social safety nets that diminish need for precautionary saving'; 'Raise wages and link wages to productivity growth by implementing a minimum wage, improving labor protections, and increasing collective bargaining via unions'; 'Increase public infrastructure investment and fill the backlog of public investment opportunities resulting from twenty-five years of neglect imposed by the neoliberal Washington consensus development model'; 'Increase the provision of public goods – like health care and education'.

9. Thus, the Australian Broadcasting Corporation, historically the public broadcaster charged with a mission of public communication and education, is now required, according to the principle of competitive neutrality, to show that it is not unfairly advantaged by public funding and government support in relation to its commercial competitors.
10. According to the Australian Department of Foreign Affairs and Trade (DFAT) website: 'The OECD's research and recommendations are useful tools in Australia's domestic policy-making process, helping to inform major decisions. OECD work has guided current Australian Government policies and programs in areas such as employment, pensions and education'.
11. 'A Sydney stockbroking firm, Constable and Bain, under the leadership of Maurice Newman, arranged and financed his trip' (Courvisanos and Millmow 2006, 9). Newman has been a long-standing member of the Mont Pèlerin Society.
12. J. Schulman (2015) claims that the Chicago School of Economics influenced the New Zealand and Australian Treasuries in the 1980s.
13. At the same time Kolev (2015, 433–34) suggests that the idea of the competitive order was the core ingredient in the climate of opinion that gradually took form as the new neoliberal political philosophy and economics:

    > Certainly a claim for an exclusive formative impact of the ordoliberals on Hayek in this respect would be too strong. Both in Walter Lippmann's *The Good Society* . . . and even more so, in the work of [Herbert] Simons within what has recently been called by James Buchanan . . . the 'Old Chicago School', one finds terminology and notions close to the ordoliberal type of reasoning regarding the competitive order. Still, correspondence on the eve of the Mont Pelèrin Society's founding between Hayek and Aaron Director, and also between Hayek and Eucken [one of the ordoliberal founders] shows that Hayek perceived the Chicago and Freiburg research programs as intimately congruent and that Simon's untimely death in 1946 hindered his intention to institutionalize these ideas at the University of Chicago. . . . Thus, inquiries into a substitute for the laissez-faire type of liberalism at Hayek's London, Eucken's Freiburg, Röpke's Geneva, and Simon's Chicago seem to be going very much in the same direction. Competitive order instead of *laissez-faire* is the programmatic aim of the new agenda; this program has to be positive in character (as opposed to the negative essence of criticizing socialism and interventionism), which Hayek underscores in correspondence with Machlup in 1953 at the beginning of *The Constitution of Liberty* project.

14. Behrens (2014, 16) surely rightly argues that the Freiburg School 'must be understood as the first attempt to integrate law and economics in order to explore the prerequisites for the proper functioning of competition on the basis of the freedom of consumers' choice'.
15. This further indication of a dynamic historical relationship between ordoliberal ideas and Hayek's social philosophy suggests where the more philosophical components of neoliberalism have resided. Kolev (2015) offers a more detailed investigation of the relationship between Hayek and ordoliberalism, suggesting that in the later stages of Hayek's intellectual trajectory his increasing focus on the evolutionary aspect of the spontaneous (market) order rather belies his earlier

emphasis on institutional design (Kolev 2015, 435). Yet as Kolev (2015, 428) remarks of the ordoliberal thinker Eucken's approach, 'the competitive order is designed and set by economic policy but simultaneously corresponds to the "spontaneous formations" of human coexistence and only protects these from power concentrations'. This kind of 'intervention', then, is justified whereas forms of intervention which interfere with such supposed spontaneous formations are not.

16. Behrens (2014, 21–22) continues here: 'Others developed the Hayekian approach to competition further into the notion of a cybernetic, self-regulating and evolutionary system based on voluntary transactions whose concrete effects can neither be anticipated nor in any way measured'.
17. This emphasis on consumer welfare over the long term is explained by the perceived need to ensure that new entrants can establish themselves in a market. Thus, consumer welfare is understood in terms of a temporal dynamic of competition where both new entrants and technological innovation represent a future horizon. In this connection, consider this passage from the *Competition Review Final Report* (2015, 25): 'New entry exerts a positive discipline on existing market players, encouraging them to be more innovative and responsive to consumer needs'.
18. That said, an efficiency dividend to reduce Commonwealth government agency budgets has been in place since the 1986–1987 budget, and Pusey (1991, 3) points out that under the Hawke Labor government in the period 1984–1989, government outlays fell. The then treasurer, Paul Keating, later boasted, 'we had outlays growing at less than the inflation rate' (O'Brien 2015, 69). So the trend was one of increasingly reduced outlays for 'human service' expenditure.
19. I argue elsewhere that 'it is a category error to think that the relationship between client and professional can be reframed so as to avoid the asymmetry that arises from the professional being able to offer something that the client needs' (Yeatman 2009, 93). The service user can readily tell whether she feels respected by the professional, whether her own lived experience is valued by the professional and whether after the fact she feels that the encounter gave her things that she values, but she cannot adjudicate the nature and quality of the judgement and expertise of the professional nor can she fully understand let alone evaluate how the professional surmised and met her need, a need she may never have known that she had.
20. In this connection, note the general disaggregating effect of the marketisation of social life as insightfully portrayed by Rodgers (2011, 41): 'In an age when words took on magical properties, no word flew higher or assumed a greater aura of enchantment than "market". . . . It stood for a way of thinking about society with a myriad of self-generated actions for its action and optimization as its natural and spontaneous outcome. It was . . . a disaggregation of society and its troubling collective presence and demands into an array of consenting, voluntarily acting individual pieces'.

Chapter 7

NAPLAN and the Role of Edu-Business

New Governance, New Privatisations and New Partnerships in Australian Education Policy[1]

Anna Hogan

A pervasive neoliberal imaginary has been working to recast education policymaking in specific ways, where contemporary policy settings now encourage the privatisation of education as a key means to improve school effectiveness and the quality of student outcomes. Such an approach to education has challenged the ideology of the traditional state-centred public provision of schooling, opening it instead to market-based processes of reform. Here not only does the state adopt neoliberal policy principles that encourage the discourses of accountability, competition and choice in education, but the state also works to open public policy processes to private sector participation. These privatisations are particularly evident in the Australian context, where the education reform initiatives introduced by the 2007 Rudd/Gillard Labor government under the pretext of an 'Education Revolution' not only introduced neoliberal performance management mechanisms into education, as evident through the National Assessment Program – Literacy and Numeracy (NAPLAN) and My School[2], but these processes have also worked to make the state more amenable to the participation of private providers in processes of test preparation, testing, data analysis and representation.

This chapter provides a critical analysis of NAPLAN as one of Australia's key policy initiatives which has worked to open the door to various amounts of privatisation in education. NAPLAN, like similar standardised test regimes in the United States (US) and United Kingdom (UK), is intended to improve student achievement and drive up education standards given these are seen as central to national success in the context of global economic competitiveness

(Rizvi and Lingard 2010; Thompson and Harbaugh 2013). As Thompson and Harbaugh (2013, 300) observe: 'Tests like NAPLAN represent a shift in the imaginary or logics of education policy, from government to governance, to practices of "auditing" schools and teachers through the production of (largely) quantitative data, and to the creation of systems that use data to steer or manage institutions, individuals and practices often at a distance'. While these particular effects have been well theorised in the literature (see Lingard 2011; Lingard and Sellar 2013), less so are the ways in which these political shifts are being leveraged by edu-businesses for commercial advantage. Indeed, Burch (2009) points out that particular segments of the education market are being reinvented around testing and accountability policies where schools and governments are now purchasing products and services from the private sector that are tied to test development and preparation, data analysis and management, and remedial services. She identifies that this is an industry worth $48 billion per year in the United States alone. Given this growth in edu-business activity is tied to changes in education policy, it is conceivable that NAPLAN may be similarly representative of new privatisations and increasing 'business opportunities' (Ball 2012) in Australian education policy.

Ball's (2007) work in particular suggests that there are a range of different privatisations 'of', 'in' and 'through' education and education policy, where edu-businesses are increasingly important in providing 'solutions' to national policy problems (Ball 2012). On this point Ball (2012, 112) notes:

> In effect, to different extents in different countries, the private sector now occupies a range of roles and relationships within the state and educational state in particular, as sponsors and benefactors, as well as working as contractors, consultants, advisers, researchers, service providers and so on and both sponsoring innovations (by philanthropic actions) *and* selling policy solutions and services to the state, sometimes in related ways.

Indeed, there is a trend in recent literature that discusses the new policy networks that emerge from these interrelations between government, edu-business and philanthropy over particular policy processes (Burch 2009; Ball 2012; Ball and Junemann 2012; Picciano and Spring 2013; Reckhow 2013; Olmedo 2014; Shiroma 2014). From these accounts we can see that neoliberal discourses of marketisation and privatisation have taken precedence, where the traditional hierarchical bureaucratic influence over the public sector has been broken down and reconfigured in ways that promote a new form of governance, or a 'polycentric' state (Ball 2012). Here, edu-businesses have gained credibility as legitimate contributors to this new policy landscape and are increasingly utilised in shaping and creating education policy.

NAPLAN exemplifies these shifting governance structures and the mix of public and private agents at work in education policy today. Understanding these evolving relationships between government institutions and edu-businesses is an important consideration in critical policy research. Thus my aim in this chapter is to document and analyse the ways in which edu-businesses are involved in NAPLAN policy processes, and the potential implications that arise from this transfer of activities from the public to the private sector. In particular, I seek to understand the motives that the Australian Curriculum, Assessment and Reporting Authority[3] (ACARA) has for contracting edu-businesses in processes of NAPLAN development, enactment and analysis. Here I reflect on tensions between public sector motives for the outsourcing of policy and the for-profit interests of edu-businesses. I argue that NAPLAN processes are indicative of new privatisations in Australia, where new policy values and new policy actors are working to redistribute power and responsibility in matters of education policy.

In what follows I first elaborate on the theoretical frameworks for analysis, which are important in understanding how new governance structures have underpinned the emergence of edu-businesses as critical to contemporary education policy processes. Here the work of Ball and Junemann (2012) on heterarchies works to characterise new networked partnerships between the public and private sectors (Robertson and Dale 2013), where shifting forms of public and private authority now mediate policy processes (Cutler 2008). Next I describe and analyse the NAPLAN policy network. Utilising the approach of 'network ethnography' (Howard 2002; Ball and Junemann 2012) I provide an account and analysis of the edu-businesses currently contributing to education policy in Australia, specifically around NAPLAN processes. My analysis suggests that edu-businesses like Pearson and the Australian Council for Educational Research (ACER) are working to construct policy problems which they can subsequently solve through their commercial activities. I see here the emergence of an Australian education policy field increasingly populated by edu-business and NAPLAN as a vector of privatisation.

THEORETICAL FRAMINGS: HETERARCHIES, NETWORKS AND PUBLIC–PRIVATE PARTNERSHIPS

A gradual shift in the form and functioning of the state has been occurring over recent years, where there now exists a genuine need to explore how educational governance is being done and by whom (Ball 2012). This uncertainty has arisen as a consequence from the move from government to governance, perhaps better conceptualised as a move from a traditional, hierarchical, bureaucratic model of command-and-control procedures to a more informal, flexible, networked form of practice (Eggers 2008). While this move has been framed by neoliberalism, it represents a move beyond conceptions of New

Public Management where the state adopts more business-like procedures. Rather, it constitutes what Ball terms (2007) privatisations of multiple kinds, where public policies are now being delivered through a strategic mix of public and private agents. These new relationships are a central feature of the contemporary state and its *modus operandi*.

Here, Ball and Junemann's (2012, 137–40) concept of 'heterarchy' is able to articulate the new 'latent structures' and relationships associated with new forms of educational governance. They define the concept in the following terms:

> Heterarchy is an organisational form somewhere between hierarchy and network that draws upon diverse horizontal and vertical links that permit different elements of the policy process to cooperate (and/or compete). Heterarchies have many of the characteristics of 'assemblages' of and for policy and governance, inasmuch as they contain heterogeneous elements placed in diverse relations to one another, in latent structures or as social morphology. (138)

As Ball and Junemann observe, heterarchies are dynamic structures that bring together bureaucratic and network relationships, which function between agencies of the government, business and civil society and extend these, in the case of contemporary education policy, to a global scale. The role of the state in these heterarchical structures varies, as Ball and Junemann (2012, 139) observe: 'Within heterarchies, public sector organisations are positioned sometimes as clients, sometimes as contractors, sometimes as partners and sometimes as competitors of private sector organisations'. Indeed, they suggest that often services are not removed from public sector control, but rather are performed in partnership or collaboration with the public sector. Heterarchies are examples of what Kickert et al. (1997; cited in Ball and Junemann 2012) refer to as 'loosely coupled, weakly tied, multi-organisational sets' – they are made up of processes and relationships rather than constituting an administrative structure.

These types of partnerships have led to a turn from hierarchy to a more complex, negotiated system, oriented to international competitiveness, innovation, flexibility and 'enterprise culture' (Jessop 1998, 35). According to Jessop (1998), the conditions for successful heterarchical governance depend on institutionalised negotiations, where actions are coordinated to secure particular outcomes which are deemed mutually beneficial. Thus, the state relinquishes part of its capacity for hierarchical, top-down, authoritative decision making in exchange for the 'policy solutions' (Ball 2012) that can be provided by the likes of edu-businesses; and edu-businesses forgo some of their autonomy in economic decision making to gain political influence and, consequently, improved system performance. What we have seen then in heterarchical governance is not an absolute change, 'but rather a shift in the balance or mix between the different elements of government – bureaucracies, markets and networks' (Ball and Junemann 2012, 5). Indeed, this hybrid mix of older and newer forms and practices of the state points to a prevailing policy landscape, where Williams (2012) argues that complex policy issues cannot be resolved by single agencies acting alone.

In heterarchies then, governments become facilitators and co-creators of policy agendas, policy texts and their deliveries. This context has important implications for thinking about and understanding policy analysis. Here, the idea of network governance has become particularly fashionable in conceptualising these complex formations, for networks provide a material basis for new forms of social organisation. By definition, networks are relational, self-organising, collaborative, non-hierarchical and flexible in nature (Barabasi 2003). This type of self-organisation means network actors form around a common goal or function and, as such, are equally subjected to change. As Newman (2001, 108) observes, 'Networks are informal and fluid, with shifting membership and ambiguous relationships and accountabilities'. Such flexible organisation represents a solid departure from rigid bureaucratic structures and heralds what Osborne and Gaebler (1992) have termed a 'reinventing of government'. Here we see the emergence of network governance where Koppenjan and Klijn (2004, 25) observe: 'In the world of network governance, government is understood to be located alongside business and civil society actors in a complex game of public policy formation, decision-making and implementation'.

This collaboration between public and private sectors is defined by Leitner and Sheppard (2002, 499) as an 'inclusive governance structure' where information can be exchanged between firms, the state and civil society. They explain that networks promote innovation and learning between the public and private sectors in ways that direct economic restructuring in positive directions and improve labour market information and training between the state and civil society in ways that deepen political participation. The result of these public/private partnerships (PPPs) is the creation of 'relational assets' (Storper 1997), where the dividing lines between state institutions and institutions of civil society are harder to draw (Amin and Thrift 1995). This is an important aspect of network governance; the state still has an important role to play, but policy networks can ensure that political decision making is flexible, dynamic and efficient (Martin and Mayntz 1991). As Wanna (2009, 266) suggests, governments are redefining themselves as 'facilitators' 'working through markets rather than acting as autarkic doers who owned, operated and produced everything themselves'. Williams (2002, 103) observes that through this mix of 'strategic alliances, joint working arrangements, partnerships and many other forms of collaboration' public services are being delivered across sectoral and organisational boundaries.

Yet these PPPs are also reworking notions of 'public authority' where market mechanisms are working to insert private sector interests into the realms of public policymaking (Robertson et al. 2012; Robertson and Dale 2013;). Cutler (2008) refers to this as the rise of 'private authority', where edu-businesses are given significant freedom to shape the ideology of education policy reform. As Burch (2009, 34) explains, in this environment the state's role has become 'highly technical' and 'organized around the management of contracts and the need for greater efficiency, while substance is shaped by the contracting private entity'. Indeed, Shiroma (2014, 335) found through her investigation of education policy networks in South America that private providers were able to apply pressure to the agenda setting and policymaking processes of the state and were able to successfully influence 'the formulation, implementation and evaluation of education policies'. So while the outsourcing of public policy may be based on the assumption that market-oriented management will lead to greater cost efficiency and improved success for governments, there are commensurate concerns here about the emerging capacity of edu-businesses to shape education policy problems and determine their solutions in ways that are commercially beneficial to themselves or their shareholders (Ball 2012; Robertson and Dale 2013).

Thus the role of edu-businesses in education policy processes is complex, still emerging and constantly evolving to take advantage of new opportunities in the education market. In this sense, there is no straightforward 'rule of thumb' that can be evoked to understand the relationships between edu-businesses, the state and education policy. Rather, as Ball (2012) contends, the resulting policy field from these interactions is complex, volatile and difficult to trace. What is clear though, as Picciano and Spring (2013) have pointed out, is that private providers are committed to the promotion of their beliefs, ideas, products and services in ways that further their own goals and objectives, that is, opportunities to profit. Picciano and Spring also suggest that it is important to remember that this new environment is not made up of one single entity conspiring to influence education policy, but rather, it is made up of multiple agents that compete with one another for contracts and sales of goods and services.

What I have been suggesting is this section, by tracing the restructuring of education governance mechanisms, is that state bureaucracies are now more heterarchical; that is, networked, horizontal relations cut across the vertical ones, as well as stretch across regions and the globe in a complex mix of the public and the private. Clearly, these new understandings necessitate research methods that are sensitive to these new forms of social organisation or educational governance. Howard (2002) and Ball and Junemann (2012) have argued that new kinds of ethnographic methods – network ethnography – enable such tracings.

METHODOLOGY: NETWORK ETHNOGRAPHY

Network ethnography is a methodological technique proposed by Howard (2002) to counter the challenges of studying organisational forms built around new media and mobilities. I would also note that the new governance structures referenced earlier, and the associated increases in the opaqueness of education policy, can be productively analysed using a network ethnography approach. Primarily network ethnography argues that the Internet can be employed as a site for research, where an increase of interactive communication technologies has provided qualitative researchers with useful techniques for collecting data on the policy networks produced through increasingly complex public–private interactions. Indeed, using the work of Kenway and Bullen (2001), I have promoted the idea of the network ethnographer as *cyberflâneur,* who can access the Internet and move through online communities, collecting information from websites, blogs, Facebook pages and twitter accounts. The *cyberflâneur* is able to move seamlessly between these spaces, travelling through what Beaulieu (2004) calls 'links of association'. The approach to research that can be undertaken by the *cyberflâneur* redefines the ways in which researchers can engage with contemporary policy issues and inspires a remapping of how one is able to trace the flows and mobilities of policy today (see Hogan 2015). Importantly, digital methods of this kind go beyond a focus on researching Internet technologies and online relationships and representations to examine what these technologies and relationships can tell us about social conditions more broadly (Rogers 2013).

Indeed, network ethnography has been applied in a small number of studies to convincingly portray changing educational governance structures in policy production and implementation (see Ball and Junemann 2012; Olmedo 2014; Shiroma 2014). As Ball and Junemann (2012, 6) observe, 'This method constitutes a mapping of the form and content of policy relations', where the network diagrams can be deployed as both 'an analytical technique for looking at the structure of policy communities and their social relationships' and a conceptual device that can be 'used to represent a set of "real" changes in the forms of governance of education, both nationally and globally'. Thus network ethnography is able to visually portray changing educational governance structures and enables recognition of the heterarchical nature of education policy processes that are produced through vertical and horizontal relations between public and private actors.

This analysis is informed by the three interrelated activities of network ethnography including: (1) Internet searches; (2) the use of these searches to construct network diagrams; and (3) the use of these diagrams to identify nodes for further analysis, primarily through semi-structured interviews. To this end, I present (below) a network diagram that was constructed using Gephi software. This network should be seen as a visual explanatory device, rather than a strict analytical representation. As such, networks encompass policy initiatives, policy actors and the interrelations between these to illustrate the complexity of contemporary policy networks. I rely upon Internet searches and a Freedom of Information (1982) request submitted to ACARA to map the policy networks associated with NAPLAN and to generate a network ethnographical account of the contexts of policy influence and production in Australia. This is supplemented with interviews conducted during 2013 as part of a broader project, and included here are three participants from ACARA, ACER and Pearson. These interviews were conducted over Skype, and all names and positions have been de-identified throughout this chapter to ensure participant anonymity.

NAPLAN POLICY NETWORK

As mentioned previously, the development and management of NAPLAN is a responsibility of ACARA. On this point ACARA (2011, 1) states: 'To ensure the delivery of a high quality and robust assessment program ACARA draws on both internal expertise and experts across Australia, all highly regarded in their relevant professional fields'. ACARA mentions that these experts include the likes of teachers, state and territory education authorities, the Australian government and other members of the non-government school sector. However, with no further information available on their website about who these experts are, or the role they play in the delivery of NAPLAN it is difficult to ascertain exactly how NAPLAN is developed and managed. Thus through both Internet searches and a Freedom of Information (1982) request I sought to unveil who these experts are and, more specifically, understand whether edu-businesses in Australia, like those in the United States and the United Kingdom, are now being contracted to produce policy texts *for* the state (Ball 2012).

From this investigation, the NAPLAN contract network (Figure 7.1) was constructed. This network diagram displays the contract arrangements that underpin NAPLAN, where both ACARA and state educational authorities contract edu-businesses in processes of developing, implementing and reporting on NAPLAN. This network is purposefully simple as it is designed to illustrate the key edu-businesses involved in this particular policy initiative.

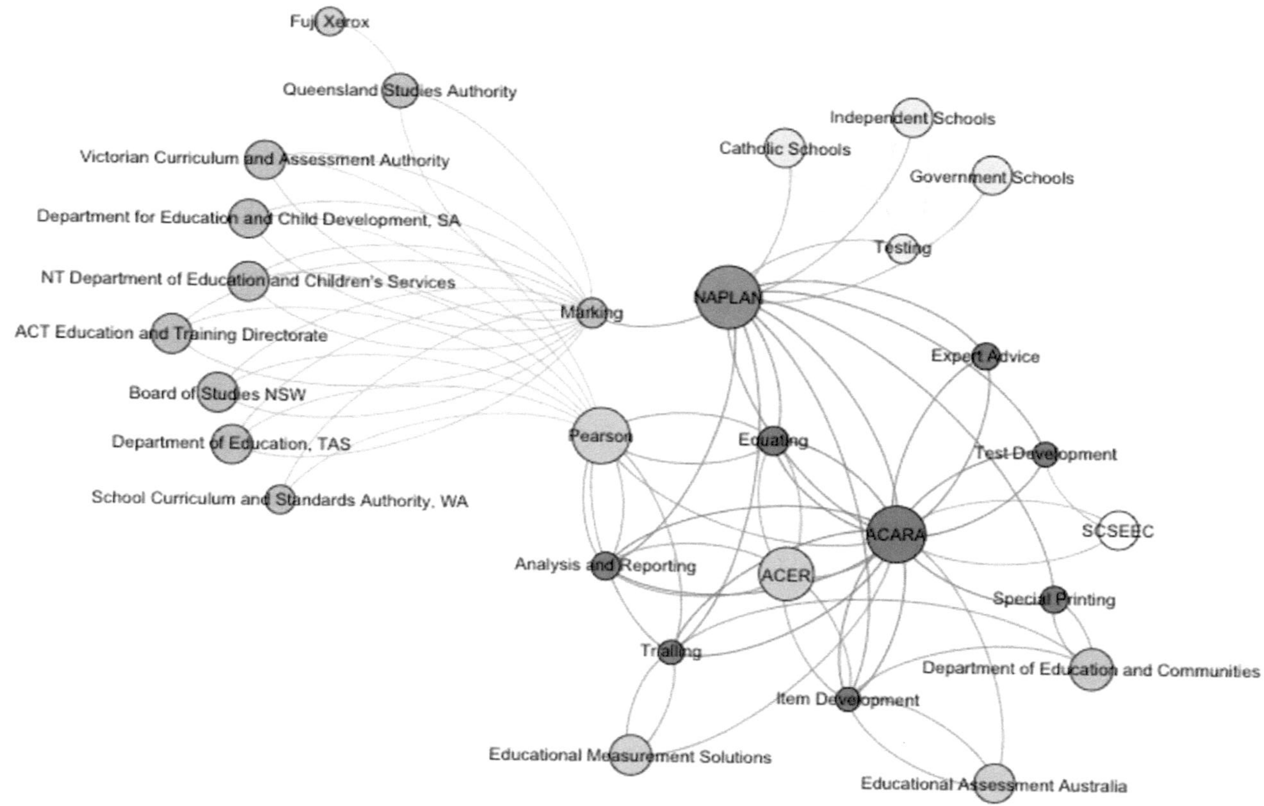

Figure 7.1 NAPLAN Contract Network

It can be observed from the diagram that there are nine lifecycle stages of NAPLAN which include:

1. Guidelines for test development
2. Item development
3. Consultation of expert advice
4. Trialling of test items
5. Equating of test items
6. Special printing of the test
7. Testing of students
8. Marking of the tests
9. Analysis and reporting of results

Out of these nine stages, ACARA is responsible for overseeing seven of them, where excluding the first stage undertaken by ACARA themselves in consultation with the Standing Council, contractors are used for the provision of all other relevant services. In 2012 the cost of these contracted services totalled $4,266,341. While ACARA did not disclose the cost of individual contracts due to concerns for their ability to achieve value for money for future NAPLAN contracts, they did provide an aggregate dollar figure for a number of the lifecycle stages. Thus, item development cost $2,075,717; trialling of the test items cost $681,253; equating of the test items cost $527,848; and the analysis and reporting of results cost $610,247.

It is clear from the network diagram that there are four significant edu-businesses utilised by ACARA, which include ACER, Educational Measurement Solutions (EMS), Educational Assessment Australia (EAA) and Pearson. Also included on the network diagram is the Department of Education and Communities from the state of New South Wales who was contracted specifically for the desktop publishing of final papers, trial papers and special printing of tests for students with disability.

Those stages not overseen by ACARA include the administering and marking of NAPLAN, which is the responsibility of the states and territories. The relevant state authority was contacted to ascertain how these processes were undertaken in their relevant jurisdiction. In every state the printing and distribution of NAPLAN materials was contracted to Pearson with the exception of Queensland who contracted Fuji Xerox for this process. The actual testing of students occurs in schools under the direction of school staff, and the subsequent marking of the test is a process overseen by most of the relevant educational authorities in the states and territories. However, in New South Wales, Victoria and the Australian Capital Territory, this process was also contracted to Pearson where it became responsible for the recruiting, training and paying of NAPLAN test markers. This presents Pearson as a central agent in the NAPLAN policy network, where it has significant contractual obligations with Commonwealth, state and territory governments.

Indeed, this NAPLAN network quite clearly represents the reconstitution of Australian educational governance, where the state has relinquished its monopoly over education policy processes in favour of private sector involvement in matters of public service delivery (Ball 2007). This has led to what Osborne and Gaebler (1992) call the 'reinvention of government' which has enabled the state to understand that what it does best is the 'leading' or 'steering' of the education system through the setting of policy frameworks, not the 'doing' or 'rowing' of the system through the provision of services. Davis, Sullivan and Yeatman (1997) argue that this move from government to governance has been mirrored by a turn to contractualism, where partnerships between the public sector and the private sector have become the new normal. In this new environment, as Patrinos, Barrera-Osorio and Guáqueta (2009, 1) observe, 'government guides policy and provides financing while the private sector delivers education services'. This has led to the emergence of the education services industry, where private actors, and edu-businesses in particular, are contributing to education policy and practice (Ball 2012). As Robertson and Verger (2012, 37) contend: 'The private sector is now deeply embedded in the heart of the state's education services at all levels, from policy and research work to delivering learning in classrooms'.

These increasing amounts of private activity have caused concern among a number of social commentators who believe that education as a public activity, serving the public interest, must remain within the control of the public domain. Yet, part of the post-Keynesian shift and the associated rise of neoliberalism and New Public Management mean that the increased role of the private sector is envisioned as being in the national interest (Ball 2007). As Christensen and Lægreid (2007b) assert, the primary aim is to modernise the public sector and render it more effective, which is based on the assumption that market-oriented management will lead to greater cost efficiency and improved success for governments. The ACARA representative I interviewed agrees with this sentiment:

> In short: No. I don't think we could operate as a modern organisation if we didn't [contract edu-businesses]. We'd become massive in terms of staff, and then because the nature of the work we do is cyclical – particularly in relation to something like NAPLAN – so you'll have an intense period where they're doing central analysis of data, you'll have an intense period where they're developing tests for a particular year, you'll have an intense period of equating. They're very different skill sets, and so if you actually employed staff – it wouldn't make much sense. You'd end up paying people to do nothing for long

> periods of time. . . . A lot of the bits of work are way too complex I suspect for a loose set of people to just pull it together. Some things you sort of need the size of an enterprise – in our case with ACER for example, they're obviously large enough to handle the complexity of the work, the quality assurance, and the risk management of the process we require.

Here ACARA clearly articulates that private sector involvement in education policy processes is a legitimate means of increasing the efficiency and effectiveness of what is now a disaggregated public practice. Indeed, this government perspective is well theorised in the literature, where many studies have examined PPPs from this perspective. What is examined to a lesser extent are the perspectives of edu-businesses on these partnerships. Given this omission in current understanding, I asked the Australian Pearson representative why they are interested in partnering with public authorities on public policy initiatives:

> No one's got the answer, the single answer. I think it comes through collaborative efforts. We have as much to gain by engaging with governments about, okay, where are you heading with your education systems? What are you thinking around assessments? How can we partner with you? Because we want the same result. We all want a positive outcome for learners. . . . That's, I think, where we see ourselves, certainly in the future, is working more in collaboration with a government perspective, with State and Federal governments around what their initiatives are for education and where they can see a for-profit organisation like Pearson fitting in. For-profit doesn't mean that we appear to take money away. It's about how you spend your money more wisely, which is also a challenge these days for any government.

In this excerpt Pearson suggests that its primary aim is improving student outcomes, that this cannot be achieved by any one organisation working alone, and that engaging in PPPs will continue to be an important aspect of its business strategy into the future.

It is worth noting here that Pearson's increasing engagement with PPPs in the Australian context is representative of its global transformation that has been occurring over recent years where it has worked to shift its business strategy from education inputs (e.g., textbooks) to education outcomes. This is indicative of the increasing business opportunities that now exist in matters of public education policy (Ball 2012). Indeed, Pearson (2012, 39) argues that as the world's leading edu-business (reporting over four billion pounds in education sales during 2012), it has a responsibility to support educational improvement and is 'committed to playing an active role in helping shape and inform the global debate around education and learning policy'. Here we see the phenomenon described by Bishop and Green (2008, 177) as 'philanthrocapitalism' in which 'corporate social responsibility . . . is being driven by the belief that doing good is profitable'. Pearson, across all of its organisational divisions, demonstrates the character of the 'new philanthropy', whereby 'organisations involved display a variety of different and changing mixes of charitable, social enterprising and business identities and commitments' (Ball 2012, 89). This blurring and hybridisation between education as a social good and education as a profit opportunity might be seen as another manifestation of what Rose (1999) and Savage (2012) have called the 'neo-social' condition, where there is a distinct elision of the social and the economic.

While the distinction between for-profit and not-for-profit edu-businesses is an issue that has received relatively little attention in contemporary analyses, Piketty (2014) has argued that in the wake of globalisation, neoliberalism, financial crises and the growth of inequality, large corporations like Pearson are facing increasing criticism from the public about their motives for public policy delivery. For example, popular and influential education policy actor Diane Ravitch, who was the former assistant secretary of education in President George W. Bush's administration, is particularly outspoken about what she sees as the 'Pearsonization' of American students and schools. In a recent blog post titled 'The United States of Pearson' (2012) she writes:

> It is difficult to remember what part of American education has not been invaded by Pearson's corporate grasp. It receives billions of dollars to test millions of students. . . . With the U.S. Department of Education now pressing schools to test children in second grade, first grade, kindergarten – and possibly earlier . . . the picture grows clear. Pearson will control every aspect of our education system.

While the Pearson representative I interviewed described this sort of criticism as a 'knee jerk reaction', it does point to potentially serious implications about the increasing trend of PPPs in matters of education policy. However, as the ACARA representative points out, this concern is not linked to the fact that Pearson is a for-profit edu-business, rather this concern emanates from the risk of the public sector becoming reliant on, or constrained by, a particular private provider:

> I guess technically a profit-making company has members, and it distributes its proceeds to the members. A not-for-profit one is just churning the money back into its own organisation, including through wages and so forth. So to some extent, I'd say we're cautious of some not-for-profits which we think are probably taking as much, or a larger margin than commercial bodies. So I guess it's really case-by-case. There's some commercial players that we are a little bit suss on, because you know, cost cutting, are they just trying to overrun the marketplace? But there's also not-for-profits that we're concerned about because they

> charge too much, in the sense of when you're trying to get value for money, it doesn't matter what happens with the margin – whether it's going to members of a company or whether it's going back into research being undertaken by an organisation – if the margin is large, we don't like it.

From this perspective then it seems too simplistic to judge an edu-business on whether it is not-for-profit or for-profit, as this is clearly not a distinction of good versus evil, nor is it one that is likely to influence with whom government authorities engage in partnership. As ACARA highlights, engaging in PPPs is a decision based on an economic assessment of 'value-for-money'. Yet, looking at the NAPLAN contract network and the centrality of Pearson and ACER, is there a concern here that ACARA and other education authorities are becoming dependent on certain edu-businesses?

PROBLEMATISING THE INCREASING USE OF PPPS

Capturing the benefits of competition is often given as a key reason for outsourcing public services. This argument derives from standard market theory, where Burch (2009), for example, proposes that the outsourcing of public services creates a competitive market for public services, increases the quality of those services and reduces costs for taxpayers. However, this economic efficiency argument is valid only if there is enough competition within the sector to ensure that the government agency doing the outsourcing is not constrained or captured by one particular provider. While ACARA believes that its procurement policy encourages competition in the Australian education market, its reliance on ACER and Pearson, two of the four edu-businesses it uses, is indicative of the prominence of these two in a national, state-based, and global web of market-oriented contractual relationships. For example, if we take ACER as an example, it has established a strong presence in the market for educational services. Beyond NAPLAN work, in 2012 ACER was contracted to work on 126 education-related projects for fifty-six different agencies. These agencies include state and federal education departments as well as national and international companies and agencies. For example, state educational authorities like the Victorian Department of Education and Early Childhood Development (VDEECD) contracted ACER to work on fifteen different projects. Also, the Department of Education, Employment and Workplace Relations (DEEWR), which since 2012 has been replaced by two separate agencies, including the Australian Government Department of Education and the Australian Government Department of Employment, contracted ACER to work on sixteen of its education projects. Similarly, there are links to international education projects headed by the like of the Organisation for

Economic Cooperation and Development (OECD), the International Association for the Evaluation of Educational Achievement (IEA), World Bank and UNICEF. ACARA is not the only agency that uses edu-businesses in matters of education policy. Examination of ACER's contract network shows that a vast majority of Australia's federal and state education authorities and governmental institutions are reliant on PPPs.

While this reliance on PPPs is not unexpected given new forms of heterarchical governance, there are concerns here about the capacity of edu-businesses to shape policy problems and their solutions in ways beneficial to their organisation. Consider the fact that edu-businesses like ACER are not only developing and enacting policy processes on national and state levels, but they are also designing textbooks, practice assessments and school reform services targeted at the local level. Indeed, ACER suggests that there are two major aspects of its work. The first is to assist educational decision makers at all levels in their collection, analysis, interpretation and use of reliable data. The second is to assist educational decision makers at all levels in their identification and implementation of evidence-based policies and practices. To this end, as one ACER representative commented:

> The products that we produce are largely in response to needs that we become aware of. . . . So for example . . . evaluations point to what's working or not working with educational programs and resources, but also to resources that may be needed to support school students.

Thus, ACER is using its policy work to inform the construction of particular education resources or what may be construed in Ball's (2012) terms as the identification of policy 'problems' to which it can sell policy 'solutions'.

It is clear that this influence arises from working in partnership with governments, government institutions and even schools, where ACER is able to identify and respond to policy needs through its work in developing, consulting, evaluating or making recommendations about public policies. Given this, these contracts and relationships are a key function for edu-businesses where ACER identifies that PPPs are:

> pretty much a key part of the landscape at this particular point in time . . . and ACER, because of all the work we do in the evaluation and the collection of evidence, is in a particularly good situation to then propose or recommend policy directions, which is ultimately all we can ever do. We can simply recommend the directions and the shape the policy might take, it is up to the government to agree.

This notion of the government 'agreeing' with policy proposals is interesting. Hogan, Sellar and Lingard (2016) have pointed to the idea that edu-businesses are working to over-simplify complicated policy issues. According to Verger (2012, 111), these simplifications or authoritative programmatic ideals act like 'cognitive locks' and work to 'restrict decision-makers to certain intellectual paths, reduce uncertainty amongst policy-makers, and constitute broad cognitive constraints on the range of solutions that they perceive and deem to be useful for solving problems'. There is a legitimate concern here about the ways in which edu-businesses might work to shape or influence education policy in specific ways.

Besussi (2006, 18) makes the point that the promise of PPPs and new heterarchical policy networks and the mode of governance they represent is to 'produce more effective and legitimate policies, without resting upon the authority and limitations of a single representative political body'. Yet if edu-businesses are working to undermine democratic policy processes for their own commercial advantage it seems that these heterarchical governance structures could equally contribute to undesirable consequences associated with the increasing privatisation of education policy processes. Rizvi and Lingard (2010, 6) argue that the policy cycle can be a messy and contested space where policies are often 'heteroglossic' in nature, which means 'they often mask whose interest they actually represent'. They make the point that this means that we must be aware of the 'discursive work that policies do in constructing problems in certain ways, perhaps differently from what the best research-based empirical and theoretical analyses might suggest' (Rizvi and Lingard 2010, 6).

I am not suggesting that edu-businesses have taken over policy processes; the power of the state remains important. As ACARA points out it sets the contracts and select the best applicant for the job. However, what we can observe with the opening up of public policy processes to private sector participation is a shift in the relationship between public and private, and a concomitant blurring over 'who does what' in matters of education policy. While the state's agenda could be interpreted simply as a desire to reform education and improve student outcomes, the question arises whether in their desire for 'solutions' to their 'problems' they are becoming acquiescent in the policy agendas of edu-businesses.

This is pertinent to consider given these agendas are tied to profit making, and moreover are largely shaped by 'generalists' with little classroom experience or formal research background in education. Edu-businesses are increasingly contributing to policy discussions and setting policy agendas in ways that have displaced traditional experts. Edu-businesses are increasingly seen as a legitimate component of the knowledge-producing community, which is resulting in new understandings of what counts as education policy research, and is contributing to a new tension around conflicting conceptions of policy evidence produced by edu-businesses and members of the academy, respectively.

CONCLUSION

In this chapter, I have attempted to map Australia's changing governance structure and highlight the mix of public and private agents at work in education policy today. While NAPLAN is indicative of these new privatisations, it is clear from analysis of ACER's contract network that PPPs are widespread and firmly entrenched in Australia. While this is not a surprising phenomenon given the new heterarchical governance structures and increasing privatisations that now shape and influence education, what is concerning are the ways in which these PPPs may work to redistribute power and responsibility in the production and implementation of education policy. This concern encompasses the democratic deficit in educational policy where edu-businesses have the capacity to shape policy processes in non-transparent and non-politically accountable ways from which they can commercially benefit.

The final issue to raise briefly here about the enhanced role of edu-businesses in policy processes is the changing notion of 'expertise' in education. Here I want to recall ACARA's statement that NAPLAN is delivered by 'experts' across the field. It seems problematic that experts in this case are not teachers, curriculum developers or even university researchers. Instead, experts are constituted in terms of their ability to offer 'value-for-money' on competitive tender applications. There is a problem here about which groups are becoming excluded from, and which groups are included in, processes of public policy, where it is increasingly obvious that edu-businesses are now closely entwined with the role and process of education policymaking. This development has not only inserted new players and new relationships into education policy processes, but it has also resulted in new understandings of what counts as 'effective' education policy. Here we are seeing an intensification of testing and accountability regimes as a logic of education reform, because I would aver, this is not only a technology of the neoliberal education imaginary, but also a means by which edu-businesses can substantially profit as part of the emergent philanthrocapitalism.

In conclusion, I have demonstrated that Ball's (2012, 112) argument can be applied to the Australian context when he observes that 'the private sector now occupies a range of roles and relationships with the state and educational state in particular'. This growing involvement of edu-businesses in education policy processes and educational governance is contributing to a blurring and hybridisation between the 'public' and the 'private', which is leading to an increase in the opacity of policymaking. Within the functioning of these new heterarchical policy networks, Ball (2012, 8) points out that it is 'unclear what may have been said to whom, where, with what effect and in exchange for what'.

NOTES

1. Reprinted with minor changes by permission from Springer Nature: Springer, Australian Educational Researcher, 'NAPLAN and the role of edu-business: New governance, new privatisations and new partnerships in Australian education policy', Anna Hogan, © *The Australian Association for Research in Education, Inc*. 2014.
2. NAPLAN tests are conducted in May each year for all students across Australia in years 3, 5, 7 and 9. All students in the same year level are assessed on the same test items in the assessment domains of Reading, Writing, Language Conventions (spelling, grammar and punctuation) and Numeracy. The results of NAPLAN for every Australian school are displayed on the My School website, which allows comparisons to be made between statistically similar schools.
3. ACARA is a Commonwealth statutory body that was established in 2008 by the Rudd/Gillard Labor government to lead the development of NAPLAN, My School and the Australian curriculum. Independent from the federal government, ACARA is jointly funded by the Commonwealth, state and territory governments and receives directions from the associated Ministers for Education through the Standing Council on School Education and Early Childhood (SCSEEC).

Chapter 8

Compassionate Care

The Managerialisation of Virtue

Kirstine Zinck Pedersen and
Anne Roelsgaard Obling

In recent years, calls for 'compassion' have been invoked around the globe as a new policy trope to improve the quality and performance of everything from healthcare services (Department of Health 2012; NHS 2014a), banking (Martin and Cahan 2013), stakeholder relationships (Hopkinson 2014), social entrepreneurship (Atkins and Parker 2012) to corporate volunteering (Grant 2012). In public sector management, compassion is increasingly viewed theoretically as well as practically as the 'antidote' to what is seen as the accumulated flaws of contemporary public sector reform.

The invocation of 'compassion' entails considerable conceptual difficulty. Compassion comes with numerous definitions and associated concepts, and is difficult to delimit. The etymological source is the Latin *compati,* which means 'to suffer with' or 'to suffer together'. This meaning is not unrelated to the everyday usage such as 'feeling sorry for somebody with problems' (Clark 1997, 30) or the ability to 'express empathy, provide emotional support and a willingness to understand and relieve another's distress and suffering' (Mannion 2014, 115). The most common synonyms for compassion are pity, sympathy and empathy.

In this chapter, our focus is on what happens when 'compassion' becomes managerialised, turned into a generic value and a new type of control mechanism in public management, specifically in healthcare governance. Here the already-broad everyday understanding of compassion is displaced by an even more wide-ranging usage that is designed to fit health care in general in all of its dimensions and roles. Compassion is evoked as an over-arching and thus abstract term that covers everything, including care, competence, communication, courage and commitment in the nursing and midwifery professions (Department of Health 2012). At other times compassion is promoted as a generic virtue or personality covering all the characteristics a healthcare leader must aspire to including emotional intelligence, resilience, integrity, authenticity, balance and motivation (NHS 2014a). The list is potentially endless. The use of compassion in policy is equalled by increased interest in compassion within management and organisation studies where a similarly abstract and all-encompassing understanding of the concept tends to prevail. For example, a series of articles on 'compassionate organization' in *Academy of Management Review* (2012) promotes compassion as an answer to the problem of 'suffering everywhere' (Rynes et al. 2012, 504) and therefore as a generalised 'organizing-principle' in any type it seems of organisational and managerial design (Rynes et al. 2012).

The empirical reference here is the comprehensive 'compassionate care' reform programme in the National Health Service (NHS) in England, which in recent years has underscored the necessity of turning to health professionals' ethical conduct and development of compassionate character as the foundation of high-quality care. The compassion agenda can be understood as a response to what is identified as two interrelated problems: on the one hand, an increase in healthcare scandals concerning breaches of safety or cases of below-standard care; and on the other, an accumulated dissatisfaction with what is identified as the dominant 'command-and-control' culture resulting from the large number of New Public Management (NPM) reforms that have swept British healthcare since the 1980s. Critics are arguing that these reforms have led to 'command-and-control' leadership practices' (de Zulueta 2013a, 2013b), shifts towards 'impersonal surveillance systems coupled with cost savings measures' (Fotaki 2015, 201), dysfunctional incentives associated with meeting external performance targets (Mannion 2014) and even 'to a reifying scientific ideology that make mere things of patients and staff alike' (Smajdor 2013, 115).

Although the turn to compassion is understood as a noble attempt to make public sector organisations more 'human' and less 'machine-like', the new attempt to 'managerialise' compassion by making it a policy concern and a new steering tool in healthcare governance is not without problems. Through empirical reference to relevant policy documents, and drawing on the idea of an 'ethics of office' that Max Weber (1978, 2004a, 2004b), among others, offers, we explore how compassion is constituted as a meta-value in current reform programmes. It represents a new area of healthcare management where compassionate character in staff, from student-nurses to hospital managers, is identified, developed and rewarded. This management reform is blind to differences between professions and tasks. The chapter reflects on the managerialisation of virtue. It argues how a seemingly value-based approach to public sector management may have unintended consequences for the quality of care and the conduct of health professionals that in some ways resemble and in some ways exceed those of the NPM, which the new paradigm is expected to humanise. In the chapter's final section we turn to Florence Nightingale (1860) who is often understood as the founding figure of not only the nursing profession but also the compassion agenda. In so doing we indicate that our critical engagement with the current managerialisation of compassion is not an argument for neglecting the ethics of nurses or other health professionals, or the centrality of compassion as an integrated component of especially the nursing role. However, Nightingale's specification of the role of the nurse enables us to understand that virtue in this context is role-specific: it concerns the ethics of a particular public office, and the ethical persona of the individual who is trained and skilled in the practice of this office.

COMPASSION IN HEALTHCARE

Of all the scandals that have paved the way for the compassion agenda in NHS, the Stafford hospital case has been the most important. The compassionate care programme has even been described as a direct result of what is termed the 'Francis effect' named after the two public inquiries by Robert Francis that investigated the scandal in 2010 and 2013 (Francis 2010, 2013). These inquiries told an uncomfortable story about appalling incidents of suffering by large number of patients at Stafford hospital between 2005 and 2009. They detailed how the Mid Staffordshire NHS hospital trust, that ran the hospital, had failed for years in its primary duty to protect its patients and maintain confidence in the healthcare system. Following the Francis reports into serious care failings at Mid Staffordshire NHS foundation trust, the mainstream UK press reported hundreds of suspicious casualties at Stafford hospital. Especially nasty were the stories of extreme neglect, where patients were left dying in their own excrement and urine, given life-threatening wrong medication, not fed properly and forced to drink water from the flower vases. In the wake of the public inquiry, politicians, NHS spokesmen and healthcare experts were outdoing each other to blame everything from David Cameron, the Tories, NHS cutbacks, amateurish management practice and leadership to the nursing profession and its lack of professional ethics for the scandal. In this blame-game, the scandal was quickly linked to the ethical conduct and character of the health professionals, the managers and not least the board members in question.

The Stafford case fed a wider call for compassionate care in the NHS in the political response to this scandal. The apparent 'characterological' flaws that had led to a supposed lack of compassion in the Stafford case were also linked to a critique of dominant ways of organising healthcare, in which, it was argued, NPM had led to a compassionless culture focused on performance targets, economy and measurement. The comprehensive compassionate care reform programme was 'to replace tick-box targets as the major focus on boards and wards' (NHS 2014a) and accordingly should be understood as a needed correction of the NPM agenda (see also Department of Health 2012).

The compassion agenda was launched as part of a turn to 'values' in the NHS. In opposition to 'cold' management ideals, Secretary of State for Health Jeremy Hunt wished to reintroduce an image of the NHS as a moral organisation driven by 'human values' expressed in the culture and character of the people working in it:

> The NHS was set up with a moral purpose and is – at its heart – a moral being. It is an institution ultimately driven not by treatment or targets or pills – but by the values of the people who work in it. And if we don't create a culture that nurtures those values, organizational change, policy change, even money will count for little. (Hunt 2014b)

So to promote human values, improve patient-safety and overhaul what inquiry chairman Robert Francis QC called a 'flawed, self-serving NHS-system' (Campbell 2013), the Francis report (2013) led to a policy process in which it was recommended that all health professionals should be trained in compassion, that compassion be considered and evaluated as a core competency of healthcare providers and that standards of compassionate care be adopted and implemented.

VALUE-BASED APPROACHES TO PUBLIC MANAGEMENT

The 'call for compassion' in public services in general, and in healthcare specifically, is part of a current public management trend in which reformers seek to correct some of the failures of earlier reform agendas by presenting 'value-based' alternatives, not least to the market-based NPM regime that has dominated most public sector reform thinking since the 1980s (e.g., Hood 2005; Hood and Dixon 2015; Pollitt and Bouckaert 2017).

Within the healthcare field, the increasing critique by medical practitioners of NPM has been backed by a large body of scholarly work documenting the unintended and often-unwanted effects of the introduction of market-type mechanisms on the professions, work systems, management and the relationships between patients and professionals (e.g., Dent 1993; Fitzgerald and Ferlie 2000; Doolin 2002; Bevan and Hood 2006; Harrison and MacDonald 2008; Waring, Dixon-Woods and Young 2010). Much of this criticism has focused particularly on the underlying rationalities and unintended effects of new kinds of externally imposed accountability and audit measures, including the widespread use of performance indicators, target setting, benchmarking and performance management (e.g., Power 1997, 2007). It is generally agreed that this 'measure-and-manage orthodoxy' (Waring 2009, 1723) has widely affected the ethos and conduct of healthcare professionals who are increasingly dominated and regulated 'through less and less visible, but more and more pervasive command and control mechanisms' (Speed 2011, 101; see also Roelsgaard Obling 2012, 2013).

The loud critiques of the ideologies and technologies of NPM have led to emergent counter-reform movements that are – despite fragmentation and variation across contexts and countries – unified by a strong focus on 'human values' and 'soft measures' in public management. Instead of focusing on competition, contracting-out and control mechanisms, these public management models attend to concepts such as governance, co-creation, trust and public value (for an overview see Pollitt and Bouckaert 2017). One of these models, Public Value Management, advocates for the strategic attention of public managers to public sector values as defined and normatively guided by the achievement of particular social missions, and understood as distinctly different from 'private sector values' guided by profit-optimisation (Moore 1995; O'Flynn 2007). With such value-based perspectives, the 'motivational force does not solely rely on rules or incentives to drive public service practice and reform' (Stoker 2006, 41). Rather, it is suggested that public servants and public managers should be understood as 'explorers commissioned by society to search for public value' (Moore 1995, 172; and see Pors, this volume) and, furthermore, that they are understood to be motivated not by profit, incentives or performance measures but by 'their relationships with others formed in the context of mutual respect and shared learning' (Stoker 2006, 41).

The increased call for values in public management fits what du Gay (2008) describes as the call for increased emotional engagement on the part of public officials. He argues that public servants in post-bureaucratic reform processes are met with two emotional injunctions: one which requires servants to be passionately responsive to the needs of their clients, and one which requires them to be enthusiastic advocates of particular policies – whether these promote efficiency and control, or 'soft currencies' such as quality, trust, charisma or compassion. The demands for responsiveness and enthusiasm include the aim to 'inculcate in bureaucratic conduct a sense of compassion or close identification with others' feelings' (2008, 336). Thus, du Gay suggests that public servants are to develop an 'ethics of enthusiasm' that brings to the forefront not the roles and obligations of their office but their 'individuality', 'humanity' and personal morality.

In this way the compassion agenda can be understood as part of a larger landscape of public management reform in which value-based approaches are introduced as correctives for market-based managerial ideology and where accordingly individual public servants are expected to bring their personalities, enthusiasms and emotions to bear on how they relate to the policy programmes and the service users.

MAX WEBER AND THE ETHICS OF OFFICE

As an evaluative analytical framework for approaching what is at stake in the managerialisation of compassion and its consequences for the organisation of healthcare and the conduct of healthcare professionals we turn to the literature on office and office-holding and to a particular tradition of ethical thought: the 'ethics of office' (Hennis 2000; Condren 2006; du Gay 2009). This is a tradition of practical ethical thought that finds no place in contemporary theories of ethics such as consequentialism, deontology or virtue ethics, but which has a long and influential history spanning Cicero's *De officiis* ([44BC] 1991); Pufendorf ([1673] 1991); Max Weber (1978, 2004a, 2004b) and sociologist Paul du Gay's recent work (e.g., du Gay 2007, 2013). Here we turn to Weber, who has been identified as one of the last greatest exponents of an ethics of office (Condren 2006, 24, 347).

Weber's conception of the ethics of office is relevant for our discussion of the compassion agenda in two important ways. Firstly, in Weber's understanding, office-holding is specific, it entails its own particular value orientation, and thus it cannot be organised by the values of another office. Weber insists on a plurality of distinct life-orders (*Lebensordnung*), each organised in terms of a specific life sphere, with its own identifiable morality, norms, responsibilities and expected life-conduct (*Lebensführung*) (Weber 2004a, 2004b). Since offices are irreducible to one another, there is no overarching virtue or meta-rationality that covers all of them. Instead, each office places specific demands and expectations on the people who are educated to occupy it. Furthermore, an office is manifested not in an individual, but in a 'persona' or role that the individual adopts when he or she serves the office. The distinction between the individual who is understood as a 'reflective' and 'autonomous' whole self (du Gay 2008, 338, see also Condren 2006, 29) and the individual who is present as a persona specific to the office he or she serves is important to understand. Thus, for example, it is the professional and procedural character of medical conduct that constitutes the practical ethos of the doctor, not the personality nor the moral convictions of this individual. Thus, the substantive ethical goals come with the specific office as this is embodied in the individual's conduct, not with the individual's subjective life.

This takes us to the second point. In Weber's account of the ethos of the office of public service, he emphasises the impersonality of how responsibility is delegated and discretion is exercised. This is an important antidote to contemporary managerialist emphasis on how the individual personality or subjectivity of the official is engaged in public service, as in the call for compassion. According to Weber, what characterises modern bureaucratic organisation was the strict separation of the office-holder's personal preferences and private moral beliefs from the conduct of the office. Thus, Weber writes in *Economy and Society*: 'Bureaucracy develops the more perfectly, the more it is "dehumanized", the more completely it succeeds in eliminating from official business love, hatred, and all purely personal, irrational, and emotional elements which escapes calculation' (1978, 975). Weber further states that public servant must act 'without regard to the person in question, *sine ira et studio*, without hate and without love . . . but sheerly in accordance with the impersonal duty imposed by his calling, and not as a result of any concrete personal relationships' (1978, 600). This separation of a civic comportment and personal principles has helped to divorce 'the administration of public life from private moral absolutism' as Paul du Gay (2008, 338) puts it.

For du Gay (2000), this stress on impersonality as a crucial feature of bureaucratic rationality is not tantamount to a denial of 'humanity' or emotion as long as 'these do not undermine the ethos governing the conduct of that office, through for example, opening the doors to corruption or encouraging inappropriate forms of patronage (2000: 75)'. From this perspective, then, Weber does not dismiss emotions as such so long as they do not interfere with the formal, and in this sense 'objective', obligations and duties of office. Thus, a good nurse or doctor, for example, is expected to be 'impersonal' so that he or she is able to attend to the matter at hand. Here, the conception of impersonality refers to the professional capacity to treat patients equally, without paying attention to their status or personal attributes. This entails a duty to decide on cases and care for patients in a way that is unaffected or unbiased by personal relations or feelings. At the same time, it might well be that a professionalised 'compassionate attitude' towards patients, for instance, is part of the health professional's official duties in certain situations.

Within the sociology of the professions, professionalism and bureaucracy are often understood as conflicting principles of organisation (see, for instance, Freidson 2001). Weber himself, however, never made a distinction between the authority of bureaucratic office and the authority of professionalism: they were both distinct forms of office. Along these lines, it is argued that healthcare organisations – especially hospitals – should be approached as 'professional bureaucracies' (e.g., Mintzberg 1979) in which the establishment of clear lines of command that enables a delineated and well-defined distribution of responsibilities and obligations through a system of office are the preconditions for the exercise of clinical discretion and professionalism (see Perrow 2014; Pedersen and du Gay forthcoming).

With these two Weberian tropes, the irreducibility of a system of offices to any kind of meta-virtue or overarching set of values, and the 'impersonality' of office in bureaucratic types of organisation, we turn now to analyse some selected parts of the compassion reform in English healthcare.

COMPASSION AS AN ABSTRACTION

> We want everyone to have greater control of their health and their well-being, and to be supported to live longer, healthier lives by high quality health and care services that are compassionate, inclusive and constantly-improving. (NHS 2018)

In the process of managerialising 'compassion', the concept has come to be defined and framed in numerous ways so that it can encompass a wide range of particular policy problems: for example, continue already-existing managerial practices, develop new types of control mechanisms, support a rhetorical strategy of change, innovation and improvement (e.g., The Kings Fund 2017b). In this process, compassion has often come to mean everything and nothing. As when then chief executive of NHS Employers Dean Royles, in his blog 'Compassion is one of our few infinite resources', defines compassion in the following way:

> Compassion can be innate and it can be taught and learned. It can be central to who we are and what we stand for, but far more importantly it can come in small doses and those small things can make a huge difference to the way people experience care. That positive experience can also help build values, it is a truly virtual circle of good . . . compassion is so close to love. (Royles 2014)

Apart from being an extraordinarily abstract value, this quote also suggests how compassion is operationalised as 'soft' and 'humanistic' reforms such as the 'Friend and Family' and 'Open and Honest Care' performance measure initiatives described earlier. So just as with the concepts and managerial programmes of patient safety and quality (see Pedersen 2018), compassion is hard to be against. Who can be against something 'so close to love'?

The abstraction of compassion is evidenced in the lack of specification of particular roles, task and care practices in the various programmes. When approaching the compassion reforms from an 'ethics of office' perspective, where an organisational persona is related to a particular office and where conduct concerns the performance of an office-specific role, such abstraction stands out as problematic. With compassion's managerialisation, it is understood as an overarching or integrating virtue – a meta-virtue – that is required for the performance of any or all of the tasks and obligations facing NHS employees whether nurse, midwife, physician, surgeon, chief executive or financial manager. The bolstering of compassion is construed as an urgent need even 'amongst commissioners and throughout arm's length bodies, assurance and oversight bodies' reaching far beyond the healthcare institutions themselves (NHS 2014c, 2). Although compassion is understood as a guiding value for the whole of NHS, most of the policies are particularly oriented to nursing, midwifery and care personnel and their managers. But even here the compassion agenda becomes one for everyone. Thus, the follow-up strategy to the *Compassion in Practice* (Department of Health 2012), the *Leading Change, Adding Value* (NHS 2016) is defined as 'a framework for all nursing, midwifery and care staff. It can be used by everyone, wherever you work and whatever your role' (2016, 1). When compassion is made to be the overriding virtue required by everyone, there is a risk of explicitly or implicitly ignoring the complex system of roles and functions that defines the instituted and official purposes of different categories of healthcare staff.

One place where this mechanism of abstraction becomes especially evident is in the NHS policy on compassionate leadership. A main finding of the public inquiries and reviews following the Stafford case was that the criminal neglect of patients and the organisational dysfunctions outlined came about because of NHS leaders' poor decision making and their prioritising of financial health and performance targets above safe and appropriate care. Within the compassionate care agenda these findings are used to develop policies that particularly target leaders, as they are understood as the change agents who can make a radical transformation of the NHS culture and environment possible. Thus a compassionate leadership programme has been introduced on the assumption 'that greater compassion within and through leadership has the potential to (re) align the NHS to its core purpose and truly transform patient care' (NHS 2014b, 10).

The leadership development programme has a high level of generality and lack of contextual specificity captured nicely in its mission statement declaring that 'compassionate leadership is everyone's business' (NHS 2014b, 3). From those at the frontline of patient care to the medical directors and board members, compassion is key to improving everything from patient experience, personal effectiveness and motivation, organisational planning activities to team performance.

But what are the consequences of promoting compassion as a guiding virtue for managers? Firstly, if compassion – and the adoption of a compassionate attitude towards others' suffering – is to be understood in relation to its original meaning, it is easy to see how in some administrative or managerial functions compassion can in some contexts and situations be a vice. For a patient flow manager, for example, it is essential to practice his or her office with a developed sense of justice, treating everyone equally independently of kith, kin or class (see Weber 1978). Here it is ethically – and often also legally – required that the flow manager prioritises and acts with a cultivated indifference to the particular patient in question, looking only to distinctive criteria (e.g., need) when deciding, for instance, who is to have the earliest slot for surgery. When fairness and equality are secured through the ethical comportment of impartiality, the demand for compassion becomes problematic, as this would make possible situations in which the patient flow manager would be likely to prioritise patients for whom he or she had the most compassion. A compassionate ethos is likely to conflict with the values of equality, equity and justice traditionally so central to the NHS.

The problem of assuming that the generalised and abstract value can guide distinctive offices and official personae is perhaps even more evident in relation to clinical work. Compassion is a more relevant virtue for a clinician involved in patient interaction than for a surgeon who spends most of his or her time in the operation theatre. But even for a surgeon, compassion may be sometimes situationally relevant. It is a virtue in the medical encounter where a surgeon is disclosing a serious diagnosis to a patient. Here exhibiting kindness, empathy and compassion is an important part of the role, and should be trained in the same manner as any other skill that relates to how surgeons conduct themselves in particular clinical situations. But compassion could be a vice in the operating theatre where the conduct of the surgeon should be guided by a mastery of surgical skill, a strict adherence to rules and protocols and an 'artificial cool-head' (Holmes 2009, 302) that secures the necessary discretionary abilities in instances where critical decision-making or swift action is needed: abilities that are not likely to be helped by overly compassionate feelings for the patient. It is therefore possible to argue that when it comes to the performance of surgery, it is potentially dangerous to instil compassion as the dominant motivational force.

The assumption that compassion should be the guiding virtue for health professionals at all organisational levels and across every position is based on the peculiar premise that if, for instance as a manager, one of your key responsibilities is to ensure the compassionate care of patients, and the compassionate character of your employees, then one of your own main virtues must also be compassion. As an implementation plan for building and strengthening leadership puts it, it is important that an individual 'distil the essential leadership behaviours, attributes and characteristics that embody a compassionate leader' (NHS 2014c, 2). The reason for this, the NHS plan states, is: 'A leader displaying compassion will win the respect of staff and allow them to deliver good quality care and feel more aligned with the organization's objectives. The leader will be more credible, more authentic, and more likely to be followed' (NHS 2014c, 22). In this way, it is no longer office-specific demands and expectations that define the virtues by which your job is to be evaluated, but rather the manner in which you positively and eagerly engage in developing a moral character based on your personal preferences and private moral beliefs. We therefore now turn to a discussion of how methods and principles of the compassionate care policy programmes are not only invoked as matters of organisational culture and change but also imply ambition in altering the conduct and modes of thinking of individual health professionals and managers.

THE FOSTERING AND TRAINING OF A COMPASSIONATE SELF

Understood as an abstract meta-virtue, compassion is rarely approached or taught in any context- or task-specific way. Rather for the individual healthcare worker compassion is a question of internalising a general value orientation, not in their roles as nurses or midwifes, for example, but as 'whole' persons and enthusiastic individuals. As Jeremy Hunt suggests, 'This is a change in culture that has to be adopted enthusiastically – not imposed unwillingly' (2014a). Thus, training courses in compassionate care, such as the NHS Compassion in Practice e-Learning programme, are said to be applying the theory of compassion 'to compassionate care through a model of the compassionate mind' and by this to be able to 'identify the core attributes and skills' needed to deliver compassionate care (Shropshire Community Health 2017). These types of training programmes are based on collaboration with compassion researcher such as the clinical psychologist Paul Raymond Gilbert who is the founder of compassion-focused therapy (CFT) and compassionate mind training (CMT).

In the NHS implementation plan 'Building and Strengthening Leadership: Leading with Compassion' (2014b), compassion is described as the 'self-awareness, resilience, mindfulness and emotional intelligence that allows you to be present and available to the needs of others' (2014b, 12). Further, 'each individual needs to: develop routine habits to stay balanced; keep rooted to core purpose; plan ahead for situations where work is personally depleting or restorative; and notice the signs and activate plans when off-balance' (2014b, 5). Thus, managers are encouraged to bolster compassion in the 'self', and various strategies are advocated for developing personal leadership as distinct from office-specific leadership. One of these concerns how to improve self-mastery through the development of 'routine habits to stay balanced' (2014b, 7). It is further argued that exercises on the 'self', for instance through the use of a coach to promote 'personal feelings', development of 'personal mission', 'ensuring a psychosocially rich life and opportunities to refresh, e.g., walking the dog; living fully in and out of work' (2014b, 6), provide a gateway to character development with the goal of enabling 'one to be present and available to the needs of others'. 'Others' seem here to include both personal–private relationships and office-specific relationships with patients, colleagues and managers.

Compassion then becomes a question of individuals looking inwards by focusing on balance, mindfulness, resilience, restoration in order to live up to externally imposed demands that they build a compassionate character. Rather than paying attention to others, especially other peoples' suffering, bolstering 'self-compassion' becomes a key concern. Therefore, healthcare managers are told to 'find those things you personally need to attend to, to ensure you are grounded and balanced, connected to what matters to you personally' (NHS 2014b, 22).

The norms embedded in the compassion agenda can thus be understood as requiring a reinvention of moral character, where compassion – and herewith increased self-awareness, mindfulness and resilience – is represented as central to the health professionals' individual selves. Compassion requires that they develop into 'reflective' and 'autonomous' human beings (e.g., du Gay 2008, 338, see also Condren 2006, 29). In this way the compassionate care policies not only signal a promotion of a more moral and 'value-based' NHS, as a corrective for the downsides of the New Public Management regime, but brings with it new all-encompassing sets of rationalities and methodologies that demand an internalisation of one particular virtue – compassion – not only to guide the conduct of everyone hired by the NHS but also to foster and cultivate more well-integrated human beings. The compassion agenda falls into a trap where morality is not embodied in and limited to a particular organisational persona, but is dependent on an abstract, undifferentiated and ultimately thoroughly personal as well as subjectively sentimental understanding of appropriate ethical behaviour.

TECHNOLOGIES OF COMPASSION MANAGEMENT

With the political focus on incentivising compassion in NHS – and with the large number of policy programmes that have been introduced under the compassion headline – 'compassion' has emerged as a management technology to improve everything from the quality of patient care and professional responsiveness towards patients to the well-being of health professionals. In some ways the compassion policies continue and extend already-existent managerial technologies in clinical practice. In other ways the compassion agenda has introduced what could be called technologies of virtue assessment, a new type of managerialism that focuses on assessing, monitoring or rewarding compassionate attitude and character in health professionals. Thus, to enable staff to act with compassion and connect with organisational goals and strategies, different technologies have been proposed to develop 'valid and realisable measures and methods to assess and reward compassionate care' (Lown 2014, 200).

As for the extension of already-existing technologies, this is mainly visible in the consistent focus on measurement. Approaching the myriad of 'compassion' policies in NHS, and multiple new managerial technologies introduced as a result of these, it quickly becomes obvious that the compassion agenda is far from a correction of the 'tick-box-mentality' that it was meant to be. Rather these policy initiatives continue the 'measure-and-manage orthodoxy' (Waring 2009) of the earlier NPM reform movement. In the strategy for nursing, midwifery and care staff, *Compassion in Practice* (Department of Health 2012), 'measurement of impact' was explicitly identified as one of six action areas. In the follow-up plans (NHS 2014a, 2016), most of the other action areas also involve a focus on measurement, not least in the use of patient experience as a new control mechanism. The measurement schemes include, for instance, 'The Friend and Family' initiative, which is a ranking of hospitals based on the patient survey question of whether patients would recommend the hospital to family and friends (NHS 2014a, 21). This initiative is based on the long-existing national patient survey programme, which has now incorporated the compassion agenda to measure 'how successfully health and care services treat people with respect, dignity and compassion, so that we can make changes, where necessary' (Department of Health 2015). In the same vein the 'Open and Honest Care: Driving Improvement' initiative 'aims to support NHS organizations become more transparent and consists in the measurement and publication of their safety, experience and improvement data; with the aim of improving practice and creating a culture of compassion' (NHS 2014a, 28).

Apart from sustaining a focus on performance measures and ranking systems, the compassion agenda also brings with it a new touch in its intense focus on the fostering and training of a compassionate self through various training programmes: for instance, through the Compassion in Practice e-Learning programme; through the introduction of a new national values-based recruitment framework to ensure 'that the NHS is recruiting the right people with the right values and behaviors to be compassionate and caring' (NHS 2014a, 42; see also, NHS 2013); and through the introduction of different types of virtue developing, accessing and rewarding technologies. One such technology is the Scottish NHS development programme, 'Valuing Feedback', that focuses on cultivating and supporting compassionate care practice by feedback processes and appreciative listening techniques generated through technologies such as Emotional Touchpoint (ET) (The Scottish Health Council 2014; Smith 2017). ET is a so-called story elicitation technique helping patients or staff to recall 'being touched emotionally (feelings) or cognitively (deep and lasting memories)' when receiving or delivering care.

The compassion agenda has led to a focus on incentive structures that support compassionate behaviour, such as employee rewards and bonus systems that are linked to quality of care measures. According to former prime minister David Cameron, 'We need a style of leadership from nurses which means poor practice is not tolerated and is driven off the wards' and one way of achieving this is that 'nurses should be hired and promoted on the basis of having compassion as a vocation' and not just academic qualifications (Campbell 2013). As a concrete example, the focus on rewards and incentives has led to 'the Leading with Compassion Recognition Scheme' where you can 'show your appreciation' by nominating NHS staff for compassion behaviour (see nhs.compassion.org/compassion).

Although this new focus on the training, fostering, assessment and rewarding of compassionate selves is often understood as a correction of 'harder' types of managerialism, it seems that with a closer look that these measures and mechanisms are not radically different. Take, for instance, the dominant policy agendas of quality improvement and patient safety governance in healthcare (see Pedersen 2018). As a mode of governance, the emphasis on quality and safety involves *both* regulation, measurement and control of instrumental aspects of clinical work procedures *and* a cultivation of what Brown and Hesketh (2004) call 'non-bureaucratic soft currencies', that is, a control of social and psychological attributes of individuals, such as interpersonal skills, humanism, charisma and appearance. This tendency is especially evident in the increased focus on user experience, where it is a political aim to make public servants personally invested in treating 'the users of services as queens not pawns' (Speed 2011, 99). In this way, the new control mechanisms to ensure 'a compassionate culture' also sit well with the new ways of thinking about the optimal use of resources in the healthcare sector. Rather than focusing just on performance enhancement and the financial health of healthcare organisations, efforts are now given to ensuring that resources are used for interventions that produce outcomes that patients most value. Compassion-based healthcare therefore aims at putting what patients value at the centre of healthcare, which is similar to other quality improvement strategies (see, for instance, the promotion of value in the King's Funds priorities for the United Kingdom [UK] National Health Service [NHS] and social care services in 2017 and onwards, The Kings Fund 2017a).

It might not come as a surprise that the development of new organisational practices and techniques link to already-established administrative and management regimes. The output focus and performance-measure strategies of NPM ideologies and methods have today become institutionalised, and thus more value-based innovations á la the compassion reform programme are likely to add yet another layer to already-existing forms. This is what is understood within institutional theory as layering, where public management agendas – in spite of the rhetoric of innovation and newness – rarely supersede earlier approaches but rather add to and build on them (Pollitt and Bouckaert 2017; see also Greve 2010).

A TASK-SPECIFIC CONCEPTION OF COMPASSION: REVISITING NIGHTINGALE

In the promotion of the compassion agenda in healthcare policy, it is often argued that compassion has always been a main – even *the* main – virtue in healthcare delivery in general, and in nursing especially. The founder of modern nursing, Florence Nightingale, is invoked as a leading figure in the establishment of compassion as the impetus for care, and the promotion of a compassionate character as the ethos of the nursing profession (see, for instance, Maben, Cornwell and Sweeney 2009; Bradshaw 2011; Bivins et al. 2017). As we turn to Nightingale now, it is to clarify that our critique of the managerialisation of compassion is not an argument for ignoring the question of the virtue or ethical comportment of healthcare professionals. On the contrary, we argue that attending to values through formulating and re-formulating the role-specific virtues, skills and duties of public offices is a continuous task. Interestingly, this is precisely what Nightingale provokes us to think.

Although Nightingale is praised as the first and foremost advocate of compassion in healthcare, words such as compassion or empathy are nowhere to be found in her influential *Notes on Nursing* (1860). Neither are any of the other 'humanistic' virtues that are often attributed to the compassionate healthcare provider such as genuineness, openness, honesty, authenticity, tolerance and kindness, to name some (see Sinclair et al. 2016). Rather Nightingale's notes constitute a detailed description of the duties and tasks of the nurse, none of which are abstracted in terms of higher or all-encompassing virtues, but rather formulated as specific guidelines on how to never speak to the invalid patient from behind, how to air the room of the patient without chilling him or her, how to reduce noise in the sickroom or how not to rush or hurry when with a patient – to name just a few. For Nightingale nursing was to be defined in task-specific terms as 'the proper use of fresh air, light, warmth, cleanliness, quiet, and the proper selection and administration of diet – all at the least expense of vital power to the patient' (1860, 8). And ensuring such 'proper use' was a question of training, not least of the important skill of observation:

> The most important practical lesson that can be given to nurses is to teach them what to observe – how to observe – what symptoms indicate improvement – what the reverse – which are of importance – which are of none – which are the

> evidence of neglect – and of what kind of neglect. All this is what ought to make part, and an essential part, of the training of every nurse. (Nightingale 1860, 105)

Thus, Nightingale argues, it is often the trained skill of observation that normatively distinguishes the good nurse from the bad nurse: the good nurse is she who meticulously observes her patient's dietary habits at every meal, for instance. And the good nurse is she who instead of asking vague, loose or leading questions such as 'did you have a good night'? asks direct and informative questions such as 'how many hours did you sleep'? (Nightingale 1860, 108).

It is not wrong to suggest that Nightingale's notes concern the training and nurturing of the compassionate character of the nurse. This is, however, only a meaningful claim if we link 'compassion' to the specific life-order of nursing and its related practical work tasks and trained abilities, or even define compassion *as* these highly specialised practices of care, and not as an inner feeling or an abstracted attitude of kindness or empathy (see also Greenhalgh 2013). From a Nightingale stance, the ethos of nursing lies not in a feeling of kindness or compassion. Rather, the ethos of nursing concerns the trained abilities and skill of the nurses, not least the skill of observation, and, she adds, 'if you cannot get the habit of observation one way or other, you had better give up being a nurse, for it is not your calling, however kind and anxious you may be' (Nightingale 1860, 113).

What is equally important is to remember the fact that the Nightingale mission was to establish nursing as a recognised profession that was not subordinate to medicine, or a mere technical skill, but a vocation, a professional calling, with its own normative and practical standards and training programmes (see Nelson and Rafferty 2010). Thus, Nightingale's understanding of nursing was office-based, and her promotion of the nursing profession was never disconnected from the hospital organisation understood as a complex system of relations between the official roles, obligations and duties needed to supply the proper treatment and care of patients. In such a system, Nightingale argued, leadership and responsibility is about ensuring that everyone fulfils his or her appointed office:

> To be 'in charge' is certainly not only to carry out the proper measures yourself but to see that every one else does so too; to see that no one either wilfully or ignorantly thwarts or prevents such measures. It is neither to do everything yourself nor to appoint a number of people to each duty, but to ensure that each does that duty to which he is appointed. (Nightingale 1860, 42)

In sharp contrast to the argument that 'compassionate leadership' result in compassionate employees, Nightingale defines clinical management as the task of ensuring that each person follows the task-specific duties linked to their particular office.

CONCLUSION

Drawing on Weber and an ethics of office perspective, we have demonstrated that the current managerialisation of compassion in the NHS leaves us with at least two types of somewhat distinct but interconnected problems: a problem of abstraction and a problem of personalisation. As for the first of these problems, the problem of abstraction, we have shown how compassion is understood as a meta-virtue, which is applicable to all forms of relationships and to every formal position in health care. Instead of tailoring compassion to office and role-specific duties in specific situations, compassion is treated as an abstract idea about creating 'whole' or 'well-integrated' human beings motivated by compassionate feelings across offices. By exploring how health professionals' are asked to work with and on themselves, and to bring practices of self-reflection and inner scrutiny into their professional work, we showed how the Weberian separation of office and person and persona and individual in practice is challenged and weakened.

The problems of medical negligence and poor standards of care identified by the Francis reports are real ones. So are the problems of the NPM tick-box-mentality. However, as we have shown it is not only uncertain but also rather naive to assume that a managerialisation of compassion – as an abstract and all-encompassing virtue that introduce new types of control in healthcare – will solve these problems. Even if we focus on the professional nursing vocation, which has historically been connected with compassion and the development of compassionate character, it cannot be understood without attending to the particular activities, responsibilities and obligations of the nursing role, which are at risk of being overlooked by more managerialist approaches to nursing care.

Chapter 9

Neoliberalism for the Common Good?

Public Value Governance and the Downsizing of Democracy[1]

Adam Dahl and Joe Soss

The language of 'public value' has emerged in recent years as an influential new idiom for efforts to reform governance. The concept blends old commitments to the common good with newer aspirations for performance-centred public management. As a political project, it mounts a challenge to the market models and interests that have transformed governance over the past several decades. This 'neoliberal turn' prevails today, public-value scholars argue, because public authorities lack a coherent alternative to discourses that frame governance in exclusively economic terms. Older notions of the public good have been too vague to provide practical direction and evaluative criteria for governance (Bozeman 2002). Public value passes this litmus test and, at the same time, allows for a robust defence of the public sector against its critics (Benington and Moore 2011). By grounding governance in the pursuit of public value, proponents aim to displace neoliberal rationalities that privilege market solutions, diminish democracy and serve private interests at the expense of the common good.

The rise of public-value models also reflects a longer historical shift in public authority from 'government' to more collaborative, multisector modes of 'governance' (Pierre 2000). Along with its many practical consequences, this shift has had significant implications for democratic theory. Dissatisfied with the limits of representative government, reformers have pursued democratising reforms in a host of extra-electoral realms such as public budgeting, service provision, planning and policy implementation (Fischer 2009, 67). In the process, they have taken up questions of participation, citizenship, inclusion and equality that have previously been of interest mainly to democratic theorists (Fung 2006; Quick and Feldman 2011). New modes of 'governance-driven democratisation' have also encouraged democratic theorists to confront new questions and practical considerations related to their concepts.

Because these governance models locate democratic politics outside the formal institutions of liberal democracy, they represent a relatively new frontier in democratic theory (Warren 2009; Bevir 2010). Thus, for democratic theorists as much as for scholars of governance, the time is ripe for dialogue regarding public-value governance and its implications.

Against this backdrop, our chapter raises questions and concerns along two dimensions. First, we question the extent to which public-value governance challenges the economistic logic of neoliberalism. Although they oppose laissez-faire efforts to roll back the state, public-value models derive much of their logic from market templates. The resulting parallels make public value less of a challenge to neoliberalism than one would surmise based on the stated intentions of its proponents. Because their logics are congruent, public-value governance is highly vulnerable to assimilation into the dominant rationality of neoliberal governance. In this manner, public-value models may ultimately reinforce and extend neoliberalism by embedding market logics more deeply in progressive uses of state power.

Second, although public value is often promoted as a democratising agenda, leading works sidestep foundational questions of power and conflict and advance prescriptions that are in tension with contemporary theories of democracy. Without attending to these problems, public-value models run a high risk of folding citizen-centred deliberative and participatory procedures into a broader mode of governance that (1) leaves political inequalities undisturbed, (2) subordinates open-ended democratic contestation to the production of specific ends and (3) substitutes 'managed democracy' for more democratic forms of rule based on shared power.

To open a space for critical thinking about public-value governance, we 'trouble the waters' a bit by presenting a reading of the literature that differs from prevailing interpretations. As many scholars in the field acknowledge, the public-value concept is ambiguous and leading arguments have been dynamic enough to be read in multiple ways. Our objective is not to debate the desirability of authors' intentions. It is to draw a more critical reading to the surface that clarifies the limits of public-value governance and its potential to be assimilated into the dominant political projects of neoliberalism.

PUBLIC VALUE AND NEOLIBERAL RATIONALITY

Public-value governance is generally understood to encompass two broad traditions (Alford and O'Flynn 2009). The 'creating public value' approach, exemplified by Moore (1995), defines 'public value' as the public sector equivalent of private value in corporate management. In this view, public managers should pursue their own visions of positive change, guided by (1) their own professional expertise and moral values and (2) citizens' desires for efficient and just public organisations that achieve collectively valued social outcomes. The second tradition, exemplified by Bozeman (2002, 2007), seeks to derive 'public values' from intersubjectively held principles that define a society's 'normative consensus' regarding (1) the rights and benefits of citizens; (2) the obligations that link state, citizen and society; and (3) broad principles of policy formation. Adopting a stance of 'pragmatic idealism' Bozeman (2007, 12–13, 143) seeks to make the public-interest ideal more tractable by expressing it in terms of public values with 'specific, identifiable content'. Under this 'procedurally oriented notion of the public interest', public values are identified and measured in the citizenry and then deployed as benchmarks for evaluating governance.

There are significant tensions between the two frameworks (e.g., on the issue of pursuing what the public values versus what is valuable for the public), yet they converge on a shared agenda (Alford and O'Flynn 2009): governance should be recast as the public-spirited pursuit of collectively valued goals, and these goals should be specified as measurable standards for evaluating performance. A chief aim of this agenda is to displace neoliberal modes of governance that privilege markets, empower self-serving economic actors and reduce the public good to an aggregation of private interests.

Public-value scholars generally equate neoliberalism with (1) laissez-faire efforts to limit state powers so that markets can flourish independently and (2) market-based innovations in governance, such as privatisation and the New Public Management (NPM). Described as a challenge to 'neo-liberal agendas to roll back the state' (Smith 2004, 69), scholars agree that public-value governance represents a sharp departure from 'the dominance of neo-liberal ideology which emphasize[s] models based on individual consumers within a private competitive market (where the state is seen as an encroachment upon, and potential threat to, individual liberty)' (Benington 2011, 31). The agenda originated, Benington and Moore (2011) explain, as an effort to contest discourses that privileged markets over politics during the Reagan and Thatcher eras.

In this regard, public-value scholarship succeeds on some important fronts. By stressing collective agency and shared values, it challenges the 'diminution of the collective as an idea' and the elevation of individuals as the 'most important arbiters of value' (Benington and Moore 2011, 7–8). By stressing the enlistment of 'citizens to co-create public value', it carves out a positive role for public engagement (Moore and Benington 2011, 273). It rejects a narrow focus on exchange value (Meynhardt 2009) and challenges the dominance of competitive market mechanisms (O'Flynn 2007). Seeking a vital role for public managers, it opposes efforts to shrink 'government so that more choices about how to use resources [are] guided by individuals acting through markets' (Benington and Moore 2011, 7–8).

On these fronts, public-value scholars restore priority to substantive commitments devalued by neoliberalism. By equating neoliberalism with a laissez-faire desire to roll back the state, however, these same scholars misconstrue its logic, and thus, the nature of challenges for contemporary governance. In Milton Friedman's (1962, 1970) vision of laissez faire, a small, constrained state keeps its hands off the market, as private firms focus on profit as their only motive. Each sector has its own distinct role to play, and society is best served when actors from each realise they cannot improve things by meddling in the other. Friedman's vision was influential but, despite perennial calls to shrink government, it was not the agenda that came to fruition in the decades surrounding the turn of the twenty-first century. The activist state was not dismantled; it was reorganised and turned to new purposes (Pierson and Skocpol 2007). The neoliberal turn in governance did not strengthen the boundary between state and market or shift its location. It *blurred* the boundary between state and market, and reorganised their relation.

Neoliberalism today operates as a *political rationality*, not an attempt to drive politically controlled institutions out of the market (Brown 2003).[2] Under neoliberal modes of governance, the state does not cede its coordinating activities and is not 'rolled back'. It is rolled out through modes of governance that fuse political and economic powers and apply market-based logics to diverse networks of governing actors (Peck and Tickell 2002). Neoliberalism does not banish politics; it uses market models to reframe politics and reorganise governance as a pursuit of 'the bottom line'. Instead of pitting state against market (or public against private) in a zero-sum relationship, neoliberalism embraces their integration. The state actively creates markets and works to foster market modes of subjectivity and governance.[3] Conversely, market actors are identified as socially responsible contributors to the achievement of societal goals previously seen as the purview of government (Sadler and Lloyd 2009). Competitive processes that pit actors against one another in quasi-market relations mesh with collaborative processes that position state, market and civil-society institutions as actors sharing power.

This account of neoliberalism – which, broadly, prevails among scholars who study it as a political rationality – runs parallel to public-value governance in ways that are rarely acknowledged. Indeed, a signature feature of public-value scholarship is its use of market templates as starting points for reconstructing governance. As Benington and Moore (2011, 9–10) point out, the concept was originally designed with 'particular attention to corporate strategy': 'Just as the private sector executive had to keep an eye focused on changing market conditions, so the public sector executive had to keep their eye on changing political, economic and social conditions'. The 'market environment' is to the corporate manager what the 'authorising environment' is to the public manager.

Mark Moore's (1995) landmark work established this parallel early on. Public value, he argued, should be seen as the public sector's categorical stand-in for private value (or shareholder value) in the corporate sector. Public managers should pursue public value by cultivating an entrepreneurial and managerial imagination modelled after the mentalities of corporate managers. The substitution of public-spirited ideals for their private-interest counterparts does, indeed, mark a significant shift in substantive goals. Emphasising this change, however, Moore (1995) offers no reflection on the ways that changes in content can coincide with deeper continuities in form and logic. To be sure, concepts and categories can be reconfigured in ways that sever them from their original uses and logics. But when scholars model one concept after another – explicitly developing B to function as a counterpart to A, encouraging new actors to think about and pursue B in just the manner that old actors thought about and pursued A, and so on – the likelihood that the logic of the original concept will leave its imprint on the derivative concept is quite high.

Barry Bozeman develops his influential model of 'public value failure' through a similar strategy of conceptual mirroring. Bozeman (2002, 150) writes: 'I suggest several criteria for identifying public failure. Where do these particular criteria come from? To some extent, they mirror the thinking of market failure'. Indeed, despite their substantive opposition (based on a public–private distinction) the logics underlying the two concepts are so parallel that Bozeman is able to construct a table illustrating how each public-failure term equates to its market-failure counterpart. Emphasising the need to place public and market value on 'commensurate levels of theory and application', Bozeman (2002, 146) summarises his project by stating: 'My goal is to develop a model that is analogous in many respects to market failure, but that eschews concerns for price efficiency and traditional utilitarianism in favor of a public value focus'.

In these and other instances, public-value theorists shift the substantive goals of governance in a way that pushes back against laissez-faire efforts to disparage public ends and roll back the state. But they also construct a new model of the public good that *incorporates* market logic – that is, a logic that organises collective endeavours around the production of value and deems these endeavours to be failures when their production of value falls short. As an analogy, consider how one can substitute new numerical terms into an algebraic equation and, thus, produce new results without disturbing the underlying relations of the equation. Or consider how rational-choice models can accommodate private *or* public goals, self-interested *or* other-regarding motives, yet retain the economic logic of a rational-choice model.[4]

Similarly, public-value theorists insert new terms into market models and, stressing the shift in what is valued, fail to note that they have extended market rationality in a novel way. They challenge the narrow focus on values set by the market but embrace the instrumental pursuit of value that is at the heart of market models of governance. This consonance of form matters because it makes it relatively easy to assimilate the public-value concept into neoliberal agendas and use it as a public-spirited frame for market-centred pursuits.

Indeed, business-minded writers who take up public-value themes demonstrate the ease of this transition. In *Unlocking Public Value,* for example, Cole and Parston (2006, 45) reduce governance to a process in which authorities are 'in the business of delivering various *public goods*'. To improve governance, they propose the 'Accenture Public Service Value Model', which 'adapts the principles of commercial shareholder value' to focus evaluations of governance on just two criteria of 'citizen value: outcomes and cost-effectiveness' (2006, xvi). Other authors work the grey areas created by value-production models in more profit-minded ways. Schwab (2008, 108, 1118) urges corporate managers to generate 'value for both the companies and the global space in which they engage' and explains how socially responsible corporations can pursue the 'transformation of socially responsible principles and ideas into commercial value'. Porter and Kramer (2011, 68) use the concept of 'shared value' to ease the tensions between public and private values and explain how socially responsible businesses can cultivate 'disadvantaged communities and developing countries . . . as viable markets'.

The compatibility of neoliberalism and public-value governance can also be seen in the latter's emphasis on collaborative problem solving as a frame for conceiving relations between state and market actors (e.g., Stoker 2006; Meynhardt 2009; Benington 2011). A striking feature of the literature to date is how little attention is devoted to the state's traditional role as a 'countervailing power' that constrains markets and limits powerful market actors (Galbraith 1952). Students of governance *should* explore the benefits of state-market collaboration and specify how such collaboration might best proceed. The problem is that most public-value scholarship ignores the other side of the coin: the desirable qualities that flow from a separation of powers and the importance of specifying how one should check the other. The imbalanced quality of public-value models is precisely the imbalance that marks neoliberalism and advances its erosion of the boundary between state and market. In this regard, the public-value movement's efforts to champion the vital role of the public sector may prove less politically consequential than its alignment with ideologies that cast government's relation to business in almost entirely collaborative and supportive (rather than countervailing) terms.

Here again, we find more business-minded scholars extending the underlying logic of public-value governance. The collaborative view of the state among public-value scholars finds its complement in new ideals of collaborative, socially responsible corporate governance.[5] Porter and Kramer (2011), for instance, present 'shared value' as a stand-in for shareholder value that aligns the pursuit of corporate profit with broader public and social goals. Calling for a 'new conception of capitalism' based on cooperation among market, state and civil society actors, they argue that corporate performance should be assessed with an eye towards 'expanding the total pool of economic and social value' (2011, 64–65). In a similar vein, Schwab (2008) advances a model of 'global corporate citizenship [that] involves the corporation acting as a stakeholder in global society, together with government and civil society'. Reframing the corporation as a citizen, Schwab provides a complement to the public-value assertion that one should 'think of citizens as shareholders in how their tax is spent' (Horner and Hazel 2005, 5). At the intersection of these makeovers, the distinction between market status (the corporation, the shareholder) and political status (the citizen) collapses.

In these and other ways, public-value governance is easily aligned with what Sheldon Wolin (1989) calls the 'economic polity'. The *marketised state* of neoliberalism does not abandon coordinating responsibilities to the market. It is a state reimagined in market terms and assimilated into collaborative relations that render it, *vis-à-vis* the market, less distinct and oppositional. Thus, while public-value scholars contest economic individualism, they extend and adapt market logics of governance as tools for pursuing the common good. Indeed, the congruence of the two suggests that public-value governance may do something its proponents do not intend at all: expand the power of neoliberal rationality in public life by wedding it to the justification of progressive state power.

PUBLIC VALUE AND THE DOWNSIZING OF DEMOCRACY

Public-value theorists intend to provide a new foundation for 'deepening democracy' and 'tackling the democratic deficit' (Horner and Hutton 2011, 116; Moore and Benington 2011, 263). As a democratising agenda, however, public-value governance faces limitations along two dimensions.

First, it fails to confront the concrete forces that have undermined American democracy in recent decades. Leading works say almost nothing about the realities of entrenched power and political bias, the barriers to democratisation or what it would take to overcome them. Second, even if barriers could be overcome, it is not clear that public-value governance would actually deepen democracy. Mechanisms of citizen inclusion are often incorporated as source material or procedural addenda to models that do little to require a democratic sharing of power (e.g., Bozeman 2002). And some prescriptive models of management are, in fact, quite hard to reconcile with democratic principles (e.g., Moore 1995).

It is helpful to begin with democracy's classical etymology, which combines *demos* (common people) with *kratos* (power). The term defines self-government as a question of power in the first instance. Power, even in its coercive forms, is essential for the functioning of democracy, and the terms of power relations stand at the heart of democratic criteria for evaluating governance (Mansbridge 1996; Piven 2006). Democracies strive for inclusive and equal political participation so that all citizens share the capacity (even if indirectly) to shape the exercise of authority. Democracies strive to position citizens so they are able to check arbitrary uses of authority and hold power accountable. Democracies strive to invest citizens with the powers needed to reconfigure their relationships with one another and with dominant institutions.

Diverse democratic values are united by a concern for the sharing of power among citizens and governing authorities. This sharing of power may occur through direct participation (Pateman 1970) or, in systems of representation, through dynamic relationships in which representatives and citizens shape, influence and mobilise one another on an ongoing basis (Disch 2011).[6] Shared power should not be confused, however, with a sharing of interests or values. Democracy necessarily entails difference and contestation in the context of power relations (Mouffe 2005; Piven 2006).

Specified in this manner, 'deficits' of democracy can be seen as central to the problems targeted by public-value scholars. The agenda is motivated, proponents emphasise, by a belief that governance is failing the public and sacrificing the common good to powerful private interests. Rarely, however, do public-value scholars discuss the root causes of the democratic deficit they seek to overcome or the kinds of political action needed to do so.

In the US context, students of politics have clarified the relevant developments in great detail. As economic inequalities have skyrocketed, political innovations have forged a tighter bond between material affluence and political influence (Gilens 2012). As labour unions and civic associations have declined, business interests have acquired unmatched abilities to shape political processes and policy outcomes (Hacker and Pierson 2011). The US polity today is structured by institutional and ideological systems of marginalisation related to race, gender and class (Soss, Fording and Schram 2011). In one policy domain after another, political rule has become dominated by contending elites who are increasingly insulated from public pressure and accountability (Soss and Jacobs 2014).

These and related developments stand at the centre of what public-value theorists rightly denounce: a system of public governance that routinely serves powerful private interests at the expense of the public interest. Yet they are roundly ignored by public-value scholars who sidestep the challenge of reorganising power in favour of promoting new languages and measurable goals for good governance. The unstated premise seems to be that better concepts, models and criteria can produce democratic, public-spirited governance within the confines of the existing political economy, without any need to challenge dominant interests and institutionalised biases in power relations.

Whatever else they may be, new idioms for specifying the common good are not effective tools for dismantling a crisis of democracy rooted in the unmooring of political power from the public. *Kratos* (power) has shifted away from the *demos* (common people) towards actors who occupy dominant managerial positions in the state and market. To offer a plausible response, public-value advocates would need to provide an analysis of the key mechanisms that sustain this system and a strategy for displacing them. By fastening their hopes to new languages and measures, these advocates embrace a weak reform strategy that risks diverting attention from the forces most responsible for undermining democracy.

Consider again the promotion of cross-sector collaboration (Moore 1995; Stoker 2006; Benington 2011). There is nothing inherently anti-democratic (or even novel) about state and market actors cooperating to achieve public purposes. The problem lies, not in collaboration *per se*, but in the pursuit of collaboration on terms that take little account of power, conflict and inequality. Market firms are far from democratic organisations. Yet scholars say little about how this fact might threaten the democratic character of collaborative governance, or about the possibility that firms themselves might need to be targeted for democratisation (cf. Dahl 1986; Pateman 1970). Market relations receive extensive discussion, but with little attention to the fact that they are, in their own right, power relations that can take oppressive and exclusive forms.

Public-value scholars are right to note the potential upsides of state-market collaboration. Too often, however, they present it as a necessary response to 'wicked problems' (or as a progressive innovation to be applauded) without reflecting on its troubled history. Although state-market collaborations varied widely in their relationship to democracy, their terms have often been shaped by market powers in ways that exploit the public and serve oligarchic ends (Winters 2011). In sidestepping this history, public-value scholars fail to ground their collaborative designs in a realistic appraisal of power relations. Yet insofar as equality in the exercise of power is a foundational democratic principle, more robust forms of democratic governance require confronting the power relations that structure the political economy and provide the setting for collaborative governance.

Here, we arrive at a more general problem in appraising the democratic potential of public-value governance. Democracy depends on conflict as much as much as cooperation. Yet whether it is through collaboration or deliberation, theories of public-value governance proceed as if democracy can subsist on one without the other – as if cooperation were an unalloyed good and conflict and contestation were not vital to democratic politics. Democracy operates, to no small degree, through 'organized combat' (Hacker and Pierson 2011) and is sustained through 'agonistic pluralism' (Mouffe 2005). It is preserved through countervailing relations between state and market institutions that provide a basis for checking abuses of power by each (Galbraith 1952). Its deliberative moments depend on coercive state action (Mansbridge 1996); its peaceable agreements must sometimes be fractured by contentious opposition (Piven 2006).

Concerns about the democratising potential of public-value governance grow deeper still when one considers the specific prescriptions advanced under one of the movement's leading variants: the 'creating public-value' framework. Neoliberalism is marked by a form of governance in which nominally democratic institutions (e.g., contested elections) coexist with managerial modes of governing the public from above. 'Managed democracy is democracy systematized', Sheldon Wolin (2008, 47) explains, 'without appearing to be suppressed'. Governance is removed from the contest of democratic politics, as managerial authorities work to tamp down and skirt conflict (Soss and Jacobs 2014). Under managed democracy, governing elites engage the public in ways primarily designed to secure the agreement and legitimacy needed to wield authority and advance preferred actions.

Against this backdrop, Moore (1995) and others are right to direct our attention to public managers as key political actors and to suggest that the vitality of democracy depends, in part, on how they engage the political process. These moves, along with calls for managers to strengthen citizen deliberation, build significant democratic dimensions into the 'creating public value' framework. Moore and Benington (2011, 273), for example, champion deliberative procedures that, quoting John Dewey, help 'call into existence a public that can understand and act on its own best interests'. Based on these observations alone, one would have to conclude that the 'creating public-value' framework advances managerial prescriptions that are quite democratic.

It is important to clarify, then, that the inclusion of deliberative procedures does not, in itself, render a mode of governance democratic. Indeed, Carole Pateman recently used her 2012 APSA Presidential Address to clarify why procedures such as participatory budgeting can be integrated into governance in ways that do not threaten dominant interests or lead to the substantive democratisation of political power. Deliberative forums can deepen an already-democratic process, but they are unlikely to democratise a broader polity defined by profound inequalities of power. As Pateman (2012, 10) explains, '"Democracy" in the wider society and political system is outside of their purview; it is largely taken for granted as an institutional background of the forums'. Citizen forums that are built on a deliberative internal logic can be assimilated into broader modes of governance that systematically deprive the public of power. Procedures for public participation can reinforce 'managed democracy' by providing a stronger foundation of knowledge and legitimacy for governance from above.

As public-value theorists such as Stoker (2006) and Bozeman (2007) have adopted deliberative procedures as a democratic fix, they have typically ignored such problems. In this respect (and many others), their agendas are hard to distinguish from deliberative models that make no use of the public-value concept at all (e.g., Richardson 2003). Some public-value theorists go further, however, by folding deliberative procedures into a 'creating public-value' model that approaches politics on terms that privilege managerial and instrumental logics. In this model of governance, advanced by Moore (1995) and others, political processes are engaged as an instrumental means towards the realisation of managerial visions of the common good. In this regard, the 'creating public-value' framework risks extending the managerial rationality that Wolin (2008) identifies as the de-democratising signature of neoliberalism.

Instrumental conceptions of governance, regardless of how they include the public, provide notoriously precarious foundations for democracy. Because democracy is defined by the open-ended nature of political contest, it cannot guarantee outcomes that are more just or effective. It holds no claim to superior performance in the production of end goals. Thus, instrumental uses of democratic forms to achieve governing ends differ fundamentally from modes of governance that are valued intrinsically for their democratic character. Once the latter is subordinated to the former, the valued ends provide grounds for judging the relative desirability of democratic processes on a case-by-case basis. They underwrite the management of democracy itself, reducing it to a tactic for producing outcomes that can often be achieved more efficiently and effectively through other means.

The instrumental logic of the 'creating public-value' model can be clarified by considering the political role it ascribes to public managers. Moore (1995) and others position public managers as what Robert Dahl (1989, 52–79) calls enlightened 'guardians' of the common good. Their task is to address difficult societal challenges as problems of design, delivery and measurement and to emulate the corporate manager in handling them with dispatch. Towards this end, Moore (1995, 38) insists that managers cannot and should not 'banish' politics; rather they should develop strategies for moving their own public-spirited plans through the political realm as an 'authorising environment'. The disruptive potential of 'external politics should be "managed"' in this model (Rhodes and Wanna 2007, 413), so it does not sidetrack the manager's pursuit of public value. In this manner, Moore's democratising intentions potentially fold into a logic of managed democracy that values public engagement but envisions open-ended clashes among empowered publics as 'tendencies that good governance should hold at bay' (Wolin 2008, 150).

The result is that Moore's (1995) text occasionally seems to work against its own grain. On a single page, for example, we find citizens presented as 'material' that managers must work on to 'fashion legitimacy and support for themselves, their policies, or their organizational strategies', and we find that 'political management' entails building a coalition 'to achieve the public purposes for which the official will be held accountable' (Moore 1995, 113). Occasional references to public accountability lie in tension with the predominantly instrumental logic of Moore's managerial model. Yet he makes no attempt to reconcile the two. Tellingly, when Moore turns to concrete cases, it is the instrumental pursuit of support and legitimacy that wins out. The public manager who fails to 'develop a constituency for his own position' is presented as the exemplar of ineffective, undesirable 'political management' (1995, 133).

By framing and evaluating governance as an instrument for 'creating public value', Moore and others create pressures to evaluate governing authorities on instrumental terms, and thus, encourage public managers to engage the citizenry with an instrumental purpose. In the process, they potentially invite governing strategies based on what Jacobs and Shapiro criticise as 'simulated' or 'instrumental' responsiveness. In this mode of politics, governing authorities engage the public not to respond to it in a substantive manner (Jacobs and Shapiro 2000), or to advance a co-constitutive dialogue (Disch 2011), but to bolster the legitimacy of their own agendas and appear responsive to relevant constituencies. Thus, one finds public-value theorists urging public managers to be creative in 'managing public expectations' (to lower the odds of arousing citizen contestation) and figure out 'how best to develop a constituency that values what the manager wants or conceives' (Horner and Hutton 2011, 117; Moore quoted in Rhodes and Wanna 2007, 406).

Politics, Moore (1995, 38) emphasises, must be 'the final arbiter of public value'. The question is: what kind of politics? Moore and colleagues' model of 'political management' has an ambiguous relationship to democratic values and, in this regard, sends conflicted signals to public managers. Moore and Benington (2011) sometimes describe open-ended deliberative processes that engage citizens in efforts to define public value. But if the goal of these processes is to constitute a new public that aligns with managerial goals and public-value benchmarks, then they are better seen as procedures defined by a *telos* (ultimate end). As such, the model is hard to square with democratic theories of political representation – both those that prioritise substantive responsiveness to the public (Dahl 1989) and those that emphasise a co-constitutive dialogue between publics and their representatives (Disch 2011).

Active efforts to engage the public and acquire political support are, to be sure, often essential for effective public management. Public managers can serve as teachers who encourage social learning in the public and as organisers of dynamic deliberative processes that bring new publics into being (Moore 1995, 179–80). But these sorts of managerial roles and endeavours can serve democracy or subvert it, depending on how they are structured and pursued. As a general matter, Moore (1995) does not reduce public value to managerial intentions. In practice, though, he urges managers to see themselves as creative entrepreneurs who envision public value, 'enlist' publics in co-production, arm themselves 'with a powerful external constituency' and 'forge new political coalitions' to advance their public-value agendas (1995, 274–75). These directives are proffered within a broader model that fails to challenge surrounding power disparities, avoids conflict and contestation and embraces instrumental approaches to governance. Taken together, these factors pose serious limitations to Moore's model as an agenda for democratising public management.

Indeed, this assessment is strengthened by a consideration of how citizens are construed in Moore's model. In public-value governance, citizens are both taxpaying shareholders in the 'authorizing environment' and the 'collective consumer' of public value. In this, Moore and others replace the individual consumer of neoclassical economics with a collective and public-spirited variant. In so doing, however, they retain an economic model in which *consumer sovereignty* overwrites political conceptions of *popular sovereignty* that stress conflict and cooperation among empowered citizens. In casting society as a 'political marketplace' in which 'we citizens' are the 'collective consumer', Moore (1995) echoes Ludwig von Mises (2009, 23), who treats the 'sovereignty of consumers' (rather than the sovereignty of democratic citizens) as the ultimate source of political authority. Citizens are decentred in the political process, recast as collective consumers of public value and shareholders in governance rather than active civic agents creating a shared future.

In the process, Moore models the state's obligation to citizens in a way that echoes the corporation's obligation to produce value for shareholders and consumers. Yet democratic theorists have routinely criticised this analogy. Dahl (1986, 199), for example, warns against conceptions of 'stockholder democracy', arguing that they violate the fundamental principle of democratic equality. Wolin (2008) stresses how 'shareholder democracy' diminishes the empowered citizenship and gives the public a 'sense of participation' without obligation (Wolin 2008, 65). Pateman (2012, 15) puts the matter bluntly: the 'conception of citizenship embodied in participatory democratic theory is that citizens are not at all like consumers'.

Moore and others thus fail to note that management in the name of shareholders is itself a 'claim to rule', *distinct from democratic claims to rule*, that entails its own political logics of accountability and legitimation (Wolin 2008, 222). Taxpaying shareholders in governance have a right to expect governing entities to efficiently produce 'returns on their investments' and report on the public value they produce (Wensley and Moore 2011, 134). Their participation may be sought out for a variety of purposes. But taxpaying shareholders are not democratic citizens defined by their inclusion in relations of shared power that shape the direction of collective life.

These and other features of public-value governance suggest that significant efforts may be needed to reconcile it with democratic values. By grafting deliberative processes onto a neoliberal framework, public-value scholars risk promoting a model that would deepen public participation in a broader project of managed democracy that diminishes citizen power. To be sure, Moore (1995) and others discuss citizens in ways that sometimes incorporate more democratic themes. Like George Frederickson (1991), they acknowledge that citizens occupy different roles at different times and should be valued not just for their self-interest but also for their understandings of the broader public interest. Nevertheless, if we ask what is distinctive about their model of citizenship, it is the image of a public that is simultaneously the collective consumer of public value, the taxpaying shareholder in governance and the occupant of a managerial authorising environment.

CONCLUSION

Despite their democratic aspirations, public-value models of governance remain in tension with democratic theories that emphasise dynamic contestation and empowered publics. By sidestepping entrenched power and institutionalised marginalisation, they obscure the most fundamental sources of the democratic deficit. By using corporate management as a template for public authority, they potentially adapt and extend the logic of neoliberal governance. Through a promotion of state-market collaborations, they fail to incorporate the countervailing powers and popular conflicts that democracies depend on. By enlisting the public as co-participants in the instrumental pursuit of public value, they risk legitimating and deepening a managerial mode of governance that creates a false impression of citizen power.

If public value prescriptions do not suffice, however, the critical question remains: What should public managers do to govern in a democratic manner that serves the public well? The question cannot be resolved in the closing lines of an essay devoted to other purposes. It can be narrowed, however, by foreclosing a retreat to a Wilsonian vision of administration divorced from politics. Calls for public managers to respect the politics-administration divide designate as 'unpolitical' some of the issues that matter most to the lives of citizens and create a realm of professional action insulated from democracy. As public-value scholars rightly reject such calls, however, they must also resist a political world view that masks the aggrandizement of bureaucratic power and casts managers as politically neutral actors – not in the Wilsonian guise but rather as enlightened entrepreneurs akin to corporate managers (Roberts 1995). By failing to address managerialism as a claim to rule, they risk bypassing democratic contestation in favour of the idea that a performance-centred technical fix can hold bureaucrats accountable for the power they exercise over citizens.

The stirrings of more democratic approaches to public governance can be seen in a host of local experiments and are being elaborated in important new scholarship on inclusion and participation (e.g., Fung 2006; Quick and Feldman 2011; Dzur 2013). To operate in a democratic manner, public managers must develop their role as participants in open-ended political processes, seeking out ways that they (and sometimes only they) can inform, represent and empower relevant publics. They must balance their collaborative problem-solving efforts with commitments to serving as countervailing powers. The work of the public manager must include discerning and promoting modes of participation that actually empower citizens in governance. As they work to ensure the achievement of policy goals and objectives, they must also work to cultivate and engage empowered, inclusive publics. Such publics are valued for their intrinsic worth and integral contributions to governance, rather than as instrumental sources of legitimacy for managerial visions of the common good.

NOTES

1. This chapter was originally published in *Public Administration Review* 74 (4, 2014): 496–504, and appears here with the permission of John Wiley & Sons.
2. A 'political rationality' (1) specifies forms of authority, the proper distribution of tasks across authorities and the goals and principles that organise governance; (2) assumes particular subjectivities and aligns practices with the ways that objects of governance are conceived; and (3) entails distinctive uses of language to frame reality and provide an idiom for the elaboration of governmental practices (see, e.g., Rose and Miller 1992, 178).
3. For illustrative applications to policy and governance, see Soss, Fording and Schram (2011).
4. As Elster (1989: 52–60) elaborates at length, rational-choice logics can be combined with diverse goals and motives because 'behavior can be rational and

instrumental and yet not be selfish, contrary to a widespread but vulgar view that equates rationality with selfishness'.

5. Nam (2011, 148), for example, suggests that a public-value system 'cultivate[s] the view of the firm as pseudo-public institutions regardless of actual ownership [and] induces a developmental motivation for CSR [corporate social responsibility]'.
6. Throughout this discussion, our use of the term 'democracy' assumes the context of a liberal, capitalist society and encompasses both representative and direct-participatory forms.

Chapter 10

Public Value and the Reframing of Citizenship[1]

Justine Grønbæk Pors

INTRODUCTION

In recent years, a stream of public management literature has turned towards what is called a new paradigm of public management, public value. The literature tackles the challenge of meeting increased demands of welfare services within a context of ever more restrictions placed on their public financing. Leading scholars and policymakers alike celebrate this paradigm of public value as a replacement of the New Public Management paradigm (NPM) and as a solution to the problems that NPM has created for public service. However, although the public-value paradigm presents itself as a much-needed attempt to renew the public sector and make public organisations more flexible and innovative, the paradigm is not unproblematic. In this chapter, I will investigate how the public-value paradigm alters and, I shall argue, ultimately impoverishes the concepts of welfare and citizenship.

The chapter combines a reading of the scholarly literature on public value with an empirical analysis of current policy attempts to implement the paradigm in welfare management, organisation and practice in Denmark. In the literature as well as in these policies, the history of the public sector is conceived as having three main phases: traditional public bureaucracy, NPM and now, today, something different, an entirely new paradigm, public value. As one of the central scholars of this paradigm, Gerry Stoker (2006, 42) puts it:

> For the public value management paradigm, the understanding of the public interest, the nature of public service ethos, the role of managers, and the contribution of democratic processes stand in contrast to traditional public administration and new public management.

A crucial part of how the public-value paradigm is represented as different from previous public administration programmes resides in the argument that it aims strictly at producing value for citizens. In the public-value paradigm, it is proposed, success lies not in following procedures as in traditional public bureaucracy or in meeting performance targets as in NPM, but in achieving a positive social and economic outcome for citizens (Stoker 2006; O'Flynn 2007; Hartley 2005; Smith 2004).

In this chapter my aim is to show how even though the public-value paradigm positions itself as different from the managerialism of NPM, it re-articulates and even intensifies the neoliberal ethos of *more-for-less* that is a core characteristic of NPM. I shall identify how the notion of value that the paradigm promotes is so general and abstract that it puts at risk the historically established ability of the welfare state and the welfare professions to specify and meet specific areas of citizen need. Moreover, I argue that the public-value paradigm turns public service delivery into a managerial hunt for identifying and harvesting more resources and possibilities in people and communities by using new forms of flexible and participatory organising. My argument is that, in their eagerness to make public service simultaneously better and cheaper, the proponents of the public-value paradigm dismantle the capacity and the idea of the welfare state where the responsibility of the public sector is to secure the standing of citizens as free from want and domination and as equal in this respect to each other. As we shall see where the welfare state takes its point of departure from the idea of citizenship rights (as in T. H. Marshall's social rights), the public-value paradigm abandons this in favour of an emphasis on the responsibilities of citizens for their own welfare.

My focus on current Danish welfare policies is because they are emblematic of the same thinking that is characteristic of the scholarly literature on public value. My claim is not that the Danish policymakers have read the literature, nor that it is their ambition to implement the thinking of this literature. Rather my contention is that both the literature and the policies are exemplary of the same set of ideas underlying current tendencies in public policy: a managerialist discourse of public value.

In what follows, I discuss first the scholarly literature on public value, focusing on how its concept of value is one that emphasises adaptability, flexibility and the production of future possibilities in what is assumed to be a context of continuous and unpredictable change. This approach pits the public-value paradigm against the welfare state where specific historically defined welfare services have been carved out in relation to areas of citizen need, and where particular areas of social policy and service professions have been institutionally demarcated as the vehicles by which these services have been guided, regulated and delivered. I then turn to discuss current Danish welfare policies with a focus on how the concept of the citizen is reinvented through the public-value paradigm. The chapter draws attention to two problematic tendencies in the paradigm. The first is that although the new public-value paradigm is offered as a better alternative to NPM, it shares with NPM the neoliberal imperative of doing more with less. The second is that although the paradigm stresses citizen involvement and the democratisation of welfare service delivery, it puts at risk the capacity and responsibility of the public sector for citizen welfare.

AN OPEN AND ABSTRACT CONCEPT OF VALUE

For the public-value paradigm, *value* is the main purpose of public policy, public management and professional work. According to the literature, the sole goal of public sector ambitions and efforts should be to produce 'social and economic value' (Stoker 2006; Moore 1994; O'Flynn 2007; Hartley 2005; Smith 2004). However, the question remains: What is *value* in the public-value paradigm? And what makes it *public*?

Value as the Solution to the Problem of Uncertainty and Constant Change

In the literature on public value, a focus on value is installed as the timely and most adaptive response in a context of fast, constant and unpredictable change. The proposition is that the public-value paradigm constitutes a solution to the problem that society changes so rapidly that even an immediate future is uncertain and unknowable. A basic and unquestioned assumption in the literature is that the only constant is change and that, therefore, the central goal of public management should be to design and adapt the organisation to a situation of ever-new challenges and conditions. As Moore (1995, 57) puts it: 'Even if they [public managers] could be sure today, they would have to doubt tomorrow, for by then the political aspirations and public needs that give point to their efforts might well have changed' (interpolation added).

Thus, a central argument in the literature is that because society is in constant flux public policy need to be characterised by flexibility and adaptability, and, that the public-value paradigm offers exactly that (e.g., Stoker 2004, 2006; Benington 2011). Scholars argue that the paradigm provides public managers with flexibility and an ability to 'deal with uncertainty, ambiguity, and unexpected change' (Stoker 2006, 47). Moreover, the paradigm is described as 'an essential coping mechanism in an uncertain and unpredictable world' (Stoker 2006, 47; see also Aldridge and Stoker 2002). Thus, flexibility and adaptability which are processes become pseudo-goals (Andersen 2013; Andersen and Pors 2016) that are treated as ends in themselves. Since such processes are not really goals, and since as we shall see they abstract from any concrete situation of or purpose for human action, they become values that are above and beyond specific policy aims (Newman 2005a, 2005b).

Conceptually situated within an understanding of society as characterised by constant change, where even an immediate future is uncertain, the celebrated quality of public value is its openness and its flexibility. Benington (2011, 31) argues that public value cannot be defined in advance but has to be generated in processes of complex interaction between state, citizens and civil society. Value is the unknown outcome of collaboration between different actors. Value is what *can be* created. Value is what *will be* valued in the future (Benington 2011, 35; Stoker 2006, 47). As Moore (1995, 57) phrases it: ‘Public managers create public value. The problem is that they cannot know for sure what that is’.

One of the Danish policies demonstrates this way of thinking about public value as an emergent phenomenon. The national association of local governments, Local Government Denmark, argues that public policy should move away from the concept of ‘welfare’ towards what they call ‘forwardfare’ (Local Government Denmark 2014). Public value is not something that can be defined today but is what emerges as public organisations move forward. Thus, for the public-value paradigm, value is always emergent. Value is the orientation to being adaptive. Value is an orientation towards an unknown future. The concept of value then is equivalent to flexibility and adaptability. It is depicted as the unknown outcome of complex collaborative processes rather than as something that is oriented and regulated by established purposes and goals. It is without specifiable attributes, and thus it is abstract. It has no past, only a future emergence.

In his writings on office and office-holding and, more particularly, the ‘ethics of office’, Paul du Gay emphasises how each different public office has its own specific purpose that follows into a specific set of tasks and responsibilities (du Gay 2009, 2013, 2017; see also Condren 2006, and Pedersen and Obling, this volume). In this tradition of thought, an ethics of office cannot be conceived of as a set of universal claims or values independent of the specific circumstances, purposes, tasks and responsibilities of particular offices. Thus there are no meta-values that can be abstracted from the specificity of office. In opposition to such an emphasis on specificity and context, public value floats free of reference to particular public office, to the purpose of a specific social policy or to the correlative purpose of a specific welfare organisation. Designed as the solution to the challenge of continuous change thought of in the abstract, and praised for its adaptability and flexibility, the concept of public value comes to suffer from what du Gay and Vikkelsø (2012, chapter 3) have called ‘the lost specification of change’. An empty pursuit of change thought of as an endless and unspecifiable process substitutes for specific purposes and tasks (see also Andersen and Pors 2017). Thus, with its open and emergent concept of value, the public-value paradigm loses all reference to and anchorage in the specific purposes and institutional fields of agency that represent the welfare services of the historically established welfare state.

Replacing Market Thinking with Possibilities

As mentioned, the literature depicting public value as the new paradigm of the public sector is keen to position itself as both the replacement of NPM and a paradigm capable of solving the problems that NPM brought in its tracks (e.g., Alford and Hughes 2008; Benington 2011). A key component of this positioning is the critique of the market approach of NPM for being too narrow, reductionist and a limited manner of understanding society. The social world, it is argued, does not consist only of market transactions, and there is more to people and their relationships than the buying and selling of commodities (Stoker 2006, 46, 51). Scholars argue that with its focus on rational choice, NPM fails to understand the complexity of human beings, in particular how citizens conceive of value in ways that go beyond an individualistic rational calculus of maximising profit and utility (Stoker 2006, 51). The problem that the literature identifies is that the NPM paradigm misses out on the possibilities that could emerge from a more nuanced and dynamic understanding of what citizens actually experience as valuable. It is worth noting that the literature does not base its argument on the proposition that it is unethical to view and treat people simply as rational market agents. Rather, the argument is that this view of people means that public organisations miss out on possibilities for creating more value. Thus, the public-value paradigm does not promote a particular conception of citizenship as a political or ethical end in itself. Rather, the paradigm aims to provide public managers with a more complex and flexible conception of citizens in order to create possibilities of relating to them in ways that can produce more social and economic value than the narrowly 'economic' approach of NPM can achieve.

Similarly, when it comes to the organisational design of public service, the market-oriented approach of NPM is criticised for being based on too simple a conception of the social world (Alford and Hughes 2008). The managerialism of the public-value approach is declared in its adoption of the classification offered by institutional economics of three coordination mechanisms or technologies of social action: hierarchies, competitive markets and networks, each treated equivalently because of having the same abstract functional or instrumental value. In this classification any identity for public bureaucratic hierarchy is lost, firstly because it is reduced to 'bureaucracy' at large, and then because, as one coordination mechanism among several, it is made to be functionally equivalent to markets and networks. The public-value approach criticises NPM and what the literature calls traditional public administration[2] for normatively championing just one organisational means of coordination: In the case of public administration this is 'hierarchy' and in the case of NPM it is 'markets' (Stoker 2006). Both paradigms, it is argued, provide public managers with too limited a repertoire of organisational possibility (Benington 2011, 39). Thus, the problem that the literature identifies in NPM is not so much the market mode of coordination as such, nor even the conception of the social world as a market (see Stoker 2006, 48). Rather, the problem with NPM is argued to be that it has *only* one way of conceiving of the social and thus that this form of organising and managing cannot reflect upon or utilise the possibilities that might emerge from conceiving of the social as involving several different forms of coordination. As Benington (2011, 39) argues, in contrast to traditional public administration and NPM, the main advantage of public-value management is its focus on diverse forms of organising and collaboration (including but not exclusively the preferred darlings of this paradigm, networks and inter-organisational partnerships). This, it is argued, can offer managers 'greater flexibility and adaptability of response' (Benington 2011, 39). Thus, the message of the literature is not a political or ethical argument against reliance for the delivery of welfare services on markets *per se*. These authors are not invoking the idea of public service and office-holding (as represented by du Gay 2017; Rohr 1998, 1989; du Gay and Lopdrup-Hjorth 2016) that is associated with a traditional public administration designed to realise distinctively *public* ends that are not reconcilable with the private ends of market action. Instead, the literature promotes the idea that public managers should utilise different forms of coordination whenever these can create more possibilities of producing social and economic values. As Stoker (2006, 44) puts it, the advantage of the public-value paradigm is that it offers a 'menu of alternatives' from which public managers can choose the organisational form they find most suited to deliver outcome.

What I want to stress is that in this 'menu of alternatives' the three forms of organising public service delivery become equivalent to each other. In particular, public and private (sectors) become equivalent, and this has the effect of cancelling the distinctiveness of government, substituting for government 'governance' as a varying form of combination of public and private organisational forms. As Stoker (2006, 44) confirms: 'No one sector has a monopoly on public service ethos'. Particular forms of organising should not, according to the literature, be seen as valuable in themselves, but instead be subjected to the question of how they produce long-term social and economic value for citizens (see Stoker 2006, 47).

Value as 'Something-More'

Finally, in the scholarly literature on public value, value does not equal specific welfare benefits and services but is an open-ended and somewhat speculative search for what might be valuable to citizens. As an often-asked rhetorical question in this literature puts it, a public hospital may perform hundreds of surgeries every year, but if it fails to improve the quality of life of citizens what is it worth (see Pedersen 2016)? Thus, the public-value paradigm brackets out questions of whether citizens have access to specific and adequate welfare services (e.g., surgical operations) from the question of value for citizens. Services are not the same as value, and the purpose of the public sector is not to define and deliver predictable services but to produce value. It is for this reason that the literature decouples its concept of value from input (amount of resources granted different sectors). Value is not just decoupled from inputs, but it is decoupled from the entire input–output relationship and ratio. It is dignified with the status of 'outcome'. The argument is that because value, as an *outcome*, depends on complex interactions between many stakeholders, it is not predictable if, how and to what extent a certain input (i.e., resources, services) may produce value (Benington 2011, 39). Value, it is argued, is always emergent and contingent, either in terms of what a specific collaborative process may produce or in terms of how it turns out that individual citizens may value a service. In installing this disconnection between input and output, the paradigm assumes that it is unpredictable how certain inputs may translate into value. The point I want to make is that this makes it possible for the proponents of the paradigm to argue that value can improve even when the resource base is reduced or cut. In the Danish welfare policies that I examine further here, Local Government Denmark (2014, 4) writes: 'The concept of value is interesting, because it moves the focus towards what the future of welfare shall entail and how it can be built rather than focusing on cut backs and retrenchments'.

Thus, the public-value paradigm serves to silence or make irrelevant questions about whether welfare services are adequately resourced. Moreover, the concept of value comes to float free of historically established definitions of citizens' need for specific services. In the public-value paradigm, the possibility of grounding welfare services in historically and objectively defined needs as well as the responsibility of the welfare state of meeting them is put at risk. Instead, the paradigm stresses the possibilities of creating more value by pointing to how new opportunities may arise from flexibility and from the ability of public managers to combine diverse actors and forms of organising. For the public-value paradigm, value is the 'extra' that may be produced in complex processes of welfare delivery. As Stoker (2006) argues, the main characteristic of public managers in pursuit of public value is that they are constantly looking for and fostering possibilities of doing and producing more than what is known in advance.

Thus, the paradigm is characterised by the idea that something extra, something more, something beyond a direct, calculable relationship between resources allocated and quality of service can (magically) emerge in complex interactions between stakeholders. In spite of how the paradigm is careful to position itself as different from NPM, it seems to be permeated by the same managerial fantasy that if only the public sector operates smarter and more flexibly, and if only public managers perform better, a situation of 'more-for-less' can be achieved.

THE REFRAMING OF CITIZENSHIP IN DANISH WELFARE POLICY

I examine now how the thinking found in the scholarly literature on public-value resonates in the case of Danish public policy. I do so by focusing on a new set of ideas currently spreading in the Danish public sector of how citizenship needs to be rethought in order to solve the problems the Danish welfare society is (allegedly) facing today.

In Denmark as in many other historically established welfare states, contemporary public sector reform policies are informed by discourses of both efficient delivery and radical service innovation (Pedersen 2016; Christensen and Lægreid 2007a; Newman and Clarke 2009; Greve 2015). Here public value emerges as a promise to combine cost-effective service delivery and radical innovation with increased citizen involvement and a reinvigoration of democratic participation. Particularly, at the level of local government where in Denmark all the main welfare types and organisations (except for hospitals) can be found, current developments are characterised by a broad political and administrative consensus that the welfare society is facing great challenges that require radical change of the historically inherited situation. By pointing to challenges such as an ageing population, increasing rates of chronic disease and more complex health diagnoses, the integration of new immigrants and the negative impact of urbanisation on rural areas, it is suggested that radical transformations of existing approaches to welfare policies and practices are called for. Across the country, local governments are experimenting with new forms of citizen participation in welfare delivery. Such initiatives occur under creative headlines such as *Local Government Rethought, Local Government 3.0* and *Local Government of Love*. In the following, I will first focus on how these policies serve to collapse boundaries between the state and civil society, and, second, how they replace a rights-based notion of citizenship with an imperative of constant self-improvement and co-creation in welfare delivery.

Collapsing the Boundaries between State and Civil Society

Resonating with the critique of NPM in the scholarly literature on public value, the new Danish citizenship policies criticise NPM for addressing citizens as consumers. What is needed instead, it is proposed, is an exploration of how citizens themselves can contribute to welfare delivery. Here is how a chief executive from a local government authority puts it in a public statement:

> We have made citizens accustomed to be consumers of public service that may consume or receive without responsibility. We have made citizens un-obliged to give something to the community. Now we have to invite citizens to once more perform as citizens and not just as consumers. We need to explore what we can achieve together. (Reiermann 2011, 16)

Fascinatingly, indicative of a move away from the NPM's emphasis on service markets, now the argument is that to invite service users to be service consumers facilitates a passive 'taker' relationship to welfare services, a relationship where the consumer does not assume any responsibility for his or her role in how service delivery functions. In place of what is now seen as the passive consumer these policies invoke an idea of active citizenship understood as a process of constant exploration of how citizens can contribute more to service delivery.

Central to initiatives under headlines such as *Local Government 3.0*, *Local Government of Love* or *Local Government Rethought* is a questioning of the state as solely responsible for the provision of welfare. The Local Government of Aarhus states:

> Welfare is not a task for the local government, we write provocatively in the introduction [to a new citizen policy]. The point of departure is that the welfare of the future cannot be sustained by the public sector. Welfare service is a task for all of us – as human beings and relations between them. (Local Government of Aarhus 2015a, 1, interpolation added)

In a somewhat polemical tone, the Local Government of Aarhus argues that it is not possible for the state to provide welfare for its citizens unless civil society is also enrolled in the task and assumes appropriate responsibility for meeting it. Pre- and well-defined boundaries between the responsibility of the state and that of citizens are described as 'old-fashioned' (Association of Development Consultants 2012). Welfare, it is argued, is something for which all citizens are responsible. Welfare is something that emerges in the relationships between human beings, rather than being provided by a state apparatus (Local Government of Aarhus 2013, 2015b). The policies provide numerous examples of how citizens might participate in welfare delivery: people who are next of kin to a resident in an elderly home can take responsibility for cooking dinner for a group of residents once a week; local companies can offer activities and training for unemployed people; and older children can walk younger children to school (a so-called walking-bus) so that the local government does not have to provide transportation (Local Government of Skanderborg 2017; Local Government of Aarhus 2013, 2015b).

The concept of 'community' stands out as something in which much hope is invested. The Local Government of Aarhus elaborates its work under the headline of *Local Government of Love*:

> We understand the Local Government of Love as the potential community, which exists and develops when people live and work together. It is the totality of a diverse community and the potential for loving relations we have as colleagues, neighbours, in sport clubs, in the city's residential home, and in the local society, we call Aarhus. (Local Government of Aarhus 2013, 6)

As expressed here, this policy aims to nurture the potentiality of communities. Responsibility for welfare provision is not placed in the public sector. Instead, the policy is oriented to the idea that something can emerge in relationships between people when they meet at work, as neighbours and in leisure time activities and that this something can be harvested and utilised.

In order to harvest the potentiality of relationships between humans and of communities, these policies promote an open exploration of what citizens may be able to contribute to welfare production. One of the core arguments in these policies is that too rigid and defined roles and divisions of tasks and responsibilities between the public sector and citizens hinder the open exploration of the potential contributions citizens and volunteer communities may make (e.g., Local Government of Aarhus 2013). Rather than organising the collaboration between citizens and public officials around well-defined roles and division of labour, the collaboration should be characterised by an ambition to contribute and take responsibility on an equal basis. As an executive chief confirms: 'We are all in the fundamental situation that we ought to help each other' (Interview with the chief executive of the Local Government of Skanderborg in the Association of Development Consultants 2012, 1). This form of organising is characterised in the following manner:

> This is organizing without boundaries. We want to dissolve the boundary between who is employed and who is a citizen. We would like everybody to be equally engaged and active. (cited in Association of Development Consultants 2012, 1)

Citizen participation in welfare delivery is thus characterised by efforts to dismantle the distinction between public officials and citizens with their different roles and responsibilities. Clarity as to what may be expected of public officials and citizens, respectively, where the former's role is to serve the latter, is dismissed with the argument that this way of thinking is outmoded: it reduces the possibilities of co-creation and of an open-ended search for potential resources.

Where NPM challenged the ethics of public office (du Gay 2017, 160), embedded as these are in a classical public bureaucratic administration and substituted for this state-oriented approach a market-based one that talked up entrepreneurship and competition, the public-value paradigm also puts the classical state-based idea of public office at risk in its enthusiasm for a civil society–based approach to welfare services. Rather than seeing distinctions between the respective responsibilities of the public official and citizens as foundational of the securing of citizen welfare considered as both a collective and an individual good, these policies dismantle such distinctions in order to search for yet-unidentified possibilities of citizens' contribution to welfare. Thus, an approach to welfare grounded upon the possibility of defining the specific responsibilities of the state and citizens, respectively, is replaced with open explorations and a never-ending game of experimenting with roles and expectations (Andersen 2011). Ultimately, the paradigm of public value makes it possible to abandon the entire tradition of conceiving of the state as the public authority responsible for securing the welfare of those citizens who come under its jurisdiction and replaces it with the neoliberal and managerialist fantasy that more value can be extracted from people and communities.

The Citizen as Co-creator

As suggested already, several local governments portray their policies and efforts as an intentional movement away from NPM and what they portray as its construction of welfare as a supermarket of services from which consumers can choose (Local Government Denmark 2014, 6; Local Government of Kolding 2012; Local Government of Aarhus 2013). Similarly, the policies are meant to challenge past welfare practices associated with public bureaucracy and depicted as structured by needs-based categories of entitlement that enable citizens to expect and get a permanent service that compensates for lost capabilities of taking care of themselves. Instead, what these policies now aim to produce is a role for citizens as active co-creators of their own welfare. As an integral part of these policies we find the argument that human beings do not thrive as 'passive receivers' of welfare services, and that therefore a central part of the work of the welfare organisations is to enable citizens to more actively take responsibility for the conduct of their own lives. Welfare practices associated with both NPM and public bureaucracy are criticised for not giving citizens possibilities of improving and developing, and for cultivating passivity and welfare dependency. What is needed instead, it is argued, are welfare policies that encourages professionals to focus on the potential of citizens to regain former capabilities with the help of rehabilitation, new welfare technologies and a newfound will on the part of citizens to take care of themselves (Local Government of Aarhus 2013). The ambition is to rehabilitate the bodies and the minds of citizens so that they can take better care of themselves again. In the Local Government of Kolding, this is framed as a movement 'from welfare to self-worth' (Local Government of Kolding 2012, 1). In its social policy it reads:

> Our local government is a self-worth society. We give possibilities and authority back to people who can manage themselves. Within a framework of community, citizenship and voluntary work we firmly believe that this makes both the individual and the society stronger. We believe that self-worth is more than welfare. Human beings want to take care of themselves all of their lives. In our self-worth society we provide space for allowing them to do so. (Local Government of Kolding 2012, 3)

The self-worth policy is based on the inherent assumption that all human beings have an inner potential to improve, to regain former strength and to take more responsibility for their own life. Thus welfare organisations and professionals should be very careful to not just provide help and services but instead focus on motivating citizens to take care of themselves. Rather than letting services be framed in terms of legislated purposes and professional knowledge, where a politically authorised professional needs-assessment gives a citizen a right to particular service supports, local governments see it as their task to identify in each citizen their inner potential to take care of themselves. The chairman of the Committee for Social Policy in the Local Government of Kolding states:

> Just like a gardener cuts a tree in order to make new sprigs trickle out, we remove the disservice and let people's self-worth grow. We believe all humans have resources and potentials that can make them capable of controlling their own life. (cit. Andersen 2012, 2)

The notion of citizenship evoked in these policies includes an effort to mobilize hitherto hidden resources in individuals and collectives. The policies assume that if only people are allowed to take more responsibility, yet unknown resources will emerge. As it is formulated in the policies from *The Local Government of Love*:

> The Local Government of Love supports, pushes and lets go. Rehabilitation and welfare technology make citizens capable of taking care of themselves as long

as possible without interference from the government. Freedom to brush your own teeth. Freedom to live by your own rhythm rather than the rhythm of others. Or just freedom to wipe your own bottom. (Local Government of Aarhus 2013, 7)

As is expressed here, welfare is not understood as something that may help people in securing a life for themselves in which they can feel free, but as something that risks taking freedom away from people.

These policies use a very particular notion of freedom and place it in a specific conceptual relationship to the notion of welfare. In her reading of T. H. Marshall's 'Citizenship and Social Class', Yeatman identifies two different concepts of freedom. One is the neoliberal understanding of freedom as a property of the individual that sees the state as inherently opposed to freedom (Yeatman 2018, 21). The other is an understanding of freedom as civic, collectivist, publicly inclusive and relational. This understanding centres on the state as the only form of social organisation that makes it possible for all individuals to be personally secure and free from domination (Yeatman 2018, 2). Here the state is not in opposition to individual freedom, but it is the key to ensuring it. Yeatman (2018, 21–22) explains:

> [T]he welfare state elaborated the idea of personal security in offering a range of publicly provided welfare services that enabled individuals to feel secure in managing their lives, parenting their children, and meeting the vicissitudes of accident, disability and old age.

The welfare policies I have presented here utilise the first rather than the second understanding of freedom. Freedom emerges in these policies in opposition to the welfare state: as freedom *from* welfare benefits. The citizen emerges as someone who would benefit from becoming independent of welfare services, hence the chairman of the Committee of Social Policy (in the Local Government of Kolding) claims that welfare is a disservice which limits the freedom and hinders the personal development of citizens (in Andersen 2012, 2). Welfare is not understood as something that helps people secure a life for themselves in which they can feel free, but as something that risks taking freedom away from people. Thus, with a neoliberal notion of freedom which equates personal freedom with independence from other people, the understanding so central to the development of the welfare state that freedom depends on state-provided welfare services (Yeatman 2018, 32) is put at risk.

This also means that, rather than seeing the citizen as someone who is granted by politically determined, legislated social policies and professional systems of welfare provision a right to certain services (what T. H. Marshall called 'a baseline of civilized living'), these policies work with a future-oriented understanding of the citizen as someone who has the inner potential to contribute more than what is currently known. In their attempt to bring out hitherto unknown resources these policies resemble what Staunæs (2011) has called 'governing the potentials of life' and what colleagues and I have termed 'the management of potentiality' (Andersen and Pors 2016; Pors 2011; Pors and Ratner 2017; Juelskjær et al. 2011). This is a form of public policy that assumes that hidden resources can be identified and harvested in people and their relationships if these are properly organised. It is based on an understanding of the human being as a store of unlimited potentialities that can be released through proper self-work. This understanding of the human also resembles what Costea, Amiridis and Crump (2012b) in their work on contemporary human resource management have called 'the principle of potentiality'. Costea, Crump and Amiridis (2007; and see also Costea chapter 4 this volume) have argued that the character of work has undergone a transformation from a focus on the object of work, that is, purposes, procedures and tasks, to a focus on the working subject itself. According to Costea, Crump and Amiridis (2007, 260) human subjectivity has become the central resource of production producing an ethos of performance where people are expected to engage themselves in a perpetual search to mobilise inner resourcefulness. With policies promoting 'self-worth' over welfare, social policy becomes a matter of governing what is seen as the unlimited potentiality of the capacities and desires of citizens to improve themselves (e.g., regain former capability to take care of themselves, become independent from welfare benefits) and, as a result, the citizen as a holder of specific rights and duties is replaced with an understanding of the citizen as unlimited inner potentiality.

Although the proponents of public-value policies are keen to position themselves both against and as an alternative to NPM, they share with NPM a rejection of the welfare state idea of citizen entitlement to welfare services, an entitlement associated with the idea that it is only if basic needs are met that people can enjoy the status of a citizen as a free being (see Yeatman on Marshall's idea of citizen status as the status of a free being) who in this respect is equal to all other citizens. While the public-value paradigm describes itself as a more 'human-' and 'people-centred' approach to public service delivery (e.g., Benington 2011, 33–34), its idea of the human is the managerial idea of human potentiality, the human as co-creator in relation to the policy aim of delivering welfare in a more cost-efficient manner. The paradigm turns out to work in a way that is similar to NPM, one that stigmatises so-called welfare dependency and that removes a rights-based conception of welfare services (Yeatman 2018).

Ultimately, with its understanding of the citizen as inner potential rather than as a politically instituted rights-based status, the public-value paradigm compromises the civic republican and social democratic ethics of public service that emphasises the importance of citizens' right to be treated equally.

It also puts at risk the ability of the professions to treat citizens equally in a professional process of needs assessment and service provision (e.g., in healthcare where particular diagnoses lead to certain treatments and care, and the more urgent cases take priority over less urgent ones). Instead, the professions are expected to search for, identify and harvest the inner potential and motivation of citizens to contribute to the managerial aim of doing more with less (Pors 2016). This is expressed in Stoker's description of the manner in which the public-value paradigm delivers equality, namely, by 'developing individual capacity so that rights and responsibilities are realized' (Stoker 2006, 50). The policy aim of equality is thus transformed into the managerial and organisational aim of developing capacity, and citizen rights and responsibilities are severely compromised by the orientation to processes that search for potentiality.

CONCLUSION

In this chapter, I have critically assessed the idea of public value in the public management literature and in Danish welfare policies with the intention of raising a set of concerns. Perhaps I have not done justice to the noble intentions of the paradigm, particularly the intention to challenge the dominance of NPM in public sectors across the globe. However, if the ambitions of the paradigm are to move beyond NPM, and to make public policy more 'human', I think it is necessary to address the ways in which the paradigm fails to free itself from the managerialism of NPM (see also Dahl and Soss this volume).

In my reading of the scholarly literature on public value, I have identified how the paradigm is based on the assumption that society is in constant change and that, therefore, its notion of value is designed to be flexible and adaptable to a yet unknown future. For the public-value paradigm, value is always emergent. Value is the orientation to being adaptive. Value is an orientation towards an unknown future. Value is portrayed as the unknown outcome of complex collaborative processes rather than as something that is oriented and regulated by established purposes and goals. With this concept of value, the purpose of public policy is no longer specific and coherently related to historically defined welfare services but is displaced by a managerial process orientation to adaptability and a search for yet unknown future possibilities. Immense hope is placed in how something more, something extra can emerge in complex interactions between different stakeholders and thus solve the problem as it is posed of an increased demand for welfare in a situation of increasingly limited public resources.

Moreover, although the literature challenges and criticises NPM's market-based approach, it does not do so in such a way as to recuperate a distinctively public conception of welfare services that translates into a set of public offices involved in both policy and service delivery. Its orientation remains relentlessly managerial, focused on how public managers can find more possibilities of doing more with less. I have sought to show how the paradigm not just impoverishes but cancels the notion of public things by swallowing them up in an economic-organisational distinction between modes of coordinating social action where one mode is commensurable with the others and ranked in terms of what value it can produce. The paradigm deprives public servants of the possibility of grounding a public sector ethics in a historical tradition of thought and practice that articulates the specificity of their professional vocation as public servants.

Thus, I have argued that, with its foundational striving to create something more, something that goes beyond a simple calculative relationship between resources and the actual quantity and quality of service they permit, the paradigm promotes the same managerialism that characterises NPM. This is the constant quest to produce more-for-less and the neoliberal-technological fantasy that something more, something extra can emerge if only the public sector is organised smarter, more in accordance with the organisational principles and possibilities of business enterprise, whether this be for profit or not for profit.

In my reading of contemporary Danish welfare policies, I have traced how an approach to welfare based upon specifically defined responsibilities of the state and citizens, respectively, is replaced with open explorations and a never-ending game of experimenting with roles and expectations with the purpose of finding and harvesting the hidden potentiality in humans and of communities. Thus, the tradition of conceiving of the state as the public authority responsible for securing the welfare of those citizens who come under its jurisdiction is challenged by the neoliberal fantasy that more value can be extracted from people and communities.

Moreover, I have shown how these policies share with NPM the specifically neoliberal notion of freedom understood as private domain (Hayek's term), as independence from the state. Thereby they reject the idea of the welfare state as the civic republican institution that secures the personal freedom and citizen standing of individuals by offering publicly provided welfare services that enable them to feel secure in their lives regardless of the vicissitudes of accident, disability and old age (Yeatman 2018, 21). The conception of citizenship is managerialised, where a rights-based understanding of citizenship is replaced by a subjectivist orientation to self-improvement and self-development, and by an understanding of the human as an unlimited horizon of potentiality (for this idea of freedom from limit, see Malpas this volume).

NOTES

1. The author wishes to thank Anna Yeatman for her thoughtful comments and careful work to help sharpen the argument of this chapter.
2. Although it is beyond this chapter to address properly, it is worth noting that the literature on public value offers a limited understanding of what it terms 'traditional public administration'. Whenever traditional public administration is referred to, it is as an antidote to the 'human' or 'people centred' approach of public value (Benington 2011, 33–34; Stoker 2006, 51). Traditional public administration, it seems, has little to offer besides rules and hierarchies. For example, Stoker (2006, 56) describes how public-value management is able to point to a motivational force that does not rely on rules (as he claims traditional bureaucracy does) or incentives (as he claims NPM does) to drive public service improvement (Stoker 2006, 56). And Hasle et al. (2014) describe how public value is able to connect to a professional sense of purpose neglected by previous forms of management. Thus, the emphasis on duty and purpose in public service and office-holding (emphasised, e.g., by Weber 1978) is disregarded.

Chapter 11

Reclaiming Professionalism in the Face of Productivism

Anna Yeatman

INTRODUCTION

In the *Call of the Reed Warbler*, Charles Massy offers an account of regenerative agriculture, one that centres on listening to earth, on developing an ecological literacy in relation to the complex interrelationships between sun, air, water, soil, plants and animals as these appear as a specific regionally bounded set of relationships, thus as constituting a particular place. His account of regenerative agriculture is provoked by the profound ecological destruction that has followed in the wake of industrial agriculture, driven as it is now by the 'productivism' of agri-business, 'the maximisation of production and the maximisation of profit' (Massy 2017, 47): 'The key difference between industrial and regenerative agriculture is that in the former humans generally believe they can control the chemical inputs while ignoring the biology. In the latter, the biology comes first' (Massy 2017, 161). Productivism is wed to what Massy calls the mechanical mind, an orientation to the world that makes it appear as so many resources to be manipulated, exploited and extracted on behalf of a human subject who has separated itself out from the life system of which it is part, a subject that thus confronts all that it makes appear (in Heidegger's phrase) as 'standing reserve' in relation to the will to power: 'Everywhere, everything is ordered to stand by, to be immediately at hand, indeed to stand there just so it may be on call for a further ordering' (Heidegger 1977a, 17). Heidegger points out that 'whatever stands by in the sense of standing-reserve no longer stands over against us as object' (Heidegger 1977a, 17). It is forced to lose its status as an object with its own reality, posing as this must a limit to the will to power. But not only this: if the object loses its own reality, so too does the human subject for, abstracted as the will to power, the human being loses all of its living specificity.

The will to power is expressed in a remorseless and relentless instrumentalism and in an end that is not strictly an end at all, for a true end is finite, specific and bounded. The ersatz end in this case has to be one that appears as an end but in fact is one without limit (see also Malpas, this volume). This is why it is expressed as the end of economic growth. Massy's eloquent call to us to heed what is at stake in our staying complicit with industrial agriculture, and to learn about what a regenerative agriculture would not just demand of us, but how it would enliven and heal us as well as the earth, is part of a more general historical awakening at this time. In this process of awakening, in calling into question the established motif of the mechanical mind – 'progress' understood as constantly new technological developments that enable a more efficient productivism – we not only can recognise how the 'proto-agriculture' and 'organic mind' of the first peoples of Australia exemplify ecological literacy, but we can also begin to practise a more nuanced and differentiated relationship to modernity itself.

Modernity is not reducible to the will to power and the mechanical mind. Apart from anything else, modernity is associated with an ethical professionalism that informs the conduct of science and turns it into service on behalf of specific human goods (including as these do the integrity of the planetary life system). Massy himself can be said to be offering a conception of regenerative agriculture as a profession that is marked out by the integration of farming with a scientific understanding of ecology and an ethics of service to not just human beings but to the entire life system for if this fails then human life becomes itself impossible to sustain. Massey's pedagogical project in his book consists of multiple examples of how professional farmers in Australia and elsewhere discovered, in the face of ecological devastation, that the mechanical world view in which they had been trained did not work, and were motivated to seek out new, regenerative practices of farming. Massy points out how a core feature of professionalism, peer support and opportunity to participate in a community of practice, was one important component of this process of change:

> For virtually all regenerative farmers who have undergone transformation, the catalyst that sent them searching for new knowledge also led them, however, serendipitously, to encounter one of the leading change organisations that have been founded by leading innovators and supporters. These organisations ultimately comprise 'communities of practice'. These are places, connections or organisations where learning occurs through social participation in the practice of a knowledge community.
>
> In my extensive research, I found it was these different communities of practice that played a double and vital role: first in providing new information counter to the unsettled person's previous world view, and, then, second, socially reinforcing that transformative learning via participation. In a non-threatening

> environment, those undergoing change received help from others in recognising perspectives and trusting their own values and beliefs. Over time, they were able to amalgamate the other perspectives and cultures of the group into a holistic, integrated, transcendent approach to knowledge. (Massy 2017, 412–13)

Massy's contrast between the mechanical mind and the organic mind is a contrast within the possibilities of modernity. As such it bears on far more than agriculture, as important as agriculture is to the question of whether life-denying or life-enhancing ways of being human come to prevail. If there are to be life-enhancing ways of being human, then we have to be able to embrace (heed, listen to, respect) the object, both living and non-living beings, as it appears to us. Such appearance cannot be forced, and it does not happen automatically; it depends on a sensibility of being open to, curious about and able to be surprised by the object appearing to us. This is a sensibility in which we invite, allow and facilitate the object in 'talking to' us, in disclosing its complex and many-faceted specificity of being, as this appears in relation to changes in perspective that we bring to it. To invite the object to 'talk to' us even when it is a non-animate object is to cultivate a practical discipline of sustained and close attention to the facticity of this object, a practice of becoming familiar with it, noticing how it changes in relation to changes of temperature, light and context, and returning to it again and again so that increasing familiarity is always mixed with wonder at both its constancy and its changes. Such respect for the object as it appears is possible only if there is respect for the object itself, for its integrity, only if there is an ethical orientation of acceptance of its given-ness. Thus, while Max Weber (1949) is right to insist that we encounter the object only in relation to a particular point of view, there is a difference between a point of view that sustains an orientation to the integrity of the object and one that does not. The ethical question of whether economics as a science stays tethered to the question of the production and distribution of resources in relation to the needs of human beings, considered as belonging to a planetary life system, or whether instead economics becomes the science of the self-regulating market economy, is in large part a question of whether economics in the second sense is able to sustain an orientation to the integrity of the object (see, e .g., Alex Zorach's Blog, 2010, on why GDP is a poor measure of wealth and prosperity).

The importance of this ethical orientation of acceptance of the 'this-ness' of the object to the question of whether a modern society is life affirming, or life denying, is a fundamental theme in the work of Hannah Arendt. In the prologue to *The Human Condition*, she emphasises how readily modern science cuts itself away from 'human existence as it has been given, a free gift from nowhere (secularly speaking)' (Arendt 1958, 2–3) in favour of technological forms of artifice that are designed to release human beings from their earth-bound existence: 'There is no reason to doubt our abilities to accomplish such an exchange, just as there is no reason to doubt our present ability to destroy all organic life on earth' (Arendt 1958, 3).

Arendt (1958, 3) declares: 'The trouble concerns the fact that the "truths" of the modern scientific world view, though they can be demonstrated in mathematical formulas, and proved technologically, will no longer lend themselves to normal expression in speech and thought'. They cannot be referred back to what is meaningful for human beings who may prefer jobs to automation, peace to nuclear war and repairing the planetary biosphere to funding exploration of the possibility of living on another planet. Meaningfulness for Arendt arises only when human beings, presenting as they always do in the plural, and as interdependent, come together to 'talk with and make sense to each other and to themselves' (Arendt 1958, 4). It is in speech that human beings encounter each other as distinct beings with different perspectives on a world that they share, and where through speech they discover a world that they have in common, thus enabling them to make sense of reality.

Arendt thought that twentieth-century science was no longer able to be held to account in normal expression in speech and thought: 'For the sciences today have been forced to adopt a "language" of mathematical symbols which, though it was originally meant only as an abbreviation for spoken statements, now contains statements that in no way can be translated back into speech' (Arendt 1958, 4). This judgement seems too wholesale; perhaps there is a distinction to be made between forms of science that are oriented by respect for 'organic life on earth' and those that are oriented to substituting technological artifice for 'human existence as it has been given'.

I want to suggest here that the professions, and professionalism, involve a form of knowledge or science that is inherently oriented to be in the service of a specific dimension of 'human existence as it has been given'. These forms of knowledge (scientific disciplines) are constructed so that they constitute practices of service to specific human goods. Like all science, these professional disciplines are informed by rigorous conceptual, logical and evidential procedure, but how they operate as sciences is directed by how they make practical provision for a specific human good. For this good to be attended to by a profession, its specificity has to be addressed – not just what this good is conceptually (e.g., health), but how it manifests in relation to the practical condition and context of individuals and their communities. In offering a conception of professionalism as both a public and an ethical phenomenon, and as will become clear in this account, I am calling into question uses and abuses of professionalism that follow upon its reduction to a form of technical expertise. Reduced to expertise, professionalism is driven by private objectives, whether these are those of the professional herself and/or her employing organisation.

Productivism abstracts from the living reality of human beings in relation to the life system of which they are part: the integrity, or wholeness, of human beings as this is expressed as a set of needs, is set to one side in favour of reconstituting reality as so many resources to be mined, exchanged, calculated and monetised. In a productivist universe the logic of the commodity form prevails: things are valued only in relation to their exchange value, and all that is specific and concrete about them in relation to the specificity of human needs disappears. There is no human being the integrity of whom the professional serves by attending to a specific good that serves this integrity. There are only productive enterprises and consumers. In the face of a productivist ethos, the professions appear as so many barriers to this radical and systematic refusal of human integrity in favour of producing and maximising monetised value. The reason for this is that the professions are nothing if they are not passionately committed stewards of distinctive goods that bear on the question of human integrity.

In what follows I elaborate on this idea of the professions as stewards of human goods. I then discuss the productivist assault on professionalism which threatens professionalism at its core. To recognise this threat requires us to develop a concept of professionalism. Just as Massy and his professional peers found the concept of regenerative agriculture in confronting the systemic destructiveness of industrial agriculture, we have the historical opportunity not just of rediscovering and reclaiming professionalism, but of allowing the provocation of its potential destruction to enable us to recognise what it is and must involve with a degree of clarity and illumination that is historically new. The final section of this chapter is given to a suggestion of how we might embrace this historical opportunity.

THE PROFESSIONS ARE STEWARDS OF DISTINCTIVE HUMAN GOODS

The idea of the professions as stewards of distinctive human goods is not new, but there are few meta-narratives of this idea. If we consult the sociology of the professions, which does offer a meta-narrative of the professions, the approach tends to be an occupational one that emphasises functionalist and/or interest-based approaches. This literature tends to reduce professionalism to a specialised form of work (e.g., Freidson 1984, 2001). Up until the 1960s it was commonplace for sociologists such as Talcott Parsons to propose that the professions involve 'the rational even-handed approach of advanced knowledge and skill to the solution of human problems in order to advance the common good' (Parsons cit. Freidson 1984, 4). But from the 1960s onwards the orientation to the professions becomes more critical: this ethical claim is viewed as an ideological mask for private interest, where professional specialisation and the control of professional associations over training and certification are used to accrue power, prestige and money to the profession.

Neither the occupational approach which suggests that it is not the legitimating norms of the professions that are relevant, rather it is what they do and its efficacy (Koehn 1994, 5), nor economism, which reduces the professions to market-oriented private interests, thereby suggesting that professional practice is just another form of commerce (Koehn 1994, 2), is adequate to conceiving the nature of professionalism. In each case, the professions are reduced to a form of expertise that has only instrumental value.

Both Daryl Koehn (1994) and the later work of Eliot Freidson (2001) argue that professionalism is something other than expertise, and a profession is more than just an occupation. Contrary to Max Weber's proposition in 'Science as a Vocation', that the ethical or value orientation of a profession such as medicine is merely the presupposition of a technical practice,[1] this ethical orientation provides the concept of the profession which is not just an external point of orientation for its practice, but its very fabric.

It was in the face of the growing attack on professionalism, far more evident in the early part of the twenty-first century than in the 1980s, that Freidson (2001) significantly qualified his occupational approach to the professions in proposing that the core defining characteristic of the professions is their 'ideology' or 'soul': 'This ideology claims both specialized knowledge that is authoritative in a functional or cognitive sense and commitment to a transcendent value that guides and adjudicates the way that knowledge is employed' (Freidson 2001, 127). Freidson offers an ideal type of professionalism consisting of five interdependent elements:

1. Specialised work in the officially recognized economy that is believed to be grounded in a body of theoretically based, discretionary knowledge and skill and that is accordingly given special status in the labor force;
2. Exclusive jurisdiction in a particular division of labor created and controlled by occupational negotiation;
3. A sheltered position in both external and internal labor markets that is based on qualifying credentials created by the occupation;
4. A formal training program lying outside the labor market that produces the qualifying credentials, which is controlled by the occupation and associated with higher education; and
5. An ideology that asserts greater commitment to doing good work than to economic gain and to the quality rather than the economic efficiency of the work. (Freidson 2001, 127)

He clarifies further:

> The ideology of professionalism asserts above all else devotion to the use of disciplined knowledge and skill for the public good. Individual disciplines are concerned with different aspects of that good, in some cases the immediate good of individual patients, students, or clients, in others of firms and groups, and in others the general good. But such service must always be judged and balanced against a still larger public good, sometimes one anticipated in the future. Practitioners and their associations have the duty to appraise what they do in light of that larger good, a duty which licences them to be more than passive servants of the state, of the firm, of the client, or even of the immediate general public. (Freidson 2001, 217)

Freidson's proposition that the ideology or, as he more aptly calls it, the soul of professionalism consists in 'devotion to the use of disciplined knowledge and skill for the public good' is congruent with Daryl Koehn's (1994) approach to the professions as 'inherently ethical practices'. For Koehn the central question is how is it that the professions merit public trust: 'Professional practices qualify as morally legitimate because, and to the extent that, they are structured to merit the trust of clients' – she explains:

> Contrary to the assertions of . . . critics, professions are not mere ideologies but inherently ethical practices. Furthermore, each of these practices has its own special ethic, one deriving its peculiar and distinctive character from its end of engendering and preserving the trust of clients who lack a specific genuine good such as health or legal justice. (Koehn 1994, 7)

Koehn makes the important point that our reliance on the professions for the provision of human goods is historically contingent. If the professions do not exist, then we will not have access to these goods: 'We should not forget that professions [she takes the three learned professions – medicine, law and theology – as her reference point] represent the only mechanism we have for collectively providing ourselves with the goods of health, legal justice and spiritual peace' (Koehn 1994, 5). The professions represent our collective commitment to ensuring that we have an institution appropriate to the provision of these goods: 'Professions represent our communally chosen response to the problem of delivering help to the ill, the injured or accused, or the sick in spirit' (Koehn 1994, 6). Freidson's (2001, 214) way of making the same point is to say that the professions historically have gained 'their protected status by a project of successful persuasion'. He continues: 'Adam Smith himself defended the privileged position of professions on the ground that their work requires trust' (Freidson 2001, 214).

The institutionalisation of the professions as distinct disciplines involves what Freidson calls 'social closure': 'their work is institutionalized by the drawing of jurisdictional boundaries so that it can be maintained and cultivated as a coherent, or at least recognizable, discipline. Without closure there can be no disciplines' (Freidson 2001, 202). Such closure is expressed in the licencing, credentialed training and professional collegium of the discipline. Freidson (2001, 203) points out that, historically, most professions achieved social closure during the nineteenth and twentieth centuries. This is the same period of the development of the modern nation state as a public and democratic jurisdictional entity, responsible for the welfare of 'the people', and there is an inherent relationship between how the state authorised and licensed particular professions, the development of the state's interest in a national higher education system and the development of the professions.[2]

The core idea of professionalism is that it represents service to the public good both as a whole and as this whole is differentiated into distinctive public goods. As a whole the public good is a modern idea. It refers to the welfare of a political-civil entity, 'the people', a public collectivity, the unit of which is the individual citizen. As Martin Loughlin (2013) proposes, the positive existence of the people is made possible only as it is institutionalised in relation to its governing institutions: this relationship is the state, or sovereignty. Understood as a system of public office, the work of government is designed to provide a public and civic container for social life, one that enables the needs of individuals considered as citizens or as free beings to be met, thereby enabling them to come together as equals within the political association of the people. In this conception the state is the embodiment of things public, and its authority is grounded in the idea of political right (this is the central insight of Loughlin's 2010 magisterial account of the foundations of public law). Loughlin draws on Rousseau's account of political right as the basis of the idea of the public good: ' "The greatest good of all" is the product of two interrelated principles: freedom and equality. Only in the civil state [the mode of human co-existence that the politically autonomous mode of being that is sovereignty makes possible] can man be elevated and realize true freedom, and such freedom cannot subsist without political equality' (2010, 115).

The professions, then, serve distinctive human goods as these constitute different facets of what it is to be a human being who is able to enjoy a civil condition of freedom and equality in relation to other human beings. When the doctor 'attends' the sick, she is not a technician intent on fixing a problem but is attending to a person in such a way that her freedom is not compromised but recognised, and, as needed, facilitated.[3]

As suggested already, the human good that a profession is designed to serve is not 'external' to the practice of the profession: as Koehn (1994, 2) puts it, it is present 'in' the professional discipline as it is practised. It is for this reason that to become a professional requires that one be trained by already-trained professionals who are recognised as having achieved a degree of mastery of their discipline. Only they are able to guide the novice in how to understand – to cognitively, ethically and emotionally integrate the science so that it becomes a living body of practical knowledge – what, without such understanding, remains lifeless, technical detail. As Lara Goitein (2015, 5) explains:

> Doctors are only as good as their training. Medical education is essentially a verbal tradition: knowledge is impaired by physicians talking and demonstrating what they mean at the patient's bedside much more than through the written word. A resident may read extensively about endocarditis (an infection of the heart valve) in a textbook, but this cannot replace the experience of watching an attending physician make this diagnosis by discovering the subtle physical signs of small infected clots and inflammatory deposits throughout the body.

Thus, it is only one's professional peers who can judge the adequacy of a professional's mode of practising his or her discipline even as such judgement must include consideration of client 'voice' in relation to whether his or her needs were met. In line with Goitein's point, William Osler, the leading figure of 'the golden age of medicine' (Freidson 2001, 182–85; Goitein 2015), offers stories of the life of exemplary physicians in *An Alabama Student and Other Biographical Essays* because: 'In what better way could I show gratitude for the extraordinary kindness experienced during twenty-one years than by a constant appeal to the students to take as their models the great men of the profession of their own country (Osler 1908, preface)?' In his account of how Dr. Oliver Wendell Holmes discovered that puerperal (childbed) fever is contagious, 'conveyed usually by the doctor or the nurse, and due to a specific infection' (Osler 1908, 61), Osler draws the reader's attention to the passionate ardour with which Holmes battled the obstetricians 'whose teachings had been for years diametrically opposed to the contagiousness of puerperal fever' (Osler 1908, 63). In the paper that Holmes read to the Boston Society for Medical Improvement in 1843, a section of which Osler quotes, the ethical orientation of medicine inheres in how Holmes addresses the error in medical knowledge that has prevailed until the point of his intervention:

> It is as a lesson rather than as a reproach that I call up the memory of these irreparable errors and wrongs. No tongue can tell the heart-breaking calamities they have caused. . . . There is no tone deep enough for record, and no voice loud enough for warning. The woman about to become a mother, or with her new-born infant upon her bosom, should be the object of trembling care and sympathy wherever she bears her tender burden, or stretches her aching limbs. (Holmes cit. Osler 1908, 62)

A full conceptual account of the professions would require an account of the scope of distinct human goods that mark out the conditions of possibility for human beings enjoying a civic and free mode of co-existence, but this is not my object here. Here I want to draw out some further implications of the proposition that the raison d'être of each professional discipline resides in its responsibility for attending to a distinct human good, and, that in so doing, this profession serves the public good (for elaboration of this argument see Koehn 1994, chapter 8). In enacting its responsibility for attending to a distinct human good, the profession publicly articulates, represents and advocates for the importance of this good for people being enabled to live a good (civil) life. In this way the profession assumes stewardship of this good; its status is that of a trustee for this good. It is for this reason that the state licenses the professions and accords them an institutional autonomy sufficient to undertake their role. It is also for this reason that the professions are invited to assume an 'independent moral voice in evaluating social policies' (Freidson 2001, 197). The societal role of the professions as it is institutionalised in these ways marks out the domain of what Freidson calls the 'institutional ethics' of a profession as distinct from the practice ethics of its individual members:

> Institutional ethics . . . deal with the economic, social, and ideological circumstances which *create* many of the moral problems of [professional] work. The issues with which they are concerned include the way practice itself is financed, administered and controlled in the concrete places where professionals work, and the social policies which establish and enforce the broader legal and economic environment within which practice takes place. Institutional ethics are concerned with the moral legitimacy of the policies and institutions that constrain the possibility to practice in a way that benefits others and serves the transcendent value of a discipline. They are animated by moral concern for the ultimate purpose of disciplines. (Freidson 2001, 216, emphasis in the original)

The professions have an integral relationship to the state understood as the embodiment of a public and civil mode of human co-existence, one that makes it possible for both individuals and communities to achieve a civic status where they are free to cooperate in the achievement of modes of being that serve them all (as the whole they constitute and as the units of this whole).[4] In their respective service to specific human/public goods, the professions enter into a relationship of collaboration with the institutions of government in how they provide for the public good. Thus, agencies that rely heavily on civil engineering, for example, have a relationship to the profession of civil engineers, agencies responsible for health policy have a relationship to the various health professions and so on. Professional public servants who are responsible for public administration in an area demarcated by what it means to secure a particular human good will often be recruited from the relevant profession, and, in any case, will bring the profession into an advisory relationship to this area of public administration.[5]

The professions *are* occupations, but they are more than just occupations. As the stewards, trustees, servants of particular human goods, the professions are perhaps better understood as a type of public office than as an occupation (this is the contribution of Paul du Gay and his colleagues, e.g., see Pedersen and Roelsgaard Obling, this volume). The intelligibility of professionalism – what it is and why we need it – depends on our being interested in sustaining the intelligibility of the argument for a public and civil mode of being. Should this weaken, it must have deleterious consequences for professionalism, and I shall turn now to this subject.

THE ATTACK ON A PUBLIC-CIVIL MODE OF BEING AND ITS CONSEQUENCES FOR PROFESSIONALISM

Summarily, over the course of the past fifty or so years, we have witnessed a sustained ideological attack on the very idea of public-civil phenomena, including the professions, as *sui generis*. The 'new' social movements of the 1960s called into being the idea of the state when they equated all power with domination, and thus made it impossible for there to be an account of 'the state and the rule of law' as precisely a public and juridical form of power that is something other than domination (for this account see Kriegel 1995). Championing the rights of individuals to participate in the decisions governing their lives, without any consideration of what kind of worldly institutional order might make this possible, these social movements helped to withdraw legitimacy from the institutions of government and the professions, which in the face of such a conception of rights, appeared as inherently 'paternalistic' and 'bureaucratic', both negatively coded terms. At the same time, the increasingly influential and organised movement of neoliberalism (Mirowski and Plehwe 2009) advocated for a form of state that was no longer public in orientation but used its power and its authority to redesign society in terms of a competitive market order that operated not just nationally but on a global scale: the goal was to institutionalise markets in such a way that they were insulated from democracy (Slobodian 2018). A central feature of these processes by which the state shifted into becoming a 'competition state' (Cerny 2010) – a mode of government that constitutes the national jurisdiction as 'open for business' – was the invitation to private corporations to advise government in how best to adapt law and policy to fit the requirements of a global competitive market order (for some indication of how this has operated, see Nik-Khah and Van Horn 2017, and consider the role of the World Economic

Forum in setting the agenda for governments).[6] More generally, the ethos of the private, capitalist corporation has come to prevail as the organisational norm for the work of government, transforming what was once a public-civil ethos into a private-civil one.

The core feature of this ethos is a trained comportment in a managerial mode of economistic rational practice: manage for competitive performance – manage for measurable 'outcomes'. These incentives are either 'carrot' (induce performance through reward) or 'stick' (induce performance through fear). Ethics and value in this context refer to rules and norms of reciprocity and exchange as these are constituted with reference to privately oriented and instrumental forms of interaction.

Productivism is legitimised in the name of 'the public', now re-calibrated as the aggregate of atomised individuals whose 'welfare' is conceived and calculated in terms of national productivity. Thus, the idea of 'public good' is both disaggregated and radically privatised as it becomes a series of monetised and marketised goods as these come together to constitute the gross national product (the activity that happens inside a national money economy). At the same time 'freedom' is reinterpreted as 'consumer sovereignty', such that individuals are free if they are free to choose in a competitive market setting. The rationale for competition is that businesses will produce cheaper and more technologically improved goods and services if they have to compete, and that the subject who benefits from this dynamic is 'the consumer'.

In the productivist universe of a competitive market order, the intelligibility of the professions disappears. The public collectivist referent for their ethical practice is no longer operable. Ben Jackson's account of the transition from 'idealism' (he is referring to British idealism in how it influenced the social liberal philosophy of the idea of the welfare state) to 'neoliberalism' in British social policy gives us some idea of how this happened. He argues that the neoliberals targeted the Beveridgean welfare state (one, we might add, that was thoroughly imbricated with the service professions of the twentieth century), making their arguments known in British policy debates in the 1960s (Jackson n.d., 3): 'The key argument of neo-liberals was that "as far as possible, state-provided services should be taken into the private sector on normal market principles except for those hard cases really needing state intervention"' (David Collard's description of the new philosophy of social welfare of the Institute of Economic Affairs, cit. Jackson n.d., 3). The attack on the Beveridge/Attlee welfare state was organised in terms of three prongs: the first attacked the universalism of a shared citizen-based entitlement to welfare state/public services (this was re-labelled middle-class welfare, inferring that people who could afford to pay for services in a private market were rorting the system) and proposed that public services should be available only selectively to those who could not afford a privately provided alternative; the second opposed what it constructed as welfare state paternalism, advocating as the alternative individual choice, enabled by public subsidy for individual purchasing power in a newly constituted service market; the third attacked public collectivism at its core by proposing there was no such thing as public service, generically considered, for individuals are always and necessarily motivated by self-interest, by private consideration, and if they claim otherwise, to be pursuing a public end, this is simply cover for the pursuit of their own private interest (Jackson n.d., 19–23).

THE REDUCTION OF PROFESSIONALISM TO EXPERTISE

This attack on all forms of public collectivism casts into doubt the entire schema of intelligibility for the professions and professionalism. In the competitive state, and in a society reconstructed as a competitive market order, the professions and their members are simply so many specialists or experts seeking to market their services to private organisations and/or consumers. As self-interested 'providers' or producers, they can be counted on to seek their interest at the expense of the public unless the discipline of competition forces them to respond to consumer preferences. Hence the rhetoric of the Commonwealth Government of Australia's social policy reform reports since the 1980s has proposed that policy has to be designed so that it ensures that the inherent tendency of providers to design services around their needs rather than the needs of consumers is effectively checked: as the recent report of the Australian Productivity Commission has it, 'There is . . . strong scope to empower people so that their needs, not those of service providers, are the key focus for policymakers' (Commonwealth of Australia 2017, 38).

Clearly within the new market-oriented schema of intelligibility, there is no way in which the professions can be understood as stewards and trustees of particular human goods. Since the ethical-purposive orientation of their work now comes under suspicion as so much redundant and self-serving cover for their own private interest as providers/producers, it is bracketed, side-lined and withdrawn from permissible speech, even as it is clear that both public and private agencies tacitly rely on a professional ethic of service that can be neither acknowledged nor made a core feature of service organisational design. Such reliance has to be made if bridges are to be built so that they are safe, if general practitioners are to attend to primary health needs, and if school teachers are to develop students' emotional, civil and cognitive competences.

The new market-oriented schema separates out the ethic of professionalism from professional work, enabling such work to be nothing other than expertise that is of instrumental value. When professional work is reduced to expertise, as Freidson argues, the professional discipline can be disaggregated, with parts of it standardised, even automated, and, consequently, the identity of profession placed at risk:

> We can assume that recent jurisdictional boundaries will be altered by reassigning many now professional tasks to less qualified workers. . . . The worst and not unlikely possibility is that professionals will be slowly transformed into especially privileged technical workers. This is what is implied by Brint's . . . careful analysis of the changes that have been taking place in the political positions of American professions. He believes that professionals, once considered trustees of socially important knowledge designed to contribute to the public good and servants of values transcending the immediate and practical, are on a course of changing into neutral technical experts. (Freidson 2001, 209–10)

Freidson proposes that greater control by both government and private firms 'over performance and cost is likely to be gained in part by intensifying the trend toward a two-tier professional system, composed of a permanent, relatively small elite corps of professionals who do research and set standards of performance in practice organisations and an often floating population of qualified practitioners who may be employed on a temporary and sometimes part-time basis' (Freidson 2001, 210).

PRODUCTIVISM AND MANAGERIALISM

Productivism subjects everything (human beings and other creaturely beings, non-animate beings and the life system of which they are part) to a single mode of valuing – 'productivity'. As Pors (this volume) suggests, the orientation to productivity, which is one of perpetually seeking to increase productivity, introduces a phantasmatic temporal dimension of 'infinite potential' of doing, performing, producing more. Performance is always relative to producing more, technological enhancement of performance can be endlessly improved and the nature of change being an open horizon of innovation, management for change is the only way to go. The only way valuing can operate in such a universe is to make things commensurable – as quantity, money, information. In this world view, as we said at the outset of this chapter, the object is displaced. It no longer has any integrity, and therefore what is involved in attending to, securing, sustaining and even regenerating it disappears from view. Instead of the given-ness of a world of objects the productivist world view supplies a simulacrum of reality that floats free of the reality to which it supposedly refers, and that constitutes a self-referential system of valuing.

This self-referential system is expressed as a managerialist ideology and discourse. Here management is no longer referrable to what it means to manage an organisation that is designed to realise a particular core task (see du Gay and Vikkelsø 2017) but is de-contextualised to become a free-standing phenomenon of management. Such de-contextualised management is expressed in the New Public Management's slogan 'let the managers manage', where it is expected that public managers will be generalists rather than having any specific area of policy expertise acquired through continuous service in a particular area and the acquisition of deep experience of its objective nature. Freidson (2001) attributes to the ideology of managerialism an 'elite generalism'. While the doctrine of consumer sovereignty cultivates a 'populist generalism', the idea that 'the customer is always right and the people are always right' (Freidson 2001, 117), the elite generalism of the managerialists has its own way of situating specialised knowledge in a relationship of subjection to their rule:

> The ideology of managerialism presents a rather different basis for resistance to specialized knowledge and skill – the celebration of what can be called *elite generalism*. Like populist generalism it does not defer to the authority of specialized knowledge, instead claiming authority over it. However, it goes beyond populist generalism by claiming the authority to command, organize, guide, and supervise both the choices of consumers[7] and the productive work of specialists. It denies authority to expertise by claiming a form of general knowledge that is superior to specialization because it can organize it rationally and efficiently. Unlike populist generalism, it does not claim merely ordinary human qualities informed by everyday knowledge and skill and the capacity to learn whatever is necessary to make economic or political decisions. Rather, even when it eschews the common claim of elites that they are endowed with superior qualities by virtue of lineage, innate ability, or character, it can fall back on its own special kind of preparation for positions of leadership – an advanced but general formal education that equips them to direct or lead specialists, consumers, and citizens. (Freidson 2001, 116–17)

A managerialised mode of being is superimposed on the world of people who have needs for human goods and the professionals who would if they could provide these human goods. In relation to professionals, managerialists practise an equable but undeniably elite *hauteur*, where it is made clear that the professional cannot possibly understand the rigor and relevance of managerialist discourse, and where a morality that is reduced to marketing slogans displaces the substantive and concrete ethical nature of the professional's task.

In their discussion of how managerialism has eviscerated the conception of professional management that is found in classical organisation theory, where management is always referrable to the task of coordinating the work of an organisation as this centres on a particular specifiable task and purpose, Paul du Gay and Signe Vikkelsø (2017, 6–7) present typical managerialist arguments for 'abandoning preoccupation with task and purpose':

a. *The world has changed* – 'Where it would earlier suffice for managers to focus on the effectiveness of the organisation's task accomplishment, it is assumed that their focus must today be directed towards the future through "strategic management", that is through positioning the organisation vis-à-vis "competitors" . . . allocating resources to areas of "competitive advantage" . . . "enacting the environment" . . . and "managing stakeholder relations" ' (du Gay and Vikkelsø 2017, 131–32);
b. *Task orientation hampers orientation* – 'a strong focus on task militates against key facets of organizational survival and flourishing, such as "creativity", "playfulness", and "innovation" ' (du Gay and Vikkelsø 2017, 133);
c. *Task offers too simplistic an understanding of organising processes* – ' "organization", "management", "task", and so on are practically and theoretically not conceivable as distinct entities and are better approached as a mutable effect of "fields", "networks", "discourses", "flows", and "processes" ' (du Gay and Vikkelsø 2017, 134);
d. *Task is power in disguise* – 'task' and 'purpose' are 'rejected as legitimate, self-evident matters and analysed as effects of power plays that should be exposed, problematized, and critiqued' (du Gay and Vikkelsø 2017, 135);
e. *Humans before tasks* – 'the focus on task has been questioned because it is considered to "instrumentalize" organizational life, thus suppressing its moral and affective dimensions through reducing "the whole human being" to a cog in an impersonal machine'. Here a rejection of the formality of bureaucratically specified task, office and span of control is rejected in favour of a more personalised and 'human' organisation (du Gay and Vikkelsø 2017, 136).

Managerialism, then, not only cancels the relevance of specific professional disciplines in the fulfilment of a particular organisation's task and purpose. In calling into question the conception of the organisation as having a primary task,[8] where the role of management is to coordinate the organisation, thought of as a system of cooperation in order to achieve this task, managerialism also destroys the professional vocation of management considered as 'a practical science of organizing' (du Gay and Vikkelsø 2017, 18). Managerialism thereby destroys the type of organisation that is built around the primary task as this is given intelligibility by a specific category of human good: the university, the university faculty, the school, the hospital and so on.

RECLAIMING PROFESSIONALISM

Du Gay and Vikkelsø (2017, 149) offer us what can only be called a generative suggestion: 'whether a discipline has the right core objects should be judged on its ability to relate practically to its phenomena'. The discipline of managerialism, oriented as it is by productivism, and the way in which it abstracts from the claims of reality, fails on this criterion. This is the point that Massy makes in relation to orthodox, industrial methods of agriculture. In transposing a productivist ethos onto the ecology of the earth, industrial agriculture requires farmers to refuse to listen to the claims of that piece of the earth that they farm, and the consequence is the destruction of the fecundity of this earth.

The subordination of the professions to managerialism does not work, and it will not work. It is leading to a profound compromise, if not the degradation, of professional practice. In professionalised settings of publicly funded services such as courts, public hospitals and public schools, the relevant professionals are increasingly over-worked, and stressed by being placed in a situation where they are neither given the discretion nor the resources to meet client needs adequately if at all.[9] In private corporate settings, privileged strata of professionals may find themselves handsomely remunerated, but they are worked hard, and expected to substitute corporate objectives for professional purpose. Other, less privileged strata of professionals, finding themselves outside career professional positions and in a casualised market for professional services, have little or no leverage ('voice') with regard to how they deliver these services, other than to 'exit'. Perhaps, most egregiously, the destruction of a professional and independent 'career public service' in government, with not just the substitution of a generalist managerialism for portfolio specific expertise, but the reduction in number of public servants, the casualisation of once-career positions and the contracting out of policy and administrative work to private consultancy firms, is leading to the breakdown in the capacity of government to do what it is expected to do. This is not a problem for those who think that a competitive market order can substitute for traditional government tasks, but it is a problem for the general public: they know that government is not working as it should. Where this translates into professionalised areas of government service – statutory social work, for example – repeated system failure cultivates in the public a distrust of all professional public officials.

We have some way to run before the accumulated impact of productivism and managerialism on professionalism becomes visible. It is like the largely invisible, slow and compounded processes of environmental devastation. Yet no one is placed better than professionals themselves to reclaim professionalism and its importance. This is the historical opportunity with which they – and we – are confronted. Such work of reclamation must be also work of clarification: just what is this professional discipline, and why is it of consequence for our shared capacity to live a civil life? It must be also work that is attune to these times when the shadow of ecological devastation is upon all kinds of human endeavour including professional work.

In confronting how our professionalism has been compromised and degraded, we have to take the next step: what actually is at stake? To take this step is to do what Charles Massy has done in relation to the profession of agriculture: to disclose and thereby clarify the precise nature of the object that the professional discipline serves.

As another example, beyond the one that Massy affords us, I want to conclude this chapter with a brief discussion of how Kristen Rundle (2012, 2018) uses the work of Lon Fuller to reveal the distinctive object of law. Against the legal positivist separation of law and morality, and in accord with the idea that the object or purpose of each profession is internal to its practice, Fuller argued that law has an 'internal morality'. What is noteworthy about Fuller's account of the internal morality of law is its relational character, and here we see a feature of professionalism that I have not highlighted until now. The object of professional practice demarcates a role-based relationship between the professional and his or her clients: in the realisation of the professional task, each has a distinctive role and responsibility, and they have to cooperate on the basis of this role differentiation (see also Koehn 1994, 143). Thus, the problem with the productivist reduction of professionalism to technical expertise is that it not only sidelines the role or office of the professional, but it does also the role or office of the client. Specifically, in regard to the latter, consumerism (consumer sovereignty) entails the same ethos of the productivism from which it derives: orient so as to get as much value for money as possible in a competitive market setting.

Let us return to Rundle's (2018, 2) account of Fuller's internal morality of law: 'Fuller was concerned, above all, to articulate the moral demands appropriate to the particular relationship between lawgiver and legal subject(s) that he saw as constitutive to the enterprise of governing through law'. Rundle sees her own task in relation to Fuller as one of 'reclamation and clarification': 'a wider view of what Fuller offered to the project of theorising the rule of law opens up novel possibilities for the application of his insights to contemporary challenges of the rule of law' (Rundle 2018, 2).

Fuller offers the morality tale of King Rex who he uses to exemplify 'how not to create and administer a legal system' (Rundle 2018, 3). King Rex's failures offered Fuller a rhetorical device by which, in contrast to these legal pathologies, he could specify eight 'basic elements' of a legal system which together constitute the internal morality of law. These are 'that law be (1) general, (2) publicly promulgated, (3) non-retroactive, (4) sufficiently clear, (5) non-contradictory, (6) possible to comply with, (7) relatively constant through time, and (8) that there be congruence between official action and declared rule' (Rundle 2018, 3).

Rundle suggests (2012, 2018) that if these eight elements are reduced (as legal positivists do) to so many technical features of law's efficacy, then the point that Fuller is making is entirely missed. Fuller is not talking about some kind of *a priori* moral or ethical orientation for the law; he sees his task as one of specifying the object that is law, 'the inner constitutive structure of the activity of governing through law' (Rundle 2018, 4). Thus, Rundle (2018, 5) proposes: 'The "morality" of Fuller's eight principles of the internal morality of law is therefore best understood as the role morality appropriate to the relationship between lawgiver and legal subject(s) that he saw as constitutive to that enterprise'.

The efficacy of law matters, but it is not a self-sufficient criterion; it refers to whether law functions as it must if it is to qualify as law, and this requires an account of the *morality* of law. Law giving, Rundle (2018, 6) suggests for Fuller, involves a ' "sense of trusteeship" (Fuller's word) for the fate of persons'. Rundle elaborates on Fuller's 'conception of the person implicit in legality' (Fuller cit. Rundle 2018, 6). Legality for Fuller makes it possible for 'man [*sic*]' to 'become a responsible agent, capable of following rules and answerable for his defaults' (Fuller cit. Rundle 2018, 6). Rundle specifies the two aspects of the argument that Fuller offers regarding how law constitutes the formal status of the person as someone capable of interacting within a legal order. The first is 'that certain capacities are needed in order to be ready to participate in legal relations' (Rundle 2018, 6). To be a legal person, the individual has to have acquired the capacity to respect the law, to know how to follow its rules and to be answerable for his defaults' (Fuller cit. Rundle 2018, 6). The second aspect concerns the ground for this respect for the law, namely, 'the distinctive kind of agency that law itself *creates*' (Rundle 2018, 7, emphasis in the original). This is the civil personhood and capacity for civil forms of action that (as early modern civil philosophers such as Hobbes argue) is made possible by means of the political-jurisprudential structuring of the state as the sovereign public authority. To return to Rundle's account of Fuller's conception of 'the distinctive kind of agency that the law itself *creates*', she cites Fuller's own elaboration of what this means and why it matters:

> A legal system does not succeed or achieve 'efficacy' simply because the citizen is willing to obey orders. It succeeds if it creates a stable order by which the citizen can orient his conduct towards his fellows . . . a functioning society is its goal, *not a subservient populace ready to do what they are told to do*. This

is not some extra-legal purpose assigned to law from without; it is intrinsic to the very notion that government act towards the citizen only in compliance with previously announced general rules. (The Fuller archive, cit. Rundle 2018, 7, emphasis in the original)

Rundle draws out the implications of this relational account of the rule of law: if citizens 'are to cooperate with those in possession of legal authority with respect to . . . laws, then the moral demands of the *relational form* of the enterprise must be met' (Rundle 2018, 8, emphasis in the original). Further: 'To secure the subject's fidelity to law . . . the lawgiver must enter into a relationship of "reciprocity" with her' (Rundle 2018, 9). If this bond of reciprocity breaks down, Fuller concludes, 'nothing is left on which to ground the citizen's duty to observe the lawgiver's rules' (Fuller cit. Rundle 2018, 9).[10]

I have discussed at some length Rundle's retrieval of Fuller's account of the rule of law, a project of reclamation and clarification that is similar to that of Martin Loughlin in retrieving the idea of public law, because it has exemplary value for those of us who could more effectively resist the tyranny and destructiveness of productivism if we reclaimed and clarified our own particular profession and its internal object. It is true as both Max Weber and Daryl Koehn suggest, that this work of (what Weber 1949, 53–54, calls 'philosophical') clarification can never issue in a self-evident (logical or factual) truth that being so commands consensus. Here it is a truth that contains within itself a question of us – do we want to live with ourselves and each other in such a way that we can enjoy a civil existence, one in which we are able to attend to our needs as human beings and to respect each other's integrity? If so, certain things follow from this, and, as I have argued here, they imply professionalism.

CONCLUSION

As Daryl Koehn suggested, the fate of professionalism and the professions is historically contingent. If collectively we are unable to understand the lethal destructiveness of productivism and to extricate itself from its seductive embrace, then, we may face the end of this distinctive ethical comportment and the way it is structured to earn public trust because of how it serves particular human goods. To pursue a professional vocation is to be called to it, and today I propose those of us who would pursue such a vocation must step up to the urgent call to reclaim and clarify the centrality of the professions to living a good life. In becoming and growing as professionals, it is (as Osler proposed) always the exemplary professionalism of our peers that assists us in confirming our intention to step up and to begin to think about what this may demand of us. But it is also the unmet human needs of those we would serve if the organisational settings in which we find ourselves not just permitted us but invited and facilitated us in so to do.

If today we find ourselves needing to provide a conception of professionalism that enables us to understand how the professions have to be structured so as to merit public trust, then it is surely because of the paradox of the creative opportunity that comes with having to face and think about how we respond to a destructive world view (what I have called productivism). Both Daryl Koehn's and Freidson's later work on professionalism were motivated by the need to answer the attacks on professionalism. Professionals now are positioned within organisations and organisational structures of public–private partnership that ask that they surrender their professionalism and conduct themselves as little more than expert guns for hire. Isabelle Stengers (2015, 92) says of this situation: 'When everyone is dependent, when everyone is linked by partnerships to industry, no one will want to "spit in the soup", to carry out research that might weaken the legitimacy of their, and everybody else's participation in the industrial redefinition of the world'. There is a certain situational truth to this statement, but this prostitution of professionalism corrodes the soul of professionals, creating an opening for being called back to their vocation of service to the public good. Just as Massy and his professional peers in the face of an ecologically devastating industrial agriculture, have creatively opened up the practice of regenerative agriculture, through building their own community of practice, all of the professions at this time need to (re)build a community of practice that enables them to call to account, and to resist, the managerialist structures of productivism that have been imposed on them and their work. As Stengers (2015, 93–95) suggests, it is a question of taking back our collective capacities to think and imagine together, in a relationship of partnership with the public, and in a shared attitude of honouring and paying attention to the life system of which we are all part.

NOTES

1. For example, these passages from 'Science as a Vocation': (1) 'Whether life is worth living and when – this question if not asked by medicine. Natural science gives us an answer to the question of what we must do if we wish to master life technically. It leaves quite aside, or assumes for its purposes, whether we should and do wish to master life technically and whether it ultimately makes sense to do so'. Here the presupposition of medicine represented by Weber as 'the task of maintaining life as such and of diminishing suffering as such to the greatest possible degree', provides an external direction for medicine as scientific technique. This leaves out the ethical substance of medicine as it attends to what it means to be a living-dying human being which is something other than a technical practice. (2) 'Whether there should be law and whether one should establish just these rules – such questions jurisprudence does not answer. It can only state: If one wishes this

result, according to the norms of our legal thought, this legal rule is the appropriate means of attaining it' (Weber 1970, 144–45). As I show later in this chapter, with reference to Fuller's account of the idea of law, Weber's legal positivism has the effect of enabling the framing normative decision to assume the status of a given, again casting legal practice as simply technical service to this given.

2. In line with this, the Wikipedia (downloaded 2018) entry on 'engineering ethics' says that the respective American societies of civil engineering, electrical engineering and mechanical engineering were created in the second half of the nineteenth century, as was the society of mining engineers. Where the first three 'were more closely identified with the engineer as learned professional', and subsequently in the early part of the twentieth century developed a formal code of ethics, the society of mining engineers did not, remaining identified with private industry and viewing the engineer as a technical employee. The development of these codes of ethics was in response to 'significant structural failures'. The entry continues: 'Over the following decades most American states and Canadian provinces either required engineers to be licensed, or passed special legislation reserving title rights to organization of professional engineers'. The first article of the code of ethics of the American Society of Civil Engineers (cited by this entry) is: 'Engineers shall hold paramount the safety, health and welfare of the public and shall strive to comply with the principles of sustainable development in the performance of their professional duties'.
3. This account of professionalism in relation to the inherently public and civil project of the modern state is my own, but it is influenced by the insufficiently elaborated proposition of both Hegel and Durkheim that the professions have an inherent relationship to the state, a shared civil and public purpose, and that it is for this reason that there has to be a careful institutional articulation of this relationship such that professional autonomy is assured but at the same time the professions play an appropriate role in the conduct of government.
4. Freedom so understood, and as already explained, is a matter of civil standing in relation to one's fellows. It is already a relationship of mutual recognition even as Hegel showed individuals, in practising freedom, have to achieve this understanding and they may fail to do this. Thus, against a 'liberal' conception of freedom as 'natural', and as pertaining to the individual considered as an atom independently of his relationships to others, this conception of freedom is predicated on the fact that the nature of human life is one of interdependency, and that, thus, the question of freedom concerns how this phenomenon of interdependence functions. If it is structured so as to invite each individual to be their own person (to assume unit status, in Winnicott's language), then in how individuals cooperate, they have to learn to respect each other as persons and what this demands of them (this is the burden of Hegel's conception of the state as ethical life as presented in his *Philosophy of Right*). Robert Pippin (2008) offers an excellent account of Hegel's idea of what it means to live a free life as a shared way of being in which individuals engage in the practice of being able to give reasons to each other for what it is they think and do. This practice is always historically contextual and inherently social: 'The quality of the reasons available to me in understanding and justifying

my deeds is not in the deepest sense "up to me", and is inextricable from the nature of the social practices (practices that inevitably involve relations of power and recognition) at a time' (Pippin 2008, 25). The professions, of course, have a major role in educating individuals in the practice of giving reasons, or of acting in such a way that they could think about how their action might be explained in terms of giving reasons.

5. It makes no sense to attempt to separate the professions (and professionalism) from bureaucracy, as Talcott Parsons, among others such as Freidson, seeks to do: they assume that the principle of bureaucracy is inherently antagonistic to professionalism (see e.g., Schudson 1980). As Paul du Gay's entire academic publishing career suggests, bureaucratic office is an inherently formal and ethical phenomenon. It is its own profession, and it is this that underwrites the idea of a professional and career public service.
6. The World Economic Forum website offers under the heading 'What makes us unique?' the following self-descriptors: 'The World Economic Forum is the International Organization for Public-Private Cooperation'. And: 'Deeply anchored in the public and private sectors, the Forum is the only global organization serving this role, bringing together the world's foremost CEOs, heads of state, ministers and policy-makers, experts and academics, international organizations, youth, technology innovators and representatives of civil society in an impartial space with the aim of driving positive change'.
7. It is worth adding Freidson's footnote here: 'While the ideology of managerialism is often accompanied by the claim that it is merely a passive servant of consumer demand, consumer desires may be taken into account in a production plan only within the constraints of the established resources and structure of the organization and agency. Furthermore, organizations often try to create or manipulate consumer demand to suit what they are equipped or prepared to supply. Thus, the organization or agency only sometimes serves consumers passively; otherwise it creates, manipulates, or constrains their choices' (Freidson 2001, 116–17).
8. In classical organisational theory, what distinguishes an organisation is 'the existence of a collective "task" or "purpose"; something that unites its members in concerted action for a shorter or longer period and which can be explained to and by them' (du Gay and Vikkelsø 2017, 137). Du Gay and Vikkelsø (2017, 147) further remark: 'It was once a core axiom in OT [Organizational Theory] that organizations should not be managed as if they are essentially alike'.
9. With reference to physicians in the USA and Britain, Eve and Hodgkin (1997, 81) comment: 'Whilst far more advanced in the USA than in Britain, in both countries physicians are under increasing pressure to keep expenditure to a minimum and in both systems this pressure is often not apparent to the patient. As this pressure for cost containment grows, so the conflict of interests becomes more pronounced: the demands of distributive justice (use this public money to the best advantage of all), and the physician's desire to maximize income conflict with the duty to do the best for each individual patient. In these circumstances it is clear that the traditional definition of professionalism (the exercise of discretion on behalf of another) no longer captures what clinicians actually do'.

10. This point is made by all the Social Contract political philosophers, for example. Hobbes, Locke, Rousseau, and it is such reciprocity that enters into the constitutive structure of 'the state and the rule of law' as Kriegel explains it. Here then it becomes clear that the idea of the state (as an inherently public phenomenon) is inseparable from the idea of the rule of law.

Chapter 12

Afterword

Bogdan Costea

Perhaps the first question readers expect to be answered at the end of any collection of studies concerns its overall claim to unity and coherence. In this spirit, it must be said from the outset that a series of studies on managerialism cannot claim either more, or less, unity or coherence than the very phenomenon under investigation. The variety of treatments, indeed the almost divergent modes of analysis, appearing here goes to show what actually unites the volume: the aim has been to raise the problems of managerialism, governance, technology and value in their multifaceted nature, to allow their manifold conceptual and empirical characters to appear side by side, without seeking to press, from an editorial position, either a unifying method, a doctrinaire stance, nor a comfortably common range of phenomena that might constitute the realities of managerialism.

What emerges cannot, therefore, be a definitive answer to the question of managerialism's triumph, nor even a more focussed, sharper, way of asking the question itself. To the contrary, we found that every time the topic is announced, new angles, new courses of inquiry, as well as new units of analysis open up to reveal yet more of its nuances and dimensions. On the other hand, asserting the manifold character of our general theme does not mean that there is no common ground or concern when the question is asked. The very fact that the question of managerialism is heard by most of the social scientific, historical and philosophic community means that its essential concern echoes much more than a mere aspect of the contemporary condition among others. Somehow, both managerialism and neoliberalism touch scholars with the most varied interests as if all regions of existence have been afflicted, or invaded, by them – whatever they actually are. There is almost no exception: individuality and the sense of self, family, community and civil society, state, as well as the planet as a whole (human and natural) have all come under the kind of scrutiny presented here. At all these levels, a sense of foreboding prevails that something corrupting, distorting and base is under way in whatever comes with the advancement of managerialism and neoliberalism – and this much is shared by all scholars preoccupied by these two 'uncanny guests', to use Nietzsche's image (1968, 7, Book One, Note 1). Sometimes, the sentiment of gloom they elicit is so urgent and so dominant that the horizon of thought shrinks into dogmatic criticism of anything that is deemed to pertain to either managerialism or neoliberalism, while this gloom turns, at the same time, into a strangely comfortable and self-certain state of mind.

This collection tries to take seriously both the task of legitimate critical reflection about all that is unfolding in the name of these two tropes, but also to set aside (in part, at least) the feeling of self-certainty that accompanies much current criticism. It is all too easy to use these two labels to dismiss everything that seems suspect and the chapters here have tried to avoid this position as much as possible. Rather, the feeling that something is indeed under way in the world (of which there is little doubt) became the basis for a different kind of question whose formulation turns out to matter substantially in any investigation. If we were to settle on the origins of this endeavour, perhaps the question could be framed as follows: who are these guests whose unwelcome visit is so disturbing us? Even if it may seem self-evident, this formulation seeks to open up a quite specific (and perhaps unusual) horizon of inquiry. Its wording is worth explaining further here, at the end, because it functioned, for us, not just as a point of entry, but also as one of our main concluding points: if 'managerialism' and 'neoliberalism' are to be our companions and foes, they cannot be defeated if they are not deciphered and identified as they cross the threshold from being mere historical episodes, to making themselves increasingly at home in every nook and cranny of contemporary order. Still, in this formula, this question reveals only one of its facets: research on managerialism and (neo)liberalism appears as a kind of search for two *intruders*, two *alien* modes of being, who have entered *our* world, otherwise pure and innocent, and have done so without welcome or consent. And some of the chapters do indeed investigate how these guests have penetrated the capillaries of the institutional and life structures we observe today.

But the question does not stop here: it can also be extended and transformed into its own questioning object. The twin presuppositions that these 'guests' are different in essence from 'us', and that their coming is 'unwelcome', are challenged and turned against themselves in several chapters (Costea, Hemming, Malpas). What if these are not alien features of modernity, but rather expressions of its very essence? And so, if the essence of modernity is the affirmation of subjectivity, are managerialism and (neo)liberalism therefore not bound up with who – and how – we ourselves are? This collection thus also explores ways in which research programmes on managerialism could widen their reach. In 1887, a couple of years after encountering nihilism 'standing at the door' as the 'uncanniest of all guests' (Nietzsche 1968, 7, Book One, Note 1), Nietzsche made a decisive, but often overlooked, note for the preface of his projected work on the transvaluation of all values:

> What I relate is the history of the next two centuries. I describe what is coming, what can no longer come differently: *the advent of nihilism*. This history can be related even now; for necessity itself is at work here. This future speaks even now in a hundred signs, this destiny announces itself everywhere; for this music of the future all ears are cocked even now. For some time now, our whole European culture has been moving as toward a catastrophe, with a tortured tension that is growing from decade to decade: restlessly, violently, headlong, like a river that wants to reach the end, that no longer reflects, that is afraid to reflect. (1968, 3, Preface, Note 2)

Which centuries did he have in mind? What are we to make of his thought if he indeed meant the twentieth and twenty-first centuries? If these two centuries have been, and are, restless, violent and thoughtless (Nietzsche's foresight in this respect was itself uncanny), they have also brought forth an unparalleled liberation of energy and human productivity. Far from being simply an effect of speculative images, this paradox is, in fact, quite decisive for any investigation of the managerial and liberal orders of human action through which the last hundred years, or so, have marked their place in history. And this matter has been, implicitly and explicitly, taken up by some of the chapters in this collection: if anything, it was through management, business, corporatism, liberalism and intense productivism that our epoch has acquired its principles of movement. When Henry Ford began, in 1908, production of the first popular car, the Model T, in a little plant in Detroit on the corner of Piquette and Beaubien Avenues deploying for the first time the then-experimental progressive assembly line, this was not simply a technical and organisational achievement for modern management, but also the founding of the absolute condition of possibility of our present. Ford's system (which is the managerial and organisational basis of 99% of any physical production process today) represents however much more than that: it is the concrete manifestation of the metaphysical process which Nietzsche announced as 'European nihilism'.

Management and managerialism are not simply technical operations, but the manner in which modern humanity claims power and freedom by bringing to full and concrete realisation the ability to produce anything, anywhere, anytime, in any quantity. The demiurgic sentiment of mastery over the genesis and generation of all values, indeed of value as such, turned out, however, to be but the beginning of a much deeper movement of 'emancipation' at the heart of the modern soul. With the conquest of power came the illusory conquest – or, as Malpas correctly calls it, the very 'erasure' – of finitude and limits. In the wake of the advent of management, there ensued a century-long euphoria with the liberation of human energy, a century in which, as Heidegger noted in 1942, humanity acquires a new law for its existence: 'Man, freely creating and fulfilling himself in creating; the genius becomes the law of being truly human' (Heidegger 1985, 31). Such is the power of humanity now fully absorbed in the workshop of endless self-production that reason itself, intoxicated by the legitimacy of its dominion, ceases to think about the kind of future humanity is forging in its new factories:

> *This will to take charge of Being in its jointure, freely shaping and knowing it*, is essentially animated and confirmed by the new experience of man as the genius. 'Genius' is only possible in the realm of Liberalism – metaphysically understood. (Heidegger 1985, 56)

Heidegger brings to light how the power of production turned into humanity's contemporary fascination with itself, with its purported 'creative', 'innovative', 'artistic', or 'aesthetic' 'potential' (or whatever other words will come to describe this category). Yet this self-appointment, and revaluation, of humanity as the centre of the modern onto-cosmological synthesis comes with a significant caveat. A profound cultural paradox defines the epoch in which we live: the paradox of the perpetually unhappy, agitated and entitled *customer* (the one who must always be served, who must always be treated as higher, as commanding), that creature who is less and less satisfied by anything, while having access to more and more of everything. In this sense, it seems that studies of managerialism and (neo)liberalism must begin to account for the possibility that their historical emergence is not simply an external visitation, but rather a profound internal movement of modern subjectivity which cannot look away from them however inconvenient their reflection of us is. As management brought into being modern production and liberated *homo faber*, it also promised new certainties and the possibility of a new cultural 'measure of things', practical as well as theoretical – as Arendt (1958, 157) explains, 'the generalization of the fabrication experience in which usefulness and utility are established as the ultimate standards for life and the world of men'. An astute reader of Nietzsche, Arendt knows however that production itself is no guarantee of value and of valuation:

> The instrumentalization of the whole world and the earth, this limitless devaluation of everything given, this process of growing meaninglessness where every end is transformed into a means and which can be stopped only by making man himself the lord and master of all things. (Arendt 1958, 157)

The conquest of the world made possible by management (as an expression of the triumph of modern reason itself) is the ultimate victory of modern humanity who cannot now simply step away from its own shadow. Arendt is right: the fabrication process, unmoored and pursued for its own sake – production *as such* – can no longer produce a stable world, while it could produce and maintain the euphoria of globalised and universalised existence after the fall of communism in 1989.

The question that arises, nearly three decades later, as the troubling indignation with globalisation has turned into political reality, is whether we are truly seeking to recover a stable world. If managerial frameworks of production, if liberal modes of understanding the human condition, are removed or renounced, what would take their place? Can we return somewhere safer? Or would we embark upon a new journey altogether? These are questions that become, or would become, pressing if radical critiques of managerialism and (neo)liberalism were to genuinely succeed. What would a new sense of stability and measure look like? Are they even possible in the realm of freedom, whose very principles are restlessness and instability (understood as mobility and continuous renewal and growth)? Is the modern soul ready to face its own countenance when it seeks to name its enemies as 'capitalism', 'corporatism', 'consumerism', 'managerialism' or '(neo)liberalism'? Is not the danger here that we always come very close when engaging in critiques of these terms to yet more rational utopias which could not be any different in their essence from those that haunted the twentieth century? If the triumph of modernity is 'the universal rule of the will to power within planetary history', as Heidegger shows, then 'in this reality stands everything today, whether it be communism, or fascism, or world-democracy' (Heidegger 2000, 375–76, BC translation).

What doctrine or system of thought would take the place of this position? In 1966, he made the following remark in a now-famous interview with the German magazine *Der Spiegel* (which Heidegger asked to be published only after his death):

> It is a decisive question for me today how a political system, and what kind of one, can at all be coordinated with the technological age. I do not know the answer to this question. I am not convinced that it is democracy. (Heidegger 1977b, 16)

To the 'technological age' corresponds the managerial spirit (it is not far-fetched to see in many instances that the two might be interchangeable in Heidegger's texts), and to this spirit corresponds the whole structure of our age – the '*one decision*' for '*thinking*', he argued already in the 1930s, is:

> . . . whether the machination of beings would unleash man as an exceedingly powerful and unbridled being of power, or whether Being would grant the

> grounding of its truth in the form of hardship from out of which the *adversity* of god and man crosses paths with the *strife* of the earth and the world. (Heidegger 2006, 11, the translation is slightly adapted to reflect some of the nuances of the original)

'Machination', Heidegger explains, 'here means the makability of beings which produces as well as makes up everything'; '*Machination* means the accordance of everything with producibility, indeed in such a way that the unceasing, unconditioned reckoning of everything is pre-directed' (Heidegger 2006, 12). The word *machination* (translating the complicated *Machenschaft* in German) indicates the way in which Heidegger understands modern humanity in relation to technology as its only manner of self-understanding, as Hemming shows in his chapter. Technology is the category that explains how modernity's only possible historical movement is decided in the metaphysics of machination, of technology and of total organisation. No other direction, no *terminus*, can appear as the horizon of the future than that pre-directed by total production. In other words, there can be no metaphysical variety among utopian programmes or systems for whom the law of movement is already determined by the promises of endless production. This is what Heidegger meant when he argued that the physical variations in the institutions of power among the regimes of communism, fascism and world-democracy (by which he meant global liberalism) are but masks for the same metaphysical essence. No contemporary thinking can move outside the realm of continuous production, exchange and consumption since they are the only manner in which the sentiment of power can now be understood. Private and public lives, work and leisure, war and peace, all appear, and are thought of, as possibilities of managed technological production. The sway of human self-assertion, therefore, finds its ultimate expression in the unstoppable movement of technology and organisation; indeed, if the instituted order of management and technology were to cease functioning (and when they occasionally do), their metaphysical primacy would become evident:

> The fascinating side of this process can, especially in conjunction with the discipline pertaining to technology, cover over to a large extent the 'misery' into which human beings are thrust by technologization. Perhaps there is no longer any such 'misery' for those human beings who are completely technological. (Heidegger 1996, 44)

In other words, one of the aspects which became increasingly apparent, and vital in the end, in the process of producing this collection is not just how critiques of managerialism can be conducted, how sharp and astute they can be, but what would follow them, what could become ground, foundation, a possible beginning? In the section preceding his announcement of the death of god, Nietzsche – one of those to whom we are bound to return if we are to read the contemporary condition critically – asks just this question:

> *In the horizon of the infinite*. – We have forsaken the land and gone to sea! We have burned our bridges behind us – indeed, we have gone farther and destroyed the land behind us. Now, tiny ship, look out! Beside you is the ocean; to be sure, it does not always roar, and at times it lies spread out like silk and gold and dreams of goodness. But there will come hours when you will realize that it is infinite and that there is nothing more awesome than infinity. Oh, the poor bird that has felt free and now strikes against the walls of this cage! Woe, when homesickness for the land overcomes you, as if there had been more *freedom* there – and there is no longer any 'land' (Nietzsche 1974, 180–81, §124, translation modified by BC)!

As modernity secured freedom by *managing* to produce and build an entirely new human world, the promised endlessness of this chain of ends and means can only lead to radical loss of value, because the freedom to appropriate the world and to transform it into a planetary factory-cum-shopping mall are bound up with an inevitable metaphysical cost:

> The process can continue only provided that no worldly durability and stability is permitted to interfere, only as long as all worldly things, all end products of the production process, are fed back into it at an ever-increasing speed. In other words, the process of wealth accumulation, as we know it, stimulated by the life process and in turn stimulating human life, is possible only if the world and the very worldliness of man are sacrificed. (Arendt 1958, 255)

Everything can be *managed, organised, controlled*, yet nothing human can any longer be rescued from homelessness and world-alienation. But, at the same time, homelessness and world-alienation are called 'freedom'. And this is the manner in which the category of freedom functions concretely in modern politics: it is, and cannot be other than, *negative*. But it does – and has done quite spectacularly for the last century – *function*. Who then is at home – and who the unwelcome guest – in the world today? Whose home is the world? These are the disturbing questions that arise when we contemplate the triumph of managerialism: 'What were we doing when we unchained this earth from its sun?', asked Nietzsche. 'Whither is it moving now? Whither are we moving (Nietzsche 1974, 181, §125)?' No answer seems to be forthcoming, and yet that itself is misleading – we are not at the end of an epoch; the present mode of existence, unsustainable though it may seem in physical terms broadly understood, has not reached its metaphysical conclusion in any way. To the contrary, we live in the age most unaware of its own brutality, an age whose self-righteousness and self-appointed goodness rings out from every corner of human self-expression. Modern humanity is convinced of itself – 'Ours is the most decent and compassionate age' after all, to use Nietzsche's (1968, 7, Book One, Note 1) devastating irony – and in no doubt about the pursuit of self-assertion. Management language has now become the ultimate framework not only for the pursuit of material production, but also for the production and reproduction of the 'self' as itself, as Heelas so astutely realised:

> Not the self as constituted by consumer culture, but the self as a self which considers itself to be something more, something much 'deeper', more natural and authentic than the self of what is taken to be involved with the superficialities of the 'merely' materialistic-cum-consumeristic; the self as a self which has to work on itself to enrich and explore itself, in the process of dealing with its problems. The self-work ethic, that is to say, treats work as something to be valued as the means to those ends espoused by expressive or therapeutic culture. This is the work ethic advocated by Abraham Maslow (1965) and E. F. Schumacher (1980), for example. (Heelas 2002, 80)

And so, we are now living out not simply the triumph of managerialism, but we find expressed in it also the triumph of the 'last man':

> Then the earth has become small, and on it hops the last man, who makes everything small. His kind is ineradicable, like the ground flea; the last man lives longest.
>
> 'We invented happiness' – say the last human beings, and they blink thereby.
> They abandoned the regions where it was hard to live: for one needs warmth. One still loves one's neighbour and rubs up against him: for one needs warmth. (Nietzsche 2006, 10)

It was David Riesman who, as early as 1950, seized with equally uncanny insight what Nietzsche meant with the thought of that human being who 'needs warmth' – what kind of warmth did Nietzsche have in mind? A social psychologist unlike others and a most gifted observer of the cultural dynamics of twentieth-century 'America' in its most intimate details, Riesman suggests – in his famous *The Lonely Crowd: A Study of the Changing American Character* (1950) – that American society was entering a phase of decline, a paradoxical notion if there ever was one. He considered the coming culture to be one of decline because the 1950s marked the inception of an age of unprecedented consumption of comforts unknown to history hitherto. But that is precisely what he wanted to indicate: decline begins when history shifts 'from an age of production to an age of consumption' (Riesman et al. 1950, 6). Riesman understood correctly that an age of consumption cannot be but an age of decline, an age of unproductive, uncreative, comfortable, lukewarm existence. To this age, he further anticipated, corresponds a weakened human type whom he called 'other-directed':

> The society of incipient decline develops in its typical members a social character hose conformity is insured by their tendency to be sensitized to the expectations and preferences of others. These I shall term *other-directed* people and the society in which they live one *dependent on other-direction*. (1950, 8)

And he showed how this becomes the central performative character of our days: the one 'who in his character is more capable of and more interested in maintaining responsive contact with others both at work and at play' (Riesman et al. 1950, 23):

> What is common to all the other-directed people is that their contemporaries are the source of direction for the individual – either those known to him or those with whom he is indirectly acquainted, through friends and through the mass media. This source is of course 'internalized' in the sense that dependence on it for guidance in life is implanted early. The goals toward which the other-directed person strives shift with that guidance: it is only the process of striving itself and the process of paying close attention to the signals from others that remain unaltered throughout life. This mode of keeping in touch with others permits a close behavioural conformity, not through drill in behaviour itself, as in the tradition-directed character, but rather through an exceptional sensitivity to the actions and wishes of others.
>
> Of course, it matters very much who these 'others' are: whether they are the individual's immediate circle or a 'higher' circle or the anonymous voices of the mass media; whether the individual fears the hostility of chance acquaintances or only of those who 'count'. But his need for approval and direction from others – and contemporary others rather than ancestors – goes beyond the reasons that lead most people in any era to care very much what others think of them. While all people want and need to be liked by some of the people some of the time, it is only the modern other-directed types who make this their chief source of direction and chief area of sensitivity.
>
> . . .
>
> The other-directed person, though he has his eye very much on the Joneses, aims to keep up with them not so much in external details as in the quality of his inner experience. That is, his great sensitivity keeps him in touch with others on many more levels than the externals of appearance and propriety. Nor does any ideal of independence or of reliance on God alone modify his desire to look to the others . . . for guidance in what experiences to seek and in how to interpret them. (Riesman et al. 1950, 22–24, emphasis in the original)

If managerialism has triumphed, the moulding of this human type – now in full historical flow – is probably one of its most significant consequences. Is it possible to set aside, then, the question of its import for the coming period? In other words, who will – and who is willing to – overcome managerialism and (neo)liberalism, if indeed such a transformation is even conceivable at the moment? Critiques of these two dimensions of contemporary life have to face this task too and, in part, this collection has sought to allow it to become explicit. What has been attempted here is also to make more explicit the need to step out of, and back from, the current intellectual resources used in these debates. Having left the original sources aside, it is probably the time now to admit that the last four or five decades have made little, if any, conceptual headway in grasping how the modern condition can be both restructured and rescued. What is to be cast aside and what rescued? Managerialism and liberalism are both involved in these two opposing gestures – how are we to articulate an intelligent stance which does not cover up the immense complexity of this question? Are we in a better position to explain how a revolution, a turning around, of the current political state of affairs is to be achieved? None of the propositions currently available with which we are familiar offers anything more than has been articulated (indeed, better articulated) in the philosophy of the nineteenth century. On the one hand, we have to contend with the same image of history as a reasonable process, as progress culminating in a rational and harmonious post-revolutionary state in which a universal, homogenous humanity could live 'forever', and where 'everything will be possible', as it were. On the other hand, we are surrounded by another kind of quasi-utopia, very much at hand, present, material, concrete: the dominion of a well fed, well clothed, very healthy, humanity, but one utterly devoid of any aspirations or ideals other than those projected and forced upon each other by a herd mentality whom Nietzsche named 'the last man'. On the one hand, Hegel; on the other, Nietzsche: however uncomfortable, the question of what, or who, has triumphed in the name of managerialism and (neo)liberalism forces us to return to their original question, as much as we have to follow their thinking back to Machiavelli, Hobbes and Rousseau. And here lies perhaps the main (implicit and explicit) conclusion of the investigations presented here: the need to grasp managerialism as part of the political philosophical problems of modernity as a whole: the question regarding the nature of the historical process, of 'history' itself, as well as the question concerning the nature of being human. As comfortable as it may be to produce utopian programmes of reform relying on the assumption that there is an endless source of 'goodness' to be discovered at the core of some global human endeavour, which, once tapped, will lead to the reconciliation of all ideals, for all people and for all time, it seems to us that a substantial gain could (and would) be made once this assumption is renounced and once Nietzsche's warnings about the impulsiveness and capricious character of human political projects can be heard again.

It seems that what is required is a recognition that the blinding success of human production in the last hundred years forces us to face once again the most pressing questions regarding modernity's essence, but that we are now at a point where our intellectual resources have been severely diminished by the political experiments of the past century. Without such a recognition, the likelihood of substantial thought is slim precisely when, as Dennis Schmidt (2001, 5) so incisively synthesised it, we live in 'a time of crisis, of exhaustion, of historical limits' and have to face (even while we are yet absolutely refusing to) the essential 'contradiction, or conflict, at the heart of the human situation': 'to suffer what is indispensable as what is impossible'. Managerialism, neoliberalism and technology have become the conditions of possibility for an epoch whose understanding of value and valuation is grounded in the primacy of human self-assertion whose expression is productivism as such. What happens when the indispensable condition of our self-understanding (the 'erasure of limits' to human self-expression) becomes the gravest danger? Perhaps this is the sternest test critical attempts to understand how managerialism, neoliberalism and technological existence have to pass.

Consolidated Bibliography

Abella, Alex. 2008. *Soldiers of Reason: The RAND Corporation and the Rise of the American Empire*. Orlando, FL: Harcourt.

ACARA. 2011. "NAPLAN." *Australian Curriculum, Assessment and Reporting Authority*. http://www.nap.edu.au/naplan/naplan.html. Accessed 21 March 2014.

ALDI. 2018. "ALDI Recruitment – Graduates." *ALDI*. https://www.aldirecruitment.co.uk/graduates/.

Aldridge, Rod, and Gerry Stoker. 2002. *Advancing a Public Service Ethos*. London: New Local Government Network.

Alford, John, and Owen Hughes. 2008. "Public Value Pragmatism as the Next Phase in Public Management." *The American Review of Public Administration* 38 (2): 130–48.

Alford, John, and Janine O'Flynn. 2009. "Making Sense of Public Value: Concepts, Critiques and Emergent Meanings." *International Journal of Public Administration* 3–4: 171–91.

Amadae, S. M. 2003. *Rationalizing Capitalist Democracy: The Cold War Origins of Rational Choice Liberalism*. Chicago: The University of Chicago Press.

———. 2015. *Prisoners of Reason: Game Theory and Neoliberal Political Economy*. Cambridge: Cambridge University Press.

Amin, Ash, and Nigel Thrift. 1995. "Institutional Issues for the European Regions: From Markets and Plans to Socioeconomics and Powers of Association." *Economy and Society* 24 (1): 41–66.

Andersen, Niels Å. 2011. "Who Is Yum-Yum? A Cartoon State in the Making." *Ephemera* 11 (4): 405–32.

———. 2013. *Managing Intensity and Play at Work: Transient Relationships*. Cheltenham: Edward Elgar Publishing.

Andersen, Niels Å., and Justine G. Pors. 2016. *Public Management in Transition: The Orchestration of Potentiality*. Bristol: Policy Press.

———. 2017. "On the History of the Form of Administrative Decisions: How Decisions Begin to Desire Uncertainty." *Management & Organizational History* 12 (2): 119–41.

Andersen, Torben K. 2012. “Kolding Viser Vej: Fra Velfærd til Selvværd [Kolding Shows the Way: From Welfare to Self-Worth].” *Mandag Morgen*, 24 October.

Arendt, Hannah. 1958. *The Human Condition*. Chicago: The University of Chicago Press.

———. 1994. “Understanding and Politics.” In *Essays in Understanding 1930–1954*, 307–28. New York: Harcourt Brace & Company.

Arnove, Robert. 1982. *Philanthropy and Cultural Imperialism: The Foundations at Home and Abroad*. Bloomington: Indiana University Press.

Association of Development Consultants. 2012. “Kommunen 30 Interview med Lisbeth Binderup [Local Government 30 Interview with Lisbeth Binderup].” http://ffuk.dk/kommune-3-0-interview-med-lisbeth-binderup/.

Atkins, Paul W. B., and Sharon K. Parker. 2012. “Understanding Individual Compassion in Organizations: The Role of Appraisals and Psychological Flexibility.” *Academy of Management Review* 37: 524–46.

Atkinson, Anthony B. 2015. *Inequality: What Can Be Done*. Cambridge, MA: Harvard University Press.

Augé, Marc. 1995. *Non-Places: Introduction to an Anthropology of Supermodernity*. London: Verso.

Australian Government Productivity Commission. 2016. “Human Services: Identifying Sectors for Reform.” *Commonwealth of Australia*. https://www.pc.gov.au/inquiries/completed/human-services/identifying-reform/report/human-services-identifying-reform.pdf.

———. 2017. *Introducing Competition and Informed User Choice into Human Services: Reforms to Human Services. Productivity Commission Inquiry Report: Overview and Recommendations*. Commonwealth of Australia.

Ball, Stephen. 2007. *Education PLC: Understanding Private Sector Participation in Public Sector Education*. Oxon: Routledge.

———. 2012. *Global Education Inc. New Policy Networks and the Neo-Liberal Social Imaginary*. Oxon: Routledge.

Ball, Stephen, and Carolina Junemann. 2012. *Networks, New Governance and Education*. Bristol: Polity Press.

Banerjee, Subhabrata. 2008. “Corporate Social Responsibility: The Good, the Bad and the Ugly.” *Critical Sociology* 34: 51–79.

Barabasi, Albert-Laszlo. 2003. *Linked: How Everything Is Connected to Everything Else and What It Means*. New York: Plume.

Barthes, Roland. 1977. *Image, Music, Text*. Translated by Stephen Heath. London: Fontana Press.

Beaulieu, Anne. 2004. “Mediating Ethnography: Objectivity and the Making of Ethnographies of the Internet.” *Social Epistemology* 18 (2–3): 139–63.

Beck, Ulrich. 1992. *Towards a New Modernity*. London: SAGE Publications.

Beeson, Mark, and Ann Firth. 1998. “Neoliberalism as a Political Rationality: Australian Public Policy Since the 1980s.” *Journal of Sociology* 34 (3): 215–31.

Behrens, Peter. 2014. “The ‘Consumer Choice’ Paradigm in German Ordoliberalism and Its Impact upon European Union Competition Law.” In Europa-Kolleg Hamburg Institute for European Integration, Discussion Paper No. 1/14.

Bell, Daniel. 1999. *The Coming of the Post-Industrial Society: A Venture in Social Forecasting*. New York: Basic Books.

Benington, John. 2011. "From Private Choice to Public Value?" In *Public Value: Theory and Practice*, edited by John Benington and Mark H. Moore, 31–51. New York: Palgrave Macmillan.

Benington, John, and Mark H. Moore. 2011. "Public Value in Complex and Changing Times." In *Public Value: Theory and Practice*, edited by John Benington and Mark H. Moore, 1–30. New York: Palgrave Macmillan.

Benjamin, Andrew. 2006. *Style and Time: Essays on the Politics of Appearance*. Evanston, IL: Northwestern University Press.

Besussi, Elena. 2006. "Mapping European Research Networks." *University College London*. https://www.ucl.ac.uk/drupal/bartlett/casa/sites/bartlett/files/migrated-files/paper103_0.pdf. Accessed 21 March 2014.

Bevan, Gwyn, and Christopher Hood. 2006. "What's Measured Is What Matters: Targets and Gaming in the English Public Healthcare System." *Public Administration* 84 (3): 517–38.

Beveridge, William. 1944. *Full Employment in a Free Society*. London: George Allen & Unwin.

Bevir, Mark. 2010. *Democratic Governance*. Princeton, NJ: Princeton University Press.

Biagioli, Mario. 2009. "Postdisciplinary Liaisons: Science Studies and the Humanities." *Critical Inquiry* 35 (4): 816–33.

Bishop, Matthew, and Michael Green. 2008. *Philanthrocapitalism: How Giving Can Save the World*. London: Black Publishers Ltd.

Bivins, Roberta, Stephanie Tierney, and Kate Seers. 2017. "Compassionate Care: Not Easy, Not Free, Not Only Nurses." *BMJ Quality & Safety*: 1–4.

Blumenberg, Hans. 1983. *The Legitimacy of the Modern Age*. Cambridge, MA: MIT Press.

———. 1985. *Work on Myth*. Cambridge, MA: MIT Press.

Boltanski, Luc, and Ève Chiapello. 2005. *The New Spirit of Capitalism*. Verso: London.

Bourdieu, Pierre. 2003. *Firing Back: Against the Tyranny of the Market 2*. London: Verso.

Bozeman, Barry. 2002. "Public Value Failure: When Efficient Markets May Not Do." *Public Administration Review* 62 (2): 145–61.

———. 2007. *Public Values and Public Interest: Counterbalancing Economic Individualism*. Washington, DC: Georgetown University Press.

Bradshaw, Ann. 2011. "Compassion: What History Teaches Us." *Ethical and Compassionate Nursing*: 4–6.

Brandom, Robert. 2011. *Perspectives on Pragmatism: Classical, Recent, and Contemporary*. Cambridge, MA: Harvard University Press.

Broadbent, Jane, Michael Dietrich, and Jennifer Roberts. 1997. "The End of the Professions." In *The End of Professions? The Restructuring of Professional Work*, edited by Jane Broadbent, Michael Dietrich, and Jennifer Roberts, 1–32. London: Routledge.

Brown, Philip, and Anthony Hesketh. 2004. *The Mismanagement of Talent: Employability and Jobs in the Knowledge Economy*. Oxford: Oxford University Press.

Brown, Wendy. 2003. "Neo-Liberalism and the End of Liberal Democracy." *Theory & Event* 7 (1). Project Muse. http://muse.jhu.edu/journals/theory_and_event/v007/7.1brown.html. Accessed 2 December 2011.

Burch, Patricia. 2009. *Hidden Markets: The New Education Privatization*. Hoboken, NJ: Routledge.

Burke, Peter. 2000. *History of Knowledge: From Gutenberg to Diderot*. New York: Wiley.

Bush, Vannevar. 1945. "Science the Endless Frontier." *Office of Scientific Research and Development*. https://www.nsf.gov/od/lpa/nsf50/vbush.htm. Accessed 9 February 2018.

Campbell, Denis. 2013. "David Cameron's Prescription for NHS Failings: Target Pay of Nurses." *The Guardian*, 6 February.

Castells, Manuel. 2011. *The Rise of the Network Society: The Information Age: Economy, Society and Culture*. Oxford: Wiley-Blackwell.

Cerny, Phillip G. 2010. "The Competition State Today: From Raison d'État to Raison du Monde." *Policy Studies* 31 (1): 5–21.

Christensen, Tom, and Per Lægreid, eds. 2007a. *Transcending New Public Management: The Transformation of Public Sector Reforms*. Aldershot: Ashgate.

———. 2007b. "The Whole-of-Government Approach to Public Sector Reform." *Public Administration Review* 67 (6): 1059–66.

Cicero, Marcus T. 1991. *On Duties*. Edited by Miriam Griffin and Margaret Atkins. Cambridge: Cambridge University Press.

Clark, Candace. 1997. *Misery and Company: Sympathy in Everyday Life*. Chicago: The University of Chicago Press.

Clarke, John, Sharon Gewirtz, and Eugene McLaughlin, eds. 2000. *New Managerialism, New Welfare?* London: SAGE Publications.

Cockburn, Andrew. 1987. "The Defense Intellectual: Edward N. Luttwak." *Grand Street* 6 (3): 161–74.

Cohen-Cole, Jamie. 2008. "Cybernetics and the Machinery of Rationality." *British Journal for the History of Science* 41 (1): 109–14.

Cole, Martin, and Greg Parston. 2006. *Unlocking Public Value*. Hoboken, NJ: Wiley and Sons.

Commonwealth of Australia. 2017. "Shifting the Dial: 5 Year Productivity Review." *Commonwealth of Australia*. https://www.pc.gov.au/inquiries/completed/productivity-review/report/productivity-review.pdf.

Condren, Conal. 2006. *Argument and Authority in Early Modern England: The Presupposition of Oaths and Offices*. Cambridge: Cambridge University Press.

Considine, Mark. 2018. "Neo-Liberal Social Policy in Australia: What Went Wrong and What Can Be Done?" Paper presented to the Academy of Social Sciences in Australia Workshop "Theorising the Dynamics of Social Service Markets," Sydney, 4–5 April.

Considine, Mark, and Martin Painter. 1997. "Introduction." In *Managerialism: The Great Debate*, edited by Mark Considine and Martin Painter, 1–12. Carlton South: Melbourne University Press.

Costea, Bogdan, Kostas Amiridis, and Norman Crump. 2012a. "In Pursuit of the Ambidextrous Graduate: Potentiality Between Exploration and Exploitation." In *Managing 'Human Resources' by Exploiting and Exploring People's Potentials: Research in the Sociology of Organizations 37*, edited by Mikael Holmqvist and André Spicer, 53–74. Bingley: Emerald Group Publishing Limited.

———. 2012b. "Graduate Employability and the Principle of Potentiality: An Aspect of the Ethics of HRM." *Journal of Business Ethics* 111 (1): 25–36.

Costea, Bogdan, Norman Crump, and Kostas Amiridis. 2007. "Managerialism and 'Infinite Human Resourcefulness': A Commentary on the 'Therapeutic Habitus', 'Derecognition of Finitude' and the Modern Sense of Self." *Journal for Cultural Research* 11 (3): 245–64.

Costea, Bogdan, Peter Watt, and Kostas Amiridis. 2015. "What Killed Moritz Erhardt? Internships and the Cultural Dangers of 'Positive' Ideas." *tripleC: Communication, Capitalism & Critique. Open Access Journal for a Global Sustainable Information Society* 13 (2): 375–89.

Courvisanos, Jerry, and Alex Millmow. 2006. "How Milton Friedman Came to Australia: A Case Study of Class-Based Political Business Cycles." *Journal of Australian Political Economy* 57 (June): 112–36.

Cutler, Claire. 2008. "Transnational Law and Privatized Governance." In *Global Ordering: Institutions and Autonomy in a Changing World*, edited by Louis Pauly and William Coleman, 144–65. Vancouver: UBC Press.

Dahl, Adam, and Joe Soss. 2018. "Neoliberalism for the Common Good? Public Value Governance and the Downsizing of Democracy." In *The Triumph of Managerialism*, edited by Anna Yeatman and Bogdan Costea. London: Rowman & Littlefield International.

Dahl, Robert. 1986. *Preface to Economic Democracy*. Berkeley: University of California Press.

———. 1989. *Democracy and Its Critics*. New Haven, CT: Yale University Press.

Davis, Glyn, Barbara Sullivan, and Anna Yeatman, eds. 1997. *The New Contractualism*. Melbourne: Macmillan Education Australia.

De Hevia, Maria, Luisa Girelli, and Viola Macchi Cassia. 2012. "Minds Without Language Represent Number Through Space: Origins of the Mental Number Line." *Frontiers in Psychology* 3: 466.

de Zulueta, Paquita. 2013a. "Compassion in Healthcare." *Clinical Ethics* 8 (4): 87–90.

———. 2013b. "Compassion in 21st Century Medicine: Is It Sustainable?" *Clinical Ethics* 8 (4): 119–28.

Deem, Rosemary, Sam Hillyard, and Michael Reed. 2008. *Knowledge, Higher Education, and the New Managerialism: The Changing Management of UK Universities*. Oxford: Oxford University Press.

Deleuze, Gilles. 1999. *Foucault*. London: Continuum.

Dent, Mike. 1993. "Professionalism, Educated Labour and the State: Hospital Medicine and the New Managerialism." *The Sociological Review* 41 (2): 244–73.

Department of Health. 2012. "Compassion in Practice: Nursing, Midwifery and Care Staff." *Our Vision and Strategy*. NHS Commissioning Board.

———. 2015. "2010–2015 Government Policy: Compassionate Care in the NHS." *Department of Health and Social Care*. https://www.gov.uk/government/

publications/2010-to-2015-government-policy-compassionate-care-in-the-nhs/2010-to-2015-government-policy-compassionate-care-in-the-nhs.
Dewey, John. 1920. *Reconstruction in Philosophy*. New York: H. Holt.
DFAT. 2018. "Australia and the OECD." *Department of Foreign Affairs and Trade*. https://dfat.gov.au/about-us/publications/Documents/australia-and-the-oecd.pdf. Accessed 2 April 2018.
Dickson, Paul. 1971. *Think Tanks*. New York: Atheneum.
Dillow, Chris. 2007. *The End of Politics: New Labour and the Folly of Managerialism*. Petersfield: Harriman House Ltd.
Disch, Lisa. 2011. "Toward a Mobilization Conception of Democratic Representation." *American Political Science Review* 105 (1): 100–14.
Dolan, Frederick M. 1990. "Representing the Political System: American Political Science in the Age of the World Picture." *Diacritics* 20 (2).
Doolin, Bill. 2002. "Enterprise Culture, Professional Identity and the Organizational Control of Hospital Clinicians." *Organization Studies* 23 (3): 369–90.
Doran, Christine. 2016. "Managerialism: An Ideology and Its Evolution." *International Journal of Management, Knowledge and Learning* 5 (1): 81–97.
Du Gay, Paul. 2000. *In Praise of Bureaucracy*. London: SAGE Publications.
———. 2007. *Organizing Identity: Persons and Organizations 'After Theory'*. London: SAGE Publications.
———. 2008. "'Without Affection or Enthusiasm': Problems of Involvement and Attachment in Responsive Public Management." *Organization* 15 (3): 335–53.
———. 2009. "Max Weber and the Ethics of Office." In *The Oxford Handbook of Sociology and Organization Studies*, edited by Paul Adler, 146–73. Oxford: Oxford University Press.
———. 2013. "New Spirits of Public Management . . . 'Post-Bureaucracy.'" In *New Spirits of Capitalism: Crises, Justifications, and Dynamics*, edited by Paul du Gay and Glenn Morgan, 274–93. Oxford: Oxford University Press.
———. 2015. "Is Office a Vocation in 'Post-Bureaucratic' Public Management?" In *Neoliberalism and the Crisis of Public Institutions, Working Papers in the Human Rights and Public Life Program no. 2*, edited by Anna Yeatman. Sydney: The Whitlam Institute.
———. 2017. "Introduction: Office as a Vocation." *European Journal of Cultural and Political Sociology* 4 (2): 156–65.
Du Gay, Paul, and Thomas Lopdrup-Hjorth. 2016. "Reclaiming Formal Organization." In *Reclaiming the Public: Working Papers in the Human Rights and Public Life Program no. 3, July 2016*, edited by Anna Yeatman, 57–85. Sydney: The Whitlam Institute.
Du Gay, Paul, and Signe Vikkelsø. 2012. "Reflections: On the Lost Specification of 'Change.'" *Journal of Change Management* 12 (2): 121–43.
———. 2017. *For Formal Organisation: The Past in the Present and Future of Organization Theory*. Oxford: Oxford University Press.
Dupré, Louis. 1993. *Passage to Modernity: An Essay on the Hermeneutics of Nature and Culture*. New Haven, CT: Yale University Press.
Dzur, Albert. 2013. "Trench Democracy: Participatory Innovation in Unlikely Places." *Boston Review*. Blog. http://www.bostonreview.net/blog/dzur-trench-democracy-1. Accessed 11 December 2013.

Edwards, Paul N. 1996. *The Closed World: Computers and the Politics of Discourse in Cold War America*. Cambridge, MA: MIT Press.

Eggers, William. 2008. "The Changing Nature of Government: Network Governance." In *Collaborative Governance: A New Era of Public Policy in Australia*, edited by Janine O'Flynn and John Wanna, 39–45. Canberra: ANU Press.

Elster, Jon. 1989. *Nuts and Bolts for the Social Science*. Cambridge: Cambridge University Press.

Enteman, Willard F. 1993. *Managerialism: The Emergence of a New Ideology*. Madison: University of Wisconsin Press.

Ericson, Richard V., and Kevin D. Haggerty. 1997. *Policing the Risk Society*. Oxford: Oxford University Press.

Eve, Rosalind, and Paul Hodgkin. 1997. "Professionalism and Medicine." In *The End of Professions? The Restructuring of Professional Work*, edited by Jane Broadbent, Michael Dietrich, and Jennifer Roberts, 69–85. London: Routledge.

Exworthy, Mark, and Susan Halford. 1999. "Professionals and Managers in a Changing Public Sector: Conflict, Compromise and Collaboration?" In *Professionals and the New Managerialism in the Public Sector*, edited by Mark Exworthy and Susan Halford, 1–18. Buckingham: Open University Press.

Fairclough, Norman. 2000. *New Labour, New Language?* New York: Routledge.

Felice, Flavio, and Massimiliano Vatiero. 2013. "Ordo and European Competition Law." http://www.siecon.org/online/wp-content/uploads/2013/09/Felice-Vatiero.pdf. Published in 2015 in *A Research Annual (Research in the History of Economic Thought and Methodology, Volume 32)*, edited by Luca Fiorito, 147–57. Bingley: Emerald Group Publishing.

Fischer, Frank. 2009. *Democracy and Expertise: Reorienting Policy Inquiry*. Oxford: Oxford University Press.

Fitzgerald, Louise, and Ewan Ferlie. 2000. "Professionals: Back to the Future." *Human Relations* 53 (5): 713–39.

Fotaki, Marianna. 2015. "Why and How Is Compassion Necessary to Provide Good Quality Healthcare?" *International Journal of Health Policy Management* 4 (4): 199–201.

Foucault, Michel. 1972. *The Archaeology of Knowledge*. London: Tavistock Publications.

———. 1980. *Power/Knowledge: Selected Interviews and Other Writing 1972–1977*. Edited by Colin Gordon. New York: Pantheon Books.

———. 1997. *Il faut défendre la société: Cours au Collège de France 1976*. Paris: Gallimard.

———. 2004. *Naissance de la biopolitique: cours au Collège de France 1978–1979*. Paris: Gallimard.

Francis, Robert. 2010. *Independent Inquiry into Care Provided by Mid Staffordshire NHS Foundation Trust January 2005 – March 2009. The Mid Staffordshire NHS Foundation Trust Inquiry*. London: The Stationery Office.

———. 2013. *Report of the Mid Staffordshire NHS Foundation Trust Public Inquiry: Executive Summary*. London: The Stationery Office.

Frederickson, George. 1991. "Toward a Theory of the Public for Public Administration." *Administration & Society* 22 (4): 395–417.

Freidson, Eliot. 1984. "Are Professions Necessary?" In *The Authority of Experts: Studies in History and Theory*, edited by Thomas Haskell, 3–27. Bloomington: Indiana University Press.

———. 2001. *Professionalism: The Third Logic*. Chicago: The University of Chicago Press.

Friedman, Milton. 1962. *Capitalism and Freedom*. Chicago: The University of Chicago Press.

———. 1970. "The Social Responsibility of Business Is to Increase Its Profits." *The New York Times Magazine*, September 13.

Fung, Archon. 2006. *Empowered Participation: Reinventing Urban Democracy*. Princeton, NJ: Princeton University Press.

Galbraith, John Kenneth. 1952. *American Capitalism: The Concept of Countervailing Power*. Boston: Houghton Mifflin.

Gilens, Martin. 2012. *Affluence and Influence: Economic Inequality and Political Power in America*. Princeton, NJ: Princeton University Press.

Ginzburg, Carlo. 1992a. *Cheese and the Worms: Cosmos of a Sixteenth-Century Miller*. Translated by John A. Tedeschi and Anne Tedeschi. Baltimore, MD: The Johns Hopkins University Press.

———. 1992b. *Clues, Myths and the Historical Method*. Baltimore, MD: The Johns Hopkins University Press.

———. 2012. *Threads and Traces*. Translated by Anne Tedeschi and John A. Tedeschi. Berkeley: University of California Press.

Goitein, Lara. 2015. "Training Young Doctors: The Current Crisis." *New York Review of Books*, 4 June. http://www.nybooks.com/articles/2015/06/04/training-young-doctors-current-crisis/.

Goot, Murray. 2010. "Labor, Government Business Enterprises and Competition Policy." *Labour History* 98 (May): 77–95.

Graeber, David. 2013. "On the Phenomenon of Bullshit Jobs: A Work Rant." *Strike*, August. https://strikemag.org/bullshit-jobs.

———. 2018. *Bullshit Jobs: A Theory*. New York: Simon & Schuster.

Grant, Adam M. 2012. "Giving Time, Time After Time: Work Design and Sustained Employee Participation in Corporate Volunteering." *Academy of Management Review* 37: 589–615.

Greenhalgh, Trisha. 2013. "The Compassionate Organization." *British Journal of General Practice* 63 (614): 481.

Greve, Carsten. 2010. "Whatever Happened to New Public Management?" Paper presented at the Danish Political Science Association meeting, 4–5 November.

———. 2015. "Ideas in Public Management Reform for the 2010s: Digitalization, Value Creation and Involvement." *Public Organization Review* 15 (1): 49–65.

Guttman, David, and Barry Willner. 1976. *The Shadow Government: The Government's Multi-Billion-Dollar Giveaway of Its Decision-Making Powers to Private Management Consultants, "Experts," and Think Tanks*. New York: Pantheon Books.

Hacker, Jacob, and Paul Pierson. 2011. *Winner-Take-All Politics: How Washington Made the Rich Richer – and Turned Its Back on the Middle Class*. New York: Simon & Schuster.

Hall, Peter. 1992. *Inventing the Nonprofit Sector and Other Essays on Philanthropy, Voluntarism, and Nonprofit Organizations*. Baltimore, MD: The Johns Hopkins University Press.

Hardt, Michael, and Antonio Negri. 2000. *Empire*. Cambridge, MA: Harvard University Press.

———. 2004. *Multitude: War and Democracy in the Age of Empire*. New York: Penguin Press.

Harper, Ian, Peter Anderson, Su McCluskey, and Michael O'Bryan QC. 2015. *Competition Policy Review: Final Report*. Commonwealth of Australia.

Harrison, Stephen, and Ruth MacDonald. 2008. *The Politics of Health Care in Britain*. London: SAGE Publications.

Hartley, Jean. 2005. "Innovation in Governance and Public Services: Past and Present." *Public Money and Management* 25 (1): 27–34.

Hasle, Peter, Ole H. Sørensen, Eva Toft, Hans Hvenegaard, and Christian U. Madsen. 2014. *Vidensgrundlag om kerneopgaven i den kommunale sektor* [Knowledge Foundation for the Core Tasks in Local Government]. Copenhagen: Team Arbejdsliv, Center for Industriel Produktion, AAU KBH for fremfærd.

Heelas, Paul. 1996. *The New Age Movement: The Celebration of the Self and the Sacralization of Modernity*. Oxford: Blackwell.

———. 2002. "Work Ethics, Soft Capitalism and the 'Turn to Life.'" In *Cultural Economy: Cultural Analysis and Commercial Life*, edited by Paul du Gay and Michael Pryke, 78–97. London: SAGE Publications.

Hegel, Georg W. F. 1938. "Differenz des Fichteschen und Schellingschen Systems der Philosophie." In *Sämtliche Werke: Jubiläumsausgabe in zwanzig Bänden (25 vols.)*, edited by Hermann Glockner, 31–168. Stuttgart: Frommans.

Heidegger, Martin. 1977a. *The Question Concerning Technology and Other Essays*. Translated by William Lovitt. New York: Garland Publishing Inc.

———. 1977b. "'Only a God Can Save Us Now': An Interview with Martin Heidegger." Translated by David Schendler. *Graduate Faculty Philosophy Journal* 6 (1): 5–27.

———. 1985. *Schelling's Treatise on the Essence of Human Freedom*. Athens, OH: Ohio University Press.

———. 1991. *Nietzsche: Volumes III and IV [Volume IV – Nihilism]*. Translated by David Farrell Krell. San Francisco, CA: HarperSanFrancisco.

———. 1996. *Hölderlin's Hymn "The Ister."* Translated by William McNeil and Julia Davies. Bloomington: Indiana University Press.

———. 2000. *Gesamtausgabe Band 16: Reden und andere Zeugnisse eines Lebensweges, 1910–1976*. Edited by Hermann Heidegger. Frankfurt am Main: Klostermann.

———. 2004. "Zu Ernst Jünger 1939/40." In *Zu Ernst Jünger (GA90)*, edited by Peter Trawny, 221–32. Frankfurt: Klostermann.

———. 2006. *Mindfulness*. Translated by Parvis Emad and Thomas Kalary, *Athlone Contemporary European Thinkers*. London: Continuum International Publishing Group.

Hennis, Wilhelm. 2000. "Personality and Life Orders: Max Weber's Theme." In *Max Weber, Rationality and Modernity*, edited by Sam Whimster and Scott Lash, 52–74. London: Routledge.

Hogan, Anna. 2015. "Network Ethnography and the Cyberflâneur: Evolving Policy Sociology in Education." *International Journal of Qualitative Studies in Education* 29 (3): 381–98.

Hogan, Anna, Sam Sellar, and Bob Lingard. 2016. "Commercialising Comparison: Pearson Puts the TLC in Soft Capitalism." *Journal of Education Policy* 31 (3): 243–58.

Holborow, Marnie. 2015. *Language and Neoliberalism*. Abingdon: Routledge.

Holmes, David. 2009. "In the Case of Emergency: Misunderstanding Tradeoffs in the War on Terror." *California Law Review* 97 (2): 301–55.

Hood, Christopher. 2005. "Public Management: The Word, the Movement, the Science." In *The Oxford Handbook of Public Management*, edited by Ewan Ferlie, Laurence E. Lynn Jr., and Christopher Pollitt. Oxford: Oxford University Press. Oxford Handbooks Online.

Hood, Christopher, and Robin Dixon. 2015. *A Government That Worked Better and Cost Less? Evaluating Three Decades of Reform and Change in the UK Central Government*. Oxford: Oxford University Press. Oxford Handbooks Online.

Hopkinson, Marley. 2014. *Compassionate Leadership: How to Create and Maintain Engaged, Committed and High-Performing Teams*. London: Piatkus.

Horner, Louise, and Louise Hazel. 2005. "Adding Public Value." *The Work Foundation*. http://www.theworkfoundation.com/assets/docs/publications/86_public_value.pdf. Accessed 6 December 2011.

Horner, Louise, and Will Hutton. 2011. "Public Value, Deliberative Democracy, and the Role of Public Managers." In *Public Value: Theory and Practice*, edited by John Benington and Mark H. Moore, 112–26. New York: Palgrave Macmillan.

Howard, Phillip. 2002. "Network Ethnography and the Hypermedia Organization: New Media, New Organizations, New Methods." *New Media & Society* 4 (4): 550–74.

Humphrys, Elizabeth, and Damien Cahill. 2016. "How Labor Made Neoliberalism." *Critical Sociology* 43 (4–5): 669–84.

Hunt, Jeremy. 2014a. "Treating Patients as People." Speech. *Department of Health*, 19 January. https://www.gov.uk/government/speeches/treating-patients-as-people.

———. 2014b. "Transparent and Accountable Healthcare: Why the Culture in the NHS Still Needs to Change." Speech. *Department of Health*, 19 November. https://www.gov.uk/government/speeches/treating-patients-as-people.

Isaac, Joel. 2007. "The Human Sciences in Cold War America." *The Historical Journal* 50 (3): 725–46.

Jackson, Ben. n.d. "Richard Titmuss Versus the IEA: The Transition from Idealism to Neo-liberalism in British Social Policy." In *Welfare and Social Policy in British Historical Perspective, 1850–2010: Essays in Honor of Professor Jose Harris*, edited by L. Goldman and S. Jones. Unpublished version.

Jacobs, Keith, and Jeff Malpas. 2017. "The Language of Resilience: Ideas and Action in Contemporary Policy-Making." *Housing, Theory and Society*: 1–16. doi:10.1080/14036096.2017.1308435.

Jacobs, Lawrence R., and Robert Y. Shapiro. 2000. *Politicians Don't Pander: Political Manipulation and the Loss of Democratic Responsiveness*. Chicago: The University of Chicago Press.

Jessop, Bob. 1998. "The Rise of Governance and the Risks of Failure." *International Social Science Journal* 155 (1): 29–45.

Jones, Evan. 2016. "Australian Trade Liberalisation Policy: The Industries Assistance Commission and the Productivity Commission." *The Economic and Labour Relations Review* 27 (2): 181–98.

Juelskjær, Malou, Hanne Knudsen, Justine G. Pors, and Dorthe Staunæs, eds. 2011. *Ledelse af uddannelse: At lede det potentielle* [Leading Education. Managing Potentiality. Knowledge]. Frederiksberg: Samfundslitteratur.

Jünger, Ernst. 1930. "Die Totale Mobilmachung." In *Krieg und Krieger*, edited by Ernst Jünger, 9–30. Berlin: Junker und Dünnhaupt.

———. 1932 [1981]. *Der Arbeiter: Herrschaft und Gestalt*. Stuttgart: Klett-Cotta.

Kaiser, David I. 2007. "The Mutual Embrace: Institutions and Epistemology." In *Positioning the History of Science*, edited by Kostas Gavroglu and Jurgen Renn, 99–103. Dordrecht, The Netherlands: Springer.

Kaplan, Fred. 1983. *The Wizards of Armageddon*. Palo Alto, CA: Stanford University Press.

Kenway, Jane, and Elizabeth Bullen. 2001. *Consuming Children: Entertainment, Advertising and Education*. Buckingham: Open University Press.

Kettl, Donald. 2002. *The Transformation of Governance: Public Administration for Twenty-First Century America*. Baltimore, MD: The John Hopkins University Press.

The Kings Fund. 2017a. "The King's Funds Priorities for the United Kingdom (UK) National Health Service (NHS) and Social Care Services in 2017 and Onwards." *The Kings Fund*. https://www.kingsfund.org.uk/publications/priorities-nhs-social-care-2017.

———. 2017b. "Innovation and Compassion in Health Care." *The Kings Fund*. https://www.kingsfund.org.uk/blog/2017/09/compassion-and-innovation-nhs.

Klikauer, Thomas. 2013. *Managerialism: A Critique of an Ideology*. Basingstoke: Palgrave Macmillan.

———. 2015. "What Is Managerialism?" *Critical Sociology* 41 (7–8): 1103–19.

Koehn, Daryl. 1994. *The Ground of Professional Ethics*. London: Routledge.

Kolev, Stefan. 2015. "Ordoliberalism and the Austrian School." In *The Oxford Handbook of Austrian Economics*, edited by Peter Boettke and Christopher Coyne, 419–44. Oxford: Oxford University Press.

Konings, Martin. 2018. *Capital and Time: For a New Critique of Neoliberal Reason*. Palo Alto, CA: Stanford University Press.

Koppenjan, Joop, and Erik-Hans Klijn. 2004. *Managing Uncertainties in Networks*. London: Routledge.

Koyré, Alexandre. 1957. *From the Closed World to the Infinite Universe*. Baltimore, MD: The John Hopkins University Press.

Kriegel, Blandine. 1995. *The State and the Rule of Law*. Princeton, NJ: Princeton University Press.

Kuklick, Bruce. 2006. *Blind Oracles: Intellectuals and War from Kennan to Kissinger*. Princeton, NJ: Princeton University Press.

Lagemann, Ellen. 1992. *The Politics of Knowledge: The Carnegie Corporation, Philanthropy, and Public Policy*. Chicago: The University of Chicago Press.

Laski, Harold. 1930. "Foundations, Universities and Research." In *The Dangers of Obedience & Other Essays*. New York: Harper & Brothers.

Leitner, Helga, and Eric Sheppard. 2002. "'The City is Dead, Long Live the Net': Harnessing European Interurban Networks for a Neoliberal Agenda." *Antipode* 34 (3): 495–518.

Lingard, Bob. 2011. "Policy as Numbers: Ac/Counting for Educational Research." *Australian Education Researcher* 38 (4): 355–82.

Lingard, Bob, and Sam Sellar. 2013. " 'Catalyst Data': Perverse Systemic Effects of Audit and Accountability in Australian Schooling." *Journal of Education Policy* 28 (5): 634–56.

Liu, Lydia H. 2010. "The Cybernetic Unconscious: Rethinking Lacan, Poe, and French Theory." *Critical Inquiry* 36 (2): 288–320.

Local Government, Denmark. 2014. "Fremfærd. Et magasin fra KL og KTO om fremtidens velfærd i kommunerne [Forwardfare. A Paper from Local Government, Denmark, and KTO]." http://fremfaerd.dk/sites/default/files/fremfaerd-magasin-enkeltsider-020614d_0_0.pdf.

Local Government of Aarhus. 2013. *Kærlig Kommune: Fremtidens sundhed og omsorg i Aarhus* [Local Government of Love: Healthcare in Aarhus]. Aarhus: Local Government of Aarhus.

———. 2015a. "Pressemeddelelse. Aarhus gentænker velfærd [Press Release. Aarhus Rethinks Welfare]." http://www.aarhus.dk/da/politik/politikker-og-planer/innovation-og-medborgerskab/Aarhus-kommune-starter-forfra.aspx.

———. 2015b. *Kommune Forfra: Aarhus gentænker velfærden* [Local Government Rethought: Aarhus Rethinks Welfare]. Aarhus: Local Government of Aarhus.

Local Government of Kolding. 2012. *Selvværd er mere end velfærd* [Selfworth Is Better than Welfare]. Kolding: Social- og Sundhedsforvaltningen.

Local Government of Skanderborg. 2017. "De Ualmindelige: Transportvane [The Unusual: Transportation Habits]." https://www.skanderborg.dk/deualmindelige#transportvane_unders%C3%B8gelse.

Locke, Robert R. 1996. *The Collapse of the American Management Mystique*. Oxford: Oxford University Press.

Locke, Robert R., and J. C. Spender. 2011. *Confronting Managerialism: How the Business Elite and Their Schools Threw Our Lives Out of Balance*. London: Zed Books.

Loughlin, Martin. 2010. *Foundations of Public Law*. Oxford: Oxford University Press.

———. 2013. "The Erosion of Sovereignty." *Netherlands Journal of Legal Philosophy* 45 (2): 57–81.

———. 2018. "Excavating Foundations." In *Questioning the Foundations of Public Law*, edited by Michael Wilkinson and Michael Dowdle, 255–76. Oxford: Hart Publishing.

Lown, Beth A. 2014. "Toward More Compassionate Healthcare Systems." *Journal of Health Policy Management* 2 (4): 199–200.

Lynch, Kathleen, Bernie Grummell, and Dympna Devine. 2012. *New Managerialism in Education: Commercialization, Carelessness and Gender*. Basingstoke: Palgrave Macmillan.

Maben, Jill, Jocelyn Cornwell, and Kieran Sweeney. 2009. "In Praise of Compassion." *Journal of Research in Nursing* 15 (1): 9–13.

Malpas, Jeff. 2012. "The Demise of Ethics." *Research in Ethical Issues in Organizations* 8: 29–46.

———. 2016. "Good Government Starts Today: On the Death of the Public, the Triumph of Private Interest, and the Loss of the Good." In *Reclaiming the Public, Working Papers in the Human Rights and Public Life Program, No. 3*, edited by Anna Yeatman, 1–23. Sydney: The Whitlam Institute.

———. 2018. *Place and Experience*. 2nd edition. Abingdon: Routledge.

Malpas, Jeff, and Gary Wickham. 1995. "Governance and Failure: On the Limits of Sociology." *Australian and New Zealand Journal of Sociology* 31: 37–50.

———. 1997. "Governance and the World: From Jo DiMaggio to Michel Foucault." *The UTS Review* 3: 91–108.

Mannion, Russell. 2014. "Enabling Compassionate Healthcare: Perils, Prospects and Perspectives." *International Journal of Health Policy Management* 2 (3): 115–17.

Mansbridge, Jane. 1996. "Using Power/Fighting Power: The Polity." In *Democracy and Difference*, edited by Seyla Benhabib, 46–66. Princeton, NJ: Princeton University Press.

Marin, Bernd, and Renate Mayntz. 1991. *Policy Networks: Empirical Evidence and Theoretical Considerations*. Frankfurt: Westview.

Martin, Daniel, and Bruce Cahan. 2013. "Building Trust and Compassion in Banking Through Transparency and Social Capital." *HuffPost*, 4 June.

Martin, Reinhold. 2005. *The Organizational Complex: Architecture, Media, and Corporate Space*. Cambridge, MA: MIT Press.

Marx, Karl. 2005. "Grundrisse." In *Ökonomische Manuskripte 1857/1858*, edited by Erich Kunderl, Roland Nietzold, Richard Sperl, Hildegard Scheibler, and others, 47–768. Berlin: Dietz Verlag (Marx Engels Werke [MEW] vol. 42, 1983).

Maslow, Abraham. 1965. *Eupsychian Management: A Journal*. Homewood, IL: Richard D. Irwin.

Massy, Charles. 2017. *Call of the Reed Warbler: A New Agriculture for a New Earth*. St. Lucia: University of Queensland Press.

Mattelart, Armand. 1994. *Mapping the World Communication: War, Progress and Culture*. Minneapolis: University of Minnesota Press.

Meagher, Gabrielle, and Susan Goodwin. 2015. "Introduction: Capturing Marketization in Australian Social Policy." In *Markets, Rights and Power in Australian Social Policy*, edited by Gabrielle Meagher and Susan Goodwin, 1–29. Sydney: Sydney University Press.

Meagher, Gabrielle, and Shaun Wilson. 2015. "The Politics of Market Encroachment: Policymaker Rationales and Voter Responses." In *Markets, Rights and Power in Australian Social Policy*, edited by Gabrielle Meagher and Susan Goodwin, 29–97. Sydney: Sydney University Press.

Meynhardt, Timo. 2009. "Public Value Inside: What Is Public Value Creation?" *International Journal of Public Administration* 32: 192–219.

Mintzberg, Henry. 1979. *The Structuring of Organizations: A Synthesis of the Research*. Saddle River, NJ: Prentice Hall.

Mirowski, Philip. 2013. *Never Let a Serious Crisis Go to Waste: How Neoliberalism Survived the Financial Meltdown*. London: Verso.

Mirowski, Philip, and Edward Nik-Khah. 2017. *The Knowledge We Have Lost in Information: The History of Information in Modern Economics*. New York: Oxford University Press.

Mirowski, Philip, and Dieter Plehwe, eds. 2009. *The Road from Mont Pelèrin: The Making of the Neoliberal Thought Collective*. Cambridge, MA: Harvard University Press.

Mitchell, Timothy. 1988. *Colonising Egypt*. Berkeley: University of California Press.

Mitchell, W. J. Thomas. 1987. *Iconology: Image, Text, Ideology*. Chicago: The University of Chicago Press.

Mondzain, Marie-Jose. 2005. *Image, Icon, Economy: The Byzantine Origins of the Contemporary Imaginary*. Translated by Rico Franses. Palo Alto, CA: Stanford University Press.

Moore, Mark, H. 1994. "Public Value as the Focus of Strategy." *Australian Journal of Public Administration* 53 (3): 296–303.

———. 1995. *Creating Public Value: Strategic Management in Government*. Cambridge, MA: Harvard University Press.

Moore, Mark H., and John Benington. 2011. "Conclusions: Looking Ahead." In *Public Value: Theory and Practice*, edited by John Benington and Mark Moore, 256–74. New York: Palgrave Macmillan.

Mouffe, Chantal. 2005. *The Return of the Political*. New York: Verso.

Nam, Young-Sook. 2011. "The Changing Landscape of Corporate Social Responsibility in Korea." *Revista de EDUCAÇÃO do Cogeime* 20 (38): 145–58.

Nelson, Sioban, and Ann Marie Rafferty. 2010. *Notes on Nightingale: The Influence and Legacy of a Nursing Icon, the Culture and Politics of Health Care Work*. New York: Cornell University Press.

Newman, Janet. 2001. *Modernising Governance: New Labour, Policy and Society*. London: SAGE Publications.

———. 2005a. "Bending Bureaucracy: Leadership and Multi-Level Governance." In *The Values of Bureaucracy*, edited by Paul du Gay, 191–209. Oxford: Oxford University Press.

———. 2005b. "Enter the Transformational Leader: Network Governance and the Micro-Politics of Modernization." *Sociology* 39 (4): 717–34.

Newman, Janet, and John Clarke. 2009. *Publics, Politics and Power: Remaking the Public in Public Services*. London: SAGE Publications.

NHS. 2013. "How to Ensure the Right People, With the Right Skills, Are in the Right Place at the Right Time: Guide to Nursing, Midwifery and Care Staffing Capacity and Capability." *National Health Service*. http://www.england.nhs.uk/wp-content/uploads/2013/11/nqb-how-to-guid.pdf.

———. 2014a. "Compassion in Practice: Two Years On." *National Health Service*. https://www.england.nhs.uk/wp-content/uploads/2014/12/nhs-cip-2yo.pdf.

———. 2014b. "Building and Strengthening Leadership: Leading with Compassion." *National Health Service*. https://www.england.nhs.uk/wp-content/uploads/2014/12/london-nursing-accessible.pdf.

———. 2014c. "Building and Strengthening Leadership: Leading with Compassion Field Guide." *National Health Service*. No longer publicly accessible.

———. 2016. "Leading Change: Adding Value." *National Health Service*. https://www.england.nhs.uk/wp-content/uploads/2016/05/nursing-framework.pdf.

———. 2018. "About NHS England." *National Health Service*. https://www.england.nhs.uk/about/about-nhs-england.

Nietzsche, Friedrich. 1911. *Wille zur Macht*. Edited by Peter Gast (Heinrich Köselitz). Vol. 15, *Nietzsche's Werke*. Leipzig: Kröner.

———. 1968. *The Will to Power*. Translated by Walter Kaufmann and R. J. Hollingdale. Edited by Walter Kaufmann. New York: Vintage Books.

———. 1974. *The Gay Science: With a Prelude in German Rhymes and an Appendix of Songs*. Translated by Walter Kaufmann. New York: Vintage Books.

———. 1999. *Friedrich Nietzsche Kritische Studienausgabe*. Edited by Giorgio Colli and Mazzino Montinari. 15 vols. Berlin: De Gruyter.

———. 2000. *Basic Writings of Nietzsche*. Translated by Walter Kaufmann. New York: Modern Library.

———. 2006. *Thus Spoke Zarathustra*. Edited by Adrian del Caro and Robert Pippin. Cambridge: Cambridge University Press.

Nightingale, Florence. 1860. *Notes on Nursing: What It Is, and What It Is Not*. New York: D. Appleton and Company.

Nik-Khah, Edward. 2016. "Economics Imperialism." Talk under auspice of Whitlam Institute given at Corrs Chambers Westgarth, Sydney, 31 May.

Nik-Khah, Edward, and Phillip Mirowski. 2016. "Making Individuals Fit for the Market – or, Hayek Comes to Orthodox Microeconomics." Paper presented at the 2016 History of Economics Society Conference, Duke University, Durham, North Carolina, 17–20 June.

———. Forthcoming. "The Ghosts of Hayek in Orthodox Microeconomics: Markets as Information Processors." In *Search of Media: Markets*, edited by A. Beverungen, Phillip Mirowski, E. Nik-Khah, and J. Schröter. Minneapolis: Meson Press and University of Minnesota Press.

Nik-Khah, Edward, and Robert Van Horn. 2012. "Inland Empire: Economics Imperialism as an Imperative of Chicago Neoliberalism." *Journal of Economic Methodology* 19 (3): 259–82.

———. 2017. "The Ties that Bond: The Evolution of the Corporate-Academic Relationship in the Rise of Neoliberalism." Paper presented at Neoliberalism and Social Democracy, Two-Day Collaborative Conference, De Paul University, Chicago, 7–8 April.

O'Brien, Kerry. 2015. *Keating*. Crows Nest: Allen & Unwin.

O'Flynn, Janine. 2007. "From New Public Management to Public Value: Paradigmatic Change and Managerial Implications." *The Australian Journal of Public Administration* 66 (3): 353–66.

Olmedo, Antonio. 2014. "From England with Love . . . ARK, Heterarchies and Global 'Philanthropic Governance.'" *Journal of Education Policy* 29 (5): 575–97.

Ormiston, Margaret E., and Elaine M. Wong. 2013. "License to Ill: The Effects of Corporate Social Responsibility and CEO Moral Identity on Corporate Social Irresponsibility." *Personnel Psychology* 66: 861–93.

Osborne, David, and Ted Gaebler. 1992. *Re-Inventing Government*. Reading: Addison-Wesley.

Osler, William. 1908. *An Alabama Student and Other Biographical Essays*. Oxford: Oxford University Press.

Palley, Thomas. 2011. "The Rise and Fall of Export-Led Growth." Working Paper No. 675, Levy Economics Institute of Bard College. http://www.levyinstitute.org/pubs/wp_675.pdf.

Panofsky, Erwin. 1962. *Studies in Iconology: Humanistic Themes in the Art of Renaissance*. New York: Harper and Row.

———. 1982. *Meaning in the Visual Arts*. Chicago: The University of Chicago Press.

———. 1997. *Perspective as Symbolic Form*. New York: Zone Books.

Pateman, Carole. 1970. *Participation and Democratic Theory*. Cambridge: Cambridge University Press.

———. 2012. "Participatory Democracy Revisited." *Perspectives on Politics* 10 (1): 7–19.

Patrinos, Harry, Felipe Barrera-Osorio, and Juliana Guáqueta. 2009. *The Role and Impact of Public-Private Partnerships in Education*. Washington, DC: World Bank Publications.

Pearson. 2012. "Annual Report and Accounts 2012." *Pearson*. https://www.pearson.com/content/dam/corporate/global/pearson-dot-com-v2/files/cosec/2013/15939_PearsonAR12.pdf.

Peck, Jamie, and Adam Tickell. 2002. "Neoliberalizing Space." *Antipode* 34 (3): 380–404.

Pedersen, Dorthe. 2016. "Leadership in Search of Public Value: Hybrid Practices and Explorative Learning." In *Developing Public Managers for a Changing World*, edited by Klaus Majgaard, Jens Carl Ry Nielsen, John W. Raine, and Brid Quinn, 103–26. Bingley: Emerald Group Publishing Limited.

Pedersen, Kirstine. 2018. *Organizing Patient Safety: Failsafe Fantasies and Pragmatic Practices*. London: Palgrave Macmillan.

Pedersen, Kirstine, and Paul du Gay. Forthcoming. "Discretion and Bureaucracy." In *Discretion and the Quest for Controlled Freedom*, edited by Tony Evans and Peter Hupe. London: Palgrave Macmillan.

Perrow, Charles. 1972 [2014]. *Complex Organizations: A Critical Essay*. 3rd edition. Brattleboro, VT: Echo Point Books.

Picciano, Anthony, and Joel Spring. 2013. *The Great American Education-Industrial Complex: Ideology, Technology and Profit*. New York: Routledge.

Pierre, Jon. 2000. *Debating Governance: Authority, Steering, and Democracy*. New York: Oxford University Press.

Pierson, Paul, and Theda Skocpol. 2007. *The Transformation of American Politics: Activist Government and the Rise of Conservatism*. Princeton, NJ: Princeton University Press.

Piketty, Thomas. 2013. *Le Capital au XXIème siècle*. Paris: Éditions de Seuil.

———. 2014. *Capital in the Twenty-First Century*. Cambridge, MA: The Belknap Press of Harvard University Press.

Pippin, Robert. 2008. *Hegel's Practical Philosophy: Rational Agency as Ethical Life*. Cambridge: Cambridge University Press.

Piven, Frances Fox. 2006. *Challenging Authority: How Ordinary People Change America*. Lanham, MD: Rowman & Littlefield.

Pollitt, Christopher, and Geert Bouckaert. 2017. *Public Management Reform: A Comparative Analysis – into the Age of Austerity*. 4th edition. Oxford: Oxford University Press.

Pors, Justine G. 2011. "Noisy Management: A History of Danish School Governing from 1970–2010." PhD Thesis, Copenhagen Business School PhD Series, Frederiksberg.

———. 2016. "Kærlig borgerledelse – om ledelse af frihed, nysgerrighed og det levede liv [Citizen Management in the Name of Love: Notes on Management of Freedom, Curiosity and Lived Life]." In *Borgernær Ledelse* [Leading Citizens], edited by Kristian Gylling-Olesen and Anja Svejgaard Pors, 20–47. Copenhagen: Akademisk Forlag.

Pors, Justine G., and Niels Å. Andersen. 2015. "Playful Organizations: Undecidability as a Scarce Resource." *Culture & Organization* 21 (4): 338–54.

Pors, Justine G., and Helene G. Ratner. 2017. "The Emergence and Workings of a Process View in Public Education Policy." *International Journal of Management Concepts and Philosophy* 10 (1): 16–31.

Porter, Michael, and Mark Kramer. 2011. "Creating Shared Value." *Harvard Business Review* (January–February): 62–77.

Power, Michael. 1997. *The Audit Society: Rituals of Verification*. Oxford: Oxford University Press.

———. 2007. "The Theory of the Audit Explosion." In *The Oxford Handbook of Public Management*, edited by Ewan Ferlie, Laurence E. Lynn Jr., and Christopher Pollitt. Oxford: Oxford University Press. Oxford Handbooks Online.

Ptak, Ralf. 2009. "Neoliberalism in Germany: Revisiting the Ordoliberal Foundations of the Social Market Economy." In *The Road from Mont Pèlerin: The Making of the Neoliberal Thought Collective*, edited by Phillip Mirowski and Dieter Plehwe, 98–139. Cambridge, MA: Harvard University Press.

Pufendorf, Samuel von. 1991. *On the Duty of Man and Citizen According to Natural Law*. Cambridge: Cambridge University Press.

Pusey, Michael. 1991. *Economic Rationalism in Canberra: A Nation Building State Changes Its Mind*. Cambridge: Cambridge University Press.

———. 2017. "Economic Rationalism in Canberra Twenty-Five Years On." In *Neoliberal Government and Its Implications for Public Office and the Welfare State, Working Papers in the Human Rights and Public Life Program*, No. 5 (May), edited by Anna Yeatman, 10–16. Sydney: The Whitlam Institute.

Quick, Kathryn S., and Martha S. Feldman. 2011. "Distinguishing Participation and Inclusion." *Journal of Planning Education and Research* 31: 272–90.

Quiggin, John. 2003. "Word for Wednesday: Managerialism (Definition)." Blog. http://johnquiggin.com/2003/07/02/word-for-wednesday-managerialism-definition/.

RAND Corporation. n.d. "History and Mission." *RAND Corporation*. http://www.RAND.org/about/history.html. Accessed 10 February 2018.

Ravitch, Diane. 2012. "The United States of Pearson?" http://dianeravitch.net/2012/05/07/the-united-states-of-pearson-2/. Accessed 21 March 2014.

Readings, Bill. 1996. *The University in Ruins*. Cambridge, MA: Harvard University Press.

Reckhow, Sarah. 2013. *Follow the Money: How Foundation Dollars Change Public School Politics*. New York: Oxford University Press.

Reiermann, Jens. 2011. "Fremtidens velfærd [Welfare in the Future]." *Mandag Morgen*, 19 January.

Rhodes, Rod A. W., and John Wanna. 2007. "The Limits to Public Value, or Rescuing Responsible Government from the Platonic Guardians." *Australian Journal of Public Administration* 66 (4): 406–21.

Richardson, Henry. 2003. *Democratic Autonomy: Public Reasoning About the Ends of Policy*. New York: Oxford University Press.

Riesman, David, Nathan Glazer, Reuel Denney, and Todd Gitlin. 1950. *The Lonely Crowd: A Study of the Changing American Character*. New Haven, CT: Yale University Press.

Rizvi, Fazal, and Bob Lingard. 2010. *Globalizing Education Policy*. Oxon: Routledge.

Roberts, Alasdair. 1995. "Civic Discovery as Rhetorical Strategy." *Journal of Policy Analysis and Management* 14 (2): 291–307.

Robertson, Susan, and Roger Dale. 2013. "The Social Justice Implications of Privatization in Education Governance Frameworks: A Relational Account." *Oxford Review of Education* 39 (4): 426–45.

Robertson, Susan, Karen Mundy, Antonio Verger, and Francine Menashy. 2012. *Public Private Partnerships in Education: New Actors and New Modes of Governance*. Cheltenham: Edward Elgar Publishing.

Robertson, Susan, and Antonio Verger. 2012. "Governing Education Through Public Private Partnerships." In *Public Private Partnerships in Education: New Actors and Modes of Governance in a Globalizing World*, edited by Susan Robertson, Karen Mundy, Antonio Verger, and Francine Menashy, 21–42. Cheltenham: Edward Elgar Publishing.

Rodgers, Daniel. 2011. *Age of Fracture*. Cambridge, MA: Belknap Press of Harvard University Press.

Roelofs, Joan. 2003. *Foundations and Public Policy: The Mask of Pluralism*. New York: SUNY Press.

Roelsgaard Obling, Anne. 2012. "Management of Emotions in Accelerated Medical Relationships." In *PhD Series 8*. Copenhagen: Copenhagen Business School.

———. 2013. "Ascribing Emotion to Reasonable Use in Accelerated Cancer Services." *Journal of Health Organization and Management* 27 (4): 432–48.

Rogers, Richard. 2013. *Digital Methods*. Cambridge, MA: MIT Press.

Rohr, John. 1989. *Ethics for Bureaucrats*. 2nd edition. New York: Marcel Dekker.

———. 1998. *Public Service, Ethics and Constitutional Practice*. Lawrence: University Press of Kansas.

Rojek, Chris. 1997. "'Leisure' in the Writings of Walter Benjamin." *Leisure Studies* 16 (3): 155–71.

Rosanvallon, Pierre. 2013. *The Society of Equals*. Cambridge, MA: Harvard University Press.

Rose, Nikolas. 1999. *Powers of Freedom: Reframing Political Thought*. New York: Cambridge University Press.

Rose, Nikolas, and Peter Miller. 1992. "Political Power Beyond the State: Problematics of Government." *British Journal of Sociology* 43 (2): 173–205.

Ross, Dorothy. 1991. *The Origins of American Social Science*. Cambridge: Cambridge University Press.

Royles, Dean. 2014. "Compassion Is One of Our Few Infinite Resources." *NHS Employers*. Blog. http://www.nhsemployers.org/blog/2014/03/compassion-is-one-of-our-few-infinite-resources.

Rundle, Kristen. 2012. *Forms Liberate: Reclaiming the Jurisprudence of Lon L. Fuller*. Oxford: Hart.

———. (forthcoming). "The Morality of the Rule of Law: Lon Fuller." In *The Cambridge Companion to the Rule of Law*, edited by Martin Loughlin and Jens Meierhenrich. Cambridge: Cambridge University Press.

Russell Sage Foundation. n.d. "History." *Russell Sage Foundation*. http://www.russellsage.org/about/history. Accessed 15 January 2018.

Ryan, James. 2012. *Lenin's Terror: The Ideological Origins of Early Soviet State Violence*. London: Routledge.

Rynes, Sara, Jean M. Bartunek, Jane E. Dutton, and Joshua D. Margolis. 2012. "Care and Compassion Through an Organizational Lens: Opening Up New Possibilities." *Academy of Management Review* 37 (4): 503–23.

Sadler, David, and Stuart Lloyd. 2009. "Neo-Liberalising Corporate Social Responsibility: A Political Economy of Corporate Citizenship." *Geoforum* 40 (4): 613–22.

Said, Edward. 1997. *Beginnings: Intention and Method*. London: Granta Books.

———. 2000. *Reflection on Exile and Other Essays*. Cambridge, MA: Harvard University Press.

Savage, Glenn. 2012. "Being Different and the Same? The Paradoxes of 'Tailoring' in Education Quasi-Markets." *Journal of Pedagogy* 3 (2): 279–302.

Scheler, Max. 1980. *Problems of a Sociology of Knowledge*. London: Routledge & Kegan Paul.

Schmidt, Dennis J. 2001. *On Germans and Other Greeks: Tragedy and Ethical Life*. Bloomington: Indiana University Press.

Schudson, M. 1980. "Reviewed Works(s): The Rise of Professionalism: A Sociological Analysis by Magali Sarfatti Larson." *Theory and Society* 9 (1): 215–29.

Schulman, Jason. 2015. *Neoliberal Labour Governments and the Union Response*. Basingstoke: Palgrave Macmillan.

Schumacher, Ernst. 1980. *Good Work*. London: Abacus.

Schwab, Klaus. 2008. "Global Corporate Citizenship: Working with Governments and Civil Society." *Foreign Affairs* 87 (1): 107–18.

The Scottish Health Council. 2014. "Why Use Emotional Touch Points." file:///C:/Users/ar.ioa/Downloads/Toolkit_2014_ET.pdf.

SDS. 1962. "Original Draft of Port Huron Statement/Port Huron Statement Draft." *Students for a Democratic Society*. http://www.sds-1960s.org/PortHuronStatement-draft.htm. Accessed 17 January 2018.

Sennett, Richard. 2008. *The Craftsman*. London: Allen Lane.

Serco. 2018. "Our Culture and Values." *Serco*. https://www.serco.com/about/culture-and-values. Accessed 18 April 2018.

Shiller, Robert J. 2012. *Finance and the Good Society*. Princeton, NJ: Princeton University Press.

Shiroma, Enedia Oto. 2014. "Networks in Action: New Actors and Practices in Education Policy in Brazil." *Journal of Education Policy* 29 (3): 323–48.

Shropshire Community Health. 2017. "Compassion in Practice e-Learning." *Shropshire Community Health*. http://www.shropscommunityhealth.nhs.uk/rte.asp?id=11144.

Sinclair, Shane, Susan McClement, Shelley Raffin-Bouchal, Thomas Hack, Neil Hagen, Shelagh McConnell, and Harvey Max Chochinov. 2016. "Compassion in Health Care: An Empirical Model." *Journal of Pain and Symptom Management* 51 (2): 193–203.

Slobodian, Quinn. 2018. *Globalists: The End of Empire and the Birth of Neoliberalism*. Cambridge, MA: Harvard University Press.

Smajdor, Anna. 2013. "Reification and Compassion in Medicine: A Tale of Two Systems." *Clinical Ethics* 8 (4): 111–18.

Smelser, Neil J. 1997. *Problematics of Sociology: The Georg Simmel Lectures, 1995*. Berkeley: University of California Press.

Smith, R. F. I. 2004. "Focusing on Public Value: Something New and Something Old." *Australian Journal of Public Administration* 63 (1): 68–79.

Smith, Sam. 2017. "Valuing Feedback: An Evaluation of a National Health Service Programme to Support Compassionate Care Practice Through Hearing and Responding to Feedback." *Journal of Research in Nursing* 22 (1–2): 112–27.

Soss, Joe, and Lawrence R. Jacobs. 2014. "Guardianship and the New Gilded Age: Insular Politics and the Perils of Elite Rule." In *Working and Living in the Shadow of Economic Fragility*, edited by Marion Crain and Michael Sherraden, 157–75. New York: Oxford University Press.

Soss, Joe, Richard Fording, and Sanford Schram. 2011. *Disciplining the Poor: Neoliberal Paternalism and the Persistent Power of Race*. Chicago: The University of Chicago Press.

Speed, Ewen. 2011. "Applying Soft Bureaucracy to Rhetorics of Choice: The UK NHS 1983–2007." In *Managing Modernity – Beyond Bureaucracy*, edited by Stewart Clegg, Martin Harris, and Höpfl Harro, 81–104. Oxford: Oxford University Press.

Spicer, André. 2018. *Business Bullshit*. Abingdon: Routledge.

Staunæs, Dorthe. 2011. "Governing the Potentials of Life Itself? Interrogating the Promises in Affective Educational Leadership." *Journal of Educational Administration and History* 43 (3): 227–47.

Stengers, Isabelle. 2015. *In Catastrophic Times: Resisting the Coming Barbarism*. n.p.: Open Humanities Press and Meson Press.

Stoker, Gerry. 2004. *Transforming Local Governance: From Thatcherism to New Labor*. Basingstoke: Palgrave Macmillan.

———. 2006. "Public Value Management: A New Narrative for Networked Governance?" *The American Review of Public Administration* 36 (1): 41–57.

Stone, Diane. 1996. *Capturing the Political Imagination: Think Tanks and the Policy Process*. London: Frank Cass.

Storper, Michael. 1997. *The Regional World: Territorial Development in a Global Economy*. New York: Guilford Press.

Sturgess, Gary. 2015. *Contestability in Public Services: An Alternative to Outsourcing*. Melbourne: ANZSOG Research Monograph.

Sztompka, Piotr. 1993. *The Sociology of Social Change*. Oxford: Blackwell.

Taylor, Charles. 1992. *Sources of the Self: The Making of the Modern Identity*. New edition. Cambridge: Cambridge University Press.

Thompson, Greg, and Allen Harbaugh. 2013. "A Preliminary Analysis of Teacher Perceptions of the Effects of NAPLAN on Pedagogy and Curriculum." *Australian Educational Researcher* 40 (3): 299–314.

Treasury. 2007. "Australian Government National Competition Policy Report 2005–07." *Commonwealth of Australia*. https://static.treasury.gov.au/uploads/sites/1/2017/06/NCP_Report_2005_07.pdf.

Van Barneveld, Kristin, and Osmond Chiu. 2018. "A Portrait of Failure: Ongoing Cuts to Australia's Cultural Institutions." *Australian Journal of Public Administration* 77 (1): 3–19.

Van Horn, Robert, Phillip Mirowski, and Thomas A. Stapleford, eds. 2011. *Building Chicago Economics: New Perspectives on the History of America's Most Powerful Economics Program*. Cambridge: Cambridge University Press.

Verger, Antonio. 2012. "Framing and Selling Global Education Policy: The Promotion of Public – Private Partnerships for Education in Low-Income Contexts." *The Journal of Education Policy* 27 (1): 109–30.

Virilio, Paul. 1999. *Politics of the Very Worst*. New York: Semiotext(e).

———. 2007. *The Original Accident*. Cambridge: Polity.

Von Karman, Theodore. n.d. "Toward New Horizons." http://archive.today/B67X6. Accessed 14 February 2018.

Von Mises, Ludwig. 1949 [1963]. *Human Action: A Treatise on Economics*. 4th revised edition. Irvington-on-Hudson: The Foundation for Economic Education.

———. 2009. *Liberty and Property*. Auburn, AL: Mises Institute.

Wanna, John. 2009. "Political Chronicles, Commonwealth of Australia July to December 2008." *Australian Journal of Politics and History* 55 (2): 261–315.

Waring, Justin. 2009. "Constructing and Re-Constructing Narratives of Patient Safety." *Social Science and Medicine* 69: 1722–31.

Waring, Justin, Mary Dixon-Woods, and Karen Young. 2010. "Modernising Medical Regulation: Where Are We Now." *Journal of Health Organization and Management* 24 (6): 540–55.

Warren, Mark E. 2009. "Governance-Driven Democratization." *Critical Policy Studies* 3 (1): 3–13.

Watson, Don. 2004. *Death Sentence: The Decay of Public Language*. New York: Vintage.

———. 2005. *Gobbledygook: How Clichés, Sludge and Management-Speak Are Strangling Our Public Language*. London: Atlantic Books.

Watts, Rob. 2017. *Public Universities, Managerialism and the Value of Higher Education*. London: Palgrave Macmillan.

Weber, Max. 1949. "'Objectivity' in Social Science and Social Policy." In *The Methodology of the Social Sciences*, 50–113. New York: The Free Press.

———. 1970. "Science as a Vocation." In *Max Weber: Essays in Sociology*, edited by Hans Gerth and C. Wright Mills, 129–59. London: Routledge & Kegan Paul.

———. 1978. *Economy and Society: An Outline of Interpretive Sociology*. Berkeley: University of California Press.

———. 2004a. "Science as a Vocation." In *The Vocation Lectures*, edited by David Owen and Tracy B. Strong. Indianapolis: Hackett Publishing Company.

———. 2004b. "Politics as a Vocation." In *The Vocation Lectures*, edited by David Owen and Tracy B. Strong. Indianapolis: Hackett Publishing Company.

———. 2004c. *The Vocation Lectures*. Edited by David Owen and Tracy B. Strong. Indianapolis: Hackett Publishing Company.

Weber, Samuel. 2001. *Institution and Interpretation*. Palo Alto, CA: Stanford University Press.

Wedel, Janine, R. 2009. *How the World's New Power Brokers Undermine Democracy, Government, and the Free Market*. New York: Basic Books.

Wensley, Robin, and Mark H. Moore. 2011. "Choice and Marketing in Public Management: The Creation of Public Value?" In *Public Value: Theory and Practice*, edited by John Benington and Mark H. Moore. New York: Palgrave Macmillan.

Wheen, Francis. 2004. *How Mumbo-Jumbo Conquered the World: A Short History of Modern Delusions*. London: Harper Perennial.

Wikipedia. 2012. "Engineering Ethics." *Wikipedia*. https://en.wikipedia.org/wiki/Engineering_ethics. Accessed 27 March 2018.

———. 2018. "Competition Law Theory." *Wikipedia*. https://en.wikipedia.org/wiki/Competition_law_theory. Accessed 15 April 2018.

Williams, Ben. 2012. "Centrifugal Schooling: Third Sector Policy Networks and the Reassembling of Curriculum Policy in England." *Journal of Education Policy* 27 (6): 775–94.

Williams, Paul. 2002. "The Competent Boundary Spanner." *Public Administration* 80 (1): 103–24.

Willmott, Robert. 2002. *Education Policy and Realist Social Theory: Primary Teachers, Child-Centred Philosophy and the New Managerialism*. London: Routledge.

Winters, Jeffrey. 2011. *Oligarchy*. New York: Cambridge University Press.

Wittel, Andreas. 2001. "Toward a Network Sociality." *Theory, Culture & Society* 18 (6): 51–76.

Wolin, Sheldon. 1989. *The Presence of the Past*. Baltimore, MD: The Johns Hopkins University Press.

———. 2008. *Democracy Incorporated*. Princeton, NJ: Princeton University Press.

Yeatman, Anna. 1997. "The Concept of Public Management and the Australian State in the 1980s." In *Managerialism: The Great Debate*, edited by Mark Considine and Martin Painter, 12–39. Carlton South: Melbourne University Press.

———. 1998. "Activism and the Policy Process." In *Activism and the Policy Process*, edited by Anna Yeatman, 16–36. St. Leonards: Allen & Unwin.

———. 2017. "Competition Policy and the Destruction of the Welfare State." In *Neoliberal Government and Its Implications for Public Office and the Welfare State, Working Papers in the Human Rights and Public Life Program no. 4*, edited by Anna Yeatman, 24–46. Sydney: Whitlam Institute.

———. 2018. "Gender, Social Policy and the Idea of the Welfare State." In *Handbook on Gender and Social Policy*, edited by Sheila Shaver, 21–37. Cheltenham: Edward Elgar Publishing.

———. 2018. "The Primacy of Speech." Paper presented at W. D. Joske Colloquium, V. I. I- Human Language and Communication, University of Tasmania, Hobart, January.

Yeatman, Anna, Gary Dowsett, Michael Fine, and Diane Gursansky. 2009. *Individualization and the Delivery of Welfare Services: Contestation and Complexity*. Basingstoke: Palgrave Macmillan.

Žižek, Slavo. 2004. "What Rumsfeld Doesn't Know that He Knows About Abu Ghraib." *In These Times*. http://inthesetimes.com/article/747.

Zorach, A. 2010. "Why GDP (Gross Domestic Product) Is a Poor Measure of Wealth and Prosperity." *Alex Zorach's Blog*. Blog. https://zorach.wordpress.com/2010/8/27/why-gdp-gross-domestic-product-is-a-poor-measure-of-wealth-and-prosperity/. Accessed 21 March 2018.

Index

About the Contributors

Bogdan Costea is Professor at Lancaster University Management School in the Department of Organisation, Work and Technology. He explores how core philosophical arguments about the nature of the self, meanings and implications of work, and human organisation reappear encoded in the contemporary culture of managerialism. He published various articles on the cultural constitution and grounds of managerialism in its various forms. He co-authored (with Laurence P. Hemming) the first English translation of Ernst Jünger's *The Worker: Dominion and Form* (2017).

Adam Dahl is Assistant Professor of Political Science at the University of Massachusetts Amherst. He is the author *Empire of the People: Settler Colonialism and the Foundations of Modern Democratic Thought* (2018). His research has appeared in *Polity*, *American Political Thought*, *Perspectives on Politics*, *New Political Science*, *Public Administration Review*, and *Political Research Quarterly*. He has also received financial support from the Mellon Foundation and the American Council of Learned Societies.

Laurence Paul Hemming is Research Professor at Lancaster University in the Politics, Philosophy and Religion Department, and the Lancaster University Management School. He was formerly Dean of Research for one of the colleges of the University of London. Among his published works are *Heidegger's Atheism* (2002), *Postmodernity's Transcending* (2005) and *Heidegger and Marx: A Productive Dialogue over the Language of Humanism* (2013). In 2017, with Bogdan Costea, he published a translation of Ernst Jünger's 1932 text *The Worker*.

Anna Hogan is Lecturer at the University of Queensland, Australia. She has been researching the role of global edu-business in education policy and practice. She is currently working on projects that investigate the privatisation of Australian public schooling, the effects of curriculum outsourcing on teachers' work and the commercialisation of student health and well-being.

Jeff Malpas is Distinguished Professor at the University of Tasmania and Distinguished Visiting Professor at Latrobe University. He is the author of many books and essays on topics in philosophy, architecture and geography. His *Place and Experience* was recently published in a new revised edition.

Anne Roelsgaard Obling is Assistant Professor in the Department of Organization at Copenhagen Business School, Denmark. Her research interests include charting the transformations of work, tasks and professional roles in bureaucratic organisations (the hospital, the army, the central administration), which are associated with contemporary reforms and reform attempts to modernise the public sector. She is part of the VELUX project 'Office as a Vocation'.

Kirstine Zinck Pedersen is Assistant Professor in the Department of Organization at Copenhagen Business School. Her research attends to the organisational, practical and ethical implications of recent managerial and technological transformations of the public sector – and in particular to the constitutive effects of quality and safety reform programmes in the healthcare sector. Kirstine is the author of the book *Organizing Patient Safety: Failsafe Fantasies and Pragmatic Practices* (2018).

Justine Grønbæk Pors is Associate Professor in the Department of Management, Politics and Philosophy at Copenhagen Business School. Her research and teaching explores current transformations of public policy and practices of governing. She is particularly interested in how regimes of change and innovation work to deconstruct foundational notions of welfare, public administration and profession. Together with Niels Åkerstrøm Andersen she has recently published *Public Management in Transition: The Orchestration of Potentiality* (2016).

Ihab Shalbak is Visiting Research Fellow at the University of Sydney. Previously Ihab worked as Lecturer in the Human Rights program and Coordinator of the Social Justice Research Network, both at the University of Sydney. In 2015, he completed his PhD on 'The Birth of Think Tank: Theory, History and Politics in the Long American Century' from the University of New South Wales.

Joe Soss is the inaugural Cowles Chair for the Study of Public Service at the University of Minnesota, where he holds faculty positions in the Hubert H. Humphrey School of Public Affairs, the Department of Political Science, and the Department of Sociology. His research and teaching explore the interplay of democratic politics, socioeconomic inequalities and public policy. He is particularly interested in the political sources and consequences of policies that govern social marginality and shape life conditions for socially marginal groups. His most recent book is *Disciplining the Poor: Neoliberal Paternalism and the Persistent Power of Race* (2011).

Anna Yeatman is Professor in the Institute for Culture and Society at Western Sydney University. She has held professorial appointments at the University of Alberta (Canada Research Chair in Political Science), Macquarie University (Chair of Sociology) and University of Waikato (Foundation Chair of Women's Studies). She has a background in political and social thought and has led public policy evaluations in the human services. She is also a Feldenkrais practitioner.

www.ingramcontent.com/pod-product-compliance
Ingram Content Group UK Ltd.
Pitfield, Milton Keynes, MK11 3LW, UK
UKHW041142300926
15471UKWH00011B/101

9 781538 158302